OXFORD IN ASIA HISTORICAL
General Editor: Wang Gungwu

THE WANDERING THOUGHTS
OF A DYING MAN

THE WANDERING THOUGHTS OF A DYING MAN

The Life and Times of
Haji Abdul Majid bin Zainuddin

Edited with an Introduction and Notes by
WILLIAM R. ROFF

KUALA LUMPUR
OXFORD UNIVERSITY PRESS
OXFORD NEW YORK MELBOURNE
1978

Oxford University Press
OXFORD LONDON GLASGOW
NEW YORK TORONTO MELBOURNE WELLINGTON
IBADAN NAIROBI DAR ES SALAAM LUSAKA CAPE TOWN
KUALA LUMPUR SINGAPORE JAKARTA HONG KONG TOKYO
DELHI BOMBAY CALCUTTA MADRAS KARACHI
● *Oxford University Press 1978*
All rights reserved. No part of this publication may be reproduced, stored in a retrieval system, or transmitted, in any form or by any means, electronic, mechanical, photocopying, recording or otherwise, without the prior permission of Oxford University Press

ISBN 0 19 580349 3

Printed in Malaysia by Sun U Book Co., Kuala Lumpur, Published by Oxford University Press, 3, Jalan 13/3, Petaling Jaya, Selangor, Malaysia

CONTENTS

Editor's Introduction	vii
TEXT	
PREFACE	1
BOOK ONE	5
BOOK TWO	51
BOOK THREE	113
BIBLIOGRAPHY OF ABDUL MAJID'S PUBLISHED WRITINGS	159
Index	161

EDITOR'S INTRODUCTION

WHEN Haji Abdul Majid b. Zainuddin died in March 1943, at the age of 56, he left a manuscript autobiography. It had been begun in September 1941, three months before the Japanese invasion of Malaya, but was not completed, probably because the war intervened. The autobiography does, however, cover the first forty years of Abdul Majid's life and most of its principal events. In particular, it gives the reader a vivid picture of, and a good deal of insight into, many central aspects of Malay life during the first quarter of the twentieth century. In this it is of unique value, for we possess no other autobiography of the period, a period formative of much that has now become modern peninsular Malaysia.

The manuscript was written in pencil, in an ordinary writing pad and two school exercise books, and, for reasons that will emerge, it was written in English. Though it is in many ways an unorganized, and indeed often rather rambling, narrative—proceeding by free association of subject matter rather than by chronological arrangement there is no question that Abdul Majid intended it for publication. Entitling it initially 'The Wandering Thoughts of a Dying Man' (he had been diagnosed as diabetic, and was gloomy about his future), he prefaces the second notebook with the suggestion that 'What I Thought of My Past Life' be added as a sub-title, and there are other remarks that make it clear that he wanted it to appear in print. As he had already published numerous books and articles this is scarcely surprising. He thought of himself as a man of letters, and was so regarded by others. Indeed there is no question that in many ways he was one of the leading English-educated Malays of his generation, and one accustomed to participating in the public debates and controversies of his time.

In bringing Abdul Majid's autobiography before the general

reader it has been thought desirable, in view of the relatively unfinished state of the manuscript, to undertake two tasks. To supply an historical introduction that will attempt to set Abdul Majid within the context of his time; and to provide the text of the autobiography with annotation that will help either to identify people and places mentioned in it or to add information that will explicate certain passages. Concerning the first of these tasks, the non-chronological form taken by the autobiography has suggested that a preliminary overview of Abdul Majid's life may be helpful, and more importantly that some attempt be made to 'complete' it by discussing in rather more detail the later part of his life, from the point at which the narrative breaks off in 1923. Concerning the second task, while efforts have been made not to overload the text with footnotes, it has seemed sensible to give as much information as possible about the individuals who peopled Abdul Majid's world during a period of Malaya's social history which is still in many ways too little known. Because of the central position he occupied in Malay society—first as a teacher at the prestigious Malay College, Kuala Kangsar, for over a decade, then as the first Malay Pilgrimage Officer to Mecca—Abdul Majid came to know, as familiars, a truly remarkable number of people, Malay, British, Chinese, and Indian. It is his lively and uninhibited presentation of this cast of characters that provides the ultimate justification, were any needed, for publication of the autobiography of what, by any measure, was an extraordinary 'ordinary man'.

Abdul Majid was born in March 1887 in Pudu, then a small settlement on the south-eastern outskirts of Kuala Lumpur. The tin mining town of Kuala Lumpur itself, though by this time the state administrative capital, was far from large, with a population of perhaps 3,000, mainly Chinese but including some Selangor Malays and a proportion of immigrant Sumatran traders. Abdul Majid's father was one of the latter, from Bonjol in Minangkabau. He kept a provision shop in the Malay quarter of town, and while he was certainly not rich he appears to have been reasonably well off. Majid began his formal education at the Pudu village school, and then in 1895 became one of the tiny handful of Malay pupils (about 10 out of 200) at the newly opened English-language Victoria Institution in Kuala Lumpur. He seems to have been clever and diligent, and in 1902, as the result of a double promotion, succeeded in passing the Cambridge Junior School Certificate examination, ordinarily the culmination of seven years' school work. At this stage, he tells us, he wanted to continue his education and eventually perhaps study medicine at a British university. His father, however, like many other Malay parents of the late century, was unenthusiastic about too much Western education, and preferred Majid to leave school and take a job in the state civil service, with a view to saving up and pursuing religious, rather than secular, learning in Mecca. Abdul Majid worked, accordingly, as a clerk for the Selangor government for two years before succumbing, for reasons he explains, to a renewed desire for education as a means of getting on in the world.

There was much talk at this time of the new boarding school that was shortly to be opened in the royal town of Perak, Kuala Kangsar, especially to train Malays from throughout the federated states for various departments of the government service. The Malay Residential School was, however, born of more than one kind of impulse, and almost at once became the preserve of the sons of the Malay nobility and aristocracy. Majid nevertheless gained admittance, by writing directly (and with some temerity) to the Federal Inspector of Schools, R.J. Wilkinson, whose idea the school had been and who was favourably disposed to able and ambitious young Malays of whatever social background, and went to Kuala Kangsar with the first intake in January 1905. Because of his previous educational experience, and no doubt his own industry and acumen, he graduated at the head of the examination list two years later, and was at once employed as the school's first (and for many years sole) Malay teacher. He remained in this post for eleven years, until 1918, and thus had thirteen years in all in Kuala Kangsar. It is scarcely surprising that he should have chosen to begin his autobiography with a series of reminiscences of those early days, nor that references to the school and the town should abound in the remainder of his narrative.

It was a time and place of considerable historical interest. Sultan Idris of Perak (reg. 1887–1916), the most able and distinguished of the Federated Malay States rulers, lived and held court there in traditional fashion (as Abdul Majid's anecdotes recount); and because of the presence of the Malay College (so renamed in 1909) the town attracted a wide range of Malay dignitaries (most of whose sons were educated there) and British officials. As Abdul Majid makes plain, it was a lively and sociable place, and though the distinctions of race and social status endemic to colonial rule were observed (as reflected, for example, in the carefully graded clubs to which one might—or might not—belong, and in the nuances of playing-field encounters), it was small enough for everyone to know everyone else and for the barriers to be defined more in terms of Malay (and British) etiquette than as a result simply of protocol and prejudice. Abdul Majid spent the whole of his twenties there, years in which he fell in love, got married, and brought up a young family (and had the beginnings of a discreet affair with a lady of position); in which he achieved fame as one of the state's champion football and billiards players; in which he became Kuala Kangsar correspondent for English-language newspapers in Penang and Ipoh, and wrote frequently for the Malay press; and in which he wrote and translated his first educational books. All these activities, and the associations with others that they brought him, are vividly reflected in the sections of the autobiography covering the Kuala Kangsar years.

And then, in 1918, Abdul Majid was chosen by the Assistant Director of Education (Malay), R.O. Winstedt, to become the first Malay Assistant Inspector of Schools. This was more than a promotion, for the job was part of a supposed 'new deal' for Malay education devised by Winstedt as the result of an overseas visit and report in 1917. Under it, selected Malays were to be given administrative and inspectorial responsibility for all vernacular schools in a particular administrative area, replacing the 'Visiting Teachers' of the past. Abdul Majid was posted to Lower Perak, with headquarters in the small town of Telok Anson part way up the Perak River. In fact he spent relatively little time here, before moving on in 1924, for in March 1919 he was sent for a year to act as principal of the Malay Teachers' Training College at Matang (Perak), while the British incumbent was on leave, and returned there again for a further eighteen months from May 1920. He describes his years at Matang as the happiest of his life, and there is no doubt that during these two periods, totalling some thirty months, he enjoyed a combination of high status (as the first Malay to hold a college principalship) and real teaching responsibility, of a kind particularly pleasing to him. Beyond everything, he was a teacher at heart, whether in formal or informal contexts (as his didactic newspaper letters and articles, his readiness to advise friends, and his harmless pedanticism demonstrate), and he was acutely aware that Malay society at this time was in need of education of all kinds. Though he took no stand on educational policy as such, he clearly felt it to be a responsibility of that small section of the Malay populace with English education to give intellectual leadership to the rest. The British had made a point of affording English education to very few Malays, holding that everyone's interests were best served by keeping peasants as peasants. Of the 10,000 boys at English schools in the federated states in 1920, fewer than 700 were Malay, and in 1922 a mere 45 Malay boys passed the Junior Cambridge examination, precisely 9 the Senior. Abdul Majid, in short, belonged to a select company, a fact of which he was acutely conscious. No social revolutionary (there were elements of both 'obliging the nobles' and *noblesse oblige* in his make-up), he nonetheless recognized that as one of the fortunate (and able) raised to high places he had a duty to help others by both example and precept.

The opportunity to further these ideals came in a peculiarly satisfying form in 1924. Abdul Majid had applied some eighteen months earlier for leave of absence to make the pilgrimage to Mecca, but had had to withdraw his application for family reasons associated with his daughter Aminah's impending marriage. It was at this point, as he records in his autobiography, that he was invited by the authorities to travel to Mecca at government expense, and report back on the conditions of the *haj*. This he readily agreed to do, and the autobiography comes to an abrupt halt in the middle of this, his first pilgrimage, in 1923. Though many later references to Mecca and the Hejaz occur elsewhere in the narrative, including discussion of his subsequent marriages, we are given no fully connected account of his life from this point forward. Returning to Malaya towards the end of 1923, however, he submitted a written report that much impressed the government, and from early in the following year was appointed first

Malayan Pilgrimage Officer (travelling to Jeddah with the first ship every year, and returning seven months later with the last), a post he was to hold for the next sixteen years.

In the mid-1920s, some 5,000 Malays annually made the pilgrimage (a sizeable proportion remaining in Mecca to study), and it had been felt for some time that more interest should be shown by the Straits and Malayan governments in what happened to them, a task that had until then been left to the British Consul in Jeddah and Indian Muslim representatives able to frequent the Holy Places. One reason for this concern was fear of the unknown, of the effects of nationalist and communist political propaganda in the Hejaz. Administration of the *haj* at the Malayan end had for some years been in the hands of the Political Intelligence Bureau of the Straits Settlement Police—which explains why, as he recounts, Abdul Majid was first recruited by a policeman, and also why, once he was formally appointed Pilgrimage Officer, he spent his annual five months in Malaya as a liaison officer with the Bureau while nominally (until 1931) a member of the Education Service. In the result, as the records show, Abdul Majid was able to provide his superiors with very little that was of interest politically, but he did perform, and extremely well, a wide range of social welfare services to Malay pilgrims in the Hejaz, for which a generation of his fellows remained grateful.*

As for his activities as a political liaison officer in Malaya, most people were aware of them (he scarcely had the personality to become an 'under-cover agent', and was indeed one of the most prominent Malays of his generation), and few are known to have resented them. While one of his tasks, for example, was to interrogate in 1935 the president of the burgeoning, essentially non-political, literary organization *Sahabat Pena* (Friends of the Pen), he was an honoured guest at its second national

---

*This phase of Abdul Majid's life is discussed in detail in the present writer's 'The Conduct of the Haj from Malaya, and the first Malayan Pilgrimage Officer,' in Amin Sweeney (ed.), *Sari Terbitan Tak Berkala* [*Occasional Papers*] No.1, Institute of Malay Language, Literature and Culture (National University of Malaysia Press, Kuala Lumpur, 1975), pp. 81–112.

conference later that year, and was subsequently appointed (with his (arch-rival as intellectual leader of the English-educated Malays, Za'ba) the organization's Adviser.

His role as confidante, adviser and friend to countless pilgrims in the Hejaz allowed full scope to Abdul Majid's talent (and liking) for putting the feet of others on the right path, and must, in addition, have done a good deal to broaden his own knowledge and understanding of Islam. In many ways he had always been a 'religious' person, as few responsible and educated Malays of his time were not. Though it is clear that his own early religious education was minimal, he showed continual concern in later years (reflected in the autobiography) for the quality of religious instruction at the Malay College, and seems for much of his life to have been of a pietistically reflective turn of mind. As with many others among the English-educated, he became greatly caught up in the Ahamadiyya movement of Khwaja Kamāl ud-Dīn (who visited Malaya in 1921, when Abdul Majid met him several times), and some of the most interesting passages in his autobiography relate to the resulting 'Qadiani' controversy. When he actually wrote the autobiography, in 1941, a sick man approaching his end, he was understandably disposed to dwell from time to time on 'last things', and it is clear that the nature of his faith, good Muslim though he was, was complex and individual. But though his views certainly changed in some respects in the course of his life, there is running through it a strong central thread of concern for the advancement of the Muslim *ummat,* community.

Towards the end of the 1930s, impressed as others were with the evident likelihood of another major international holocaust, Abdul Majid wrote the manuscript of a book (never published, and subsequently lost during the war itself) entitled 'Factors for World Peace in Islam', and in May 1940, shortly after relinquishing his post as Malay Pilgrimage Officer, he embarked on his last major task, the founding, and effectively the editing (though his son, Latiph, was nominal editor), of a monthly journal in English, *The Modern Light*. Calling itself (not altogether accurately) 'The first and only Malay Organ in English', it was markedly Islamic in interest, its masthead describing it as 'An Islamic Study of Eastern and Western Culture... Devoted to the material and spiritual welfare of the Malay in particular and of the Malayan Muslims in general', with the motto, 'To remind each other to the ways of Islam is the duty of every Muslim'. Thus were set out—as they are so clearly illustrated in the autobiography—the abiding themes of Abdul Majid's life: his role as a cultural broker between East and West, modernity and tradition; his combination of economic pragmatism (often embarked upon, seldom successful) and other-worldly earnestness; his eternal didacticism (not always or wholly removed from self-righteousness) and personal sense of duty. The journal ran for some eighteen issues (though copies of only the first twelve are now extant), dealing with everything from the then acute controversy over 'Who is a Malay?', to the need for a Malay National Bank and the nature of Wahhabism. Much of it Abdul Majid wrote himself, having previously toured the country in the face of ill health (as he says in the preface to the autobiography) to arouse support for it amongst his 'old boys' and others. Its back files deserve more critical scrutiny than they have yet received, just as the autobiography itself ought to (and hopefully now will) be better known.

In sum, then, what follows are the rich personal memories of a more than ordinary man, though one perhaps possessed of as much spirit and ambition as intellect, certainly one subject in full measure to the common human frailties, displaying frequently an immodesty so artless that few could take more than momentary exception to his personal strictures upon others, his conceits about himself, or his small pomposities—but a man, too, very much the creation of his time and with the courage to come to terms with it, the time being one in which the Malay people as a whole were faced with the major and on occasion overwhelming problems of colonial rule and social change. As a personal document it is always revealing, often amusing and frequently moving; as an historical one it is illustrative of a generation, a glass held up to the lives of some hundreds of men (and not a few women) whose being and whose concerns in the Malaya of the first forty years of this century touched upon those of Haji Abdul Majid bin Zainuddin, teacher and preacher, father and founder, guide, philosopher and friend.

Treatment of the Text

As has been stated, the manuscript exists in the form of three notebooks (now deposited with the National Archives of Malaysia), the first a red-covered writing pad, in which Abdul Majid worked from the front to the rear and then, on the verso, back again; the second and third buff-covered school exercise books. In preparing the text for publication, simple errors in spelling have been corrected where clearly accidental, but in all other respects, including those of paragraph arrangement, handling of proper names, and the like, the original has been let stand. The pagination of the original (as numbered by Abdul Majid) has been inserted in the margin of the printed text (with a slash in the text indicating the juncture proper), in order to allow reference to the original. Occasional additions by the editor, to resolve ambiguities or make the text clear, have been enclosed in square brackets, and any omissions (there are very few) have been indicated by three or four full points at the appropriate gap in the text. Alterations or omissions by Abdul Majid himself (of which, again, there are few) are signified in the footnotes.

Acknowledgements

The greatest measure of gratitude is due to Haji Muhammad Zin b. Ayub, who, as Abdul Majid's son-in-law (married to the late Hajjah Aminah) looked after the manuscript with every possible care for very many years, allowed me to prepare it for publication, and has now presented it to the Malaysian National Archives. In addition I owe to him, as I do to Abdul Majid's son, Haji Latiph, a lasting debt for supplying vast amounts of oral information about the family, for use in the notes. I hope that the result does not disappoint or in any way offend them. I am grateful, too, to a great many other people who helped me with identifications and other information concerning people mentioned in the text, and in particular to the late Raja Razman b. Raja Abdul Hamid (Kuala Kangsar), Datuk Abdullah b. Muhammad (Johore Bahru), and Datuk Wan Ibrahim b. Wan Suloh (Alor Setar). The many others who have contributed are too numerous to list, but not too numerous for me to continue to feel gratitude towards. I am also, as on so many other occasions, especially grateful to the archives and libraries that have assisted me, in particular the National Archives of Malaysia, the University of Malaya and University of Singapore Libraries, and the Library of the Royal Commonwealth Society, London. Finally, I wish to thank the Institute of South-east Asian Studies, Singapore, for affording typing assistance in preparing the final draft while holding a Visiting Fellowship there, and to the National Endowment for the Humanities, Washington, which gave me a grant enabling me to spend part of 1972 at the Institute.

Columbia University,   WILLIAM R. ROFF
New York

The Wandering Thoughts of a Dying Man

PREFACE

'If I get into the mud and fall, it should be my
duty to warn others of the muddy place ——'

H.A.M.

It took me some time to decide upon the above title for what I am going to write. It certainly sounds strange to call myself a dying man; but how can I think otherwise. For one thing, I have never heard of any friend or acquaintance afflicted with the same disease as I am ever recover fully and be his old self again.

Somehow or other, he succumbs to it sooner or later. There was the case of Sheikh Yahya Afifi who went to Europe for treatment; and yet he died within two or three years after his return. He only lived up to about 50 years of age. Then there was the case of Dato Stia (Noordin) of Perak. He also lived up to about 50. I mention these two cases because in both cases, it could not be due to want of money with which to get the best of treatment that Science could offer. On the other hand, there is the case of Mohamed Tahir, Senior Co-operative Officer, Pahang. He is said to have kept down the sugar in his system by the regular use of insulin with the daily test of his urine. If he lives up to 70 or there about, then all sufferers of this terrible scourge should be told to follow his example faithfully!

In my case, although I have managed to control the disease for some considerable time by the/use of Pan-Melitus pills and such like, I became worse with the shock of bad news about my Fate! I was two months in hospital being treated with injections of insulin. But on the day I left the hospital, in spite of the doctor's assurance that there was no more sugar in my system, I did not feel myself. For two or three months I tried to keep healthy by taking long walks and doing changkol work.[1] When one morning whilst at the latter exercise I fainted; and so henceforth stopped all physical strain.

[1] I.e., gardening; a *cangkul* is a hoe.

About this time, mental work in the shape of writing seemed to get hold of my spirit. For over a year I was at it. It was about this time that one night I got up to find that I could not raise my legs and hands. Even speech seemed to have left me for when I tried to talk to my family who had come around me, I found I could not utter the words properly. I revived by taking some hot drinks. And next day, Dr. Samuels of Johore prescribed Mendaco for me. I got on alright after that, and soon felt fit to go on tour round Malaya.[2]

I think it must be my spirit that urged me to take the trip. For my health or physical self was evidently not up to the task, as when I got to Alor Star/I collapsed and fainted for nearly seven hours. My host, Inche Laidin, was very kind to me and got two doctors to attend to me. I must not forget though that one of the doctors was paid by Tunku Yaacob, Agricultural Officer for the State. Tunku Yaacob was one of my old boys.

But this did not send me home immediately as advised by the doctors. Instead, I continued the journey. Again, and again I collapsed. At Taiping, at Tapah, at Kuala Pilah and lastly at Kota Bharu. Still, I went on doggedly. The thought that I was doing a national service kept me up. Before I started from home the idea that I might fail in my mission did occur to me; but it was weighed down with the belief that at least I might waken up the people to a responsibility of their economic progress. One thing seems remarkable and that is the thought that I might not stand the strain never occurred to my mind.

I should not forget to mention that at Kota Bharu, Nik Ahmad Kamil was particularly kind to me as his guest.[3] He got the services of Dr. K.L. Mah to attend to my case.

In spite of all the care of the various doctors I got back to Johore feeling very wretched. I can remember the morning I arrived at the Station, waited/by Latiff and his children: but I was not my old self again in many respects.

[2]This tour was undertaken to introduce and publicize his monthly magazine, *The Modern Light* (May, 1940–? Sept. 1941). See Editorial Introduction, above, pp. xiii–xiv.

[3]Nik Ahmad Kamil b. Nik Mahmud (b. 1909), son of the then Datuk Perdana Mentri of Kelantan, was at the time deputy chief minister of the state, having returned in 1931 from studying law in Britain.

In time I felt that my eye-sight was affected. And later, I remember being taken to Dr. D'Cotta for consultation. He advised me to get glasses.

So, glasses were bought for me by Ali. And Dr. Thompson of the Thompson Optical Co. told me that the cause for my bad eye-sight was diabetes. Dr. D'Cotta said there was acidity in my urine, besides the usual sugar.

I was told to have insulin injections and Latiff[4] gave me tablets of the Milk of Magnesia—the latter for the acidity.

It must be about three months now that I have been having the above; but I feel that I am getting worse and worse. There is nothing which I can describe as signs of improvement. Indeed, I often believe that when I feel giddy, I lie down to. . . .[5] Indeed, recovery will be a miracle! But of course, as long as there is life, there is hope!

SINGAPORE
1ST RAMADHAN 1360 A.H.
22ND SEPTEMBER 1941 A.D.

---

[4]His elder son (b. 1909), more often in later years spelt Latiph. See below, note 27.

[5]Omission in original.

BOOK ONE

HAVING written the Preface, I found it difficult how (or rather *where*) to start writing these Memoirs: I was thinking practically all day yesterday without coming to a decision on what subject I should write first.

It appeared to me that every subject I could think of claimed my first attention.

However, as this is the month of Ramadhan, my thoughts naturally centre round it and the fasting that I observed in the past. I remember clearly that I seldom missed my fast during this month every year. It was in Kuala Kangsar early in my life that I enjoyed this month. I was then a teacher in the Malay College, Kuala Kangsar. The school always closed for about six weeks for Puasa and Hari Raya.[1] Haji Mohammad Nur who was the College Qur'an and Religious teacher was the Imam of the town.[2] He was a great Qari (Qur'an Reader) with a sweet voice and a favourite of H.H. Sultan Idris of Perak. This Ruler was a great man and patronised Qaris who came from all over Malaya to Kuala Kangsar during Ramadhan.[3]

---

[1] Abdul Majid taught at the Malay Residential School (as it was then called) from 1907. *Bulan Puasa* is Malay for 'fasting month'; *Hari Raya* is the *'Id al-Fiṭr,* the feast that follows.

[2] A Mandailing from Tapanuli, Sumatra, Muhammad Nur appears to have been brought to Pusing, Perak, as a child, later becoming a Qur'ān teacher there. Sultan Idris invited him to Kuala Kangsar as a *qāri,'* and as Imam of the town mosque, and he was later (c. 1908 or 1909) appointed district *kathi,* becoming also College Qur'an teacher in 1909 (see below, p. 64). He died aged about sixty, possibly in the early 1920s. (Interviews with Raja Razman b. Raja Abdul Hamid, Kuala Kangsar, and Haji Abdullah b. Haji Muhammad Salleh, Ipoh, 1967.)

[3] Raja Idris b. Raja Iskandar became Sultan of Perak in 1887, and died in 1916.

Of the people who thus came to Kuala Kangsar, I remember being told of Haji Sulaiman Johore. I saw this man some years afterwards in Singapore and I learnt that he was a brother-in-law of the late/Hon.Inche Eunos, whose father was a Dato and Head of the Police in Johore. The old man's photograph appears in my book: *The Malayan Kaleidoscope* where he is shown as a Malay Police Officer. His name was Dato Abdullah. Haji Sulaiman must have commanded great respect as a Qari to be able to marry a daughter of the Head of Police in Johore.[4]

When I saw him, he was already an old man,—somewhere about sixty years of age. And I know that there were gramophone records of his Qur'an reading. I remember he had a big voice.

During the time I was in Kuala Kangsar, there was no more of the Ramadhan Qur'an-party, although Sultan Idris still paid the Qaris who read the Qur'an during the fasting month. In my time the Qaris were paid $30 to $100 each which was paid three or four days before the Hari Raya. I must mention that the Qur'an-reading took place in the Kuala Kangsar Mosque, whereas during the time when Haji Sulaiman Johore came, it took place at Bukit Chandan in the Sultan's palace.

There was another famous Qari, a Patani man, who came to Kuala Kangsar about that time; but I cannot remember his name, although it was mentioned to me before. I suppose I forgot his name as I never saw him in person as I did Haji Sulaiman Johore: But during the time in which I took part in the Qur'an-reading parties and of which I now write, the people who came to the mosque regularly were the mosque officials, the religious officials and some old men religiously inclined. Their names were Haji Mohammad Nur, Bilal Manap, Bilal Din who formed the first group;[5] Haji Mohamed Tahir, Kathi, and his brother Haji Abdul

---

[4]Nothing is known of Haji Sulaiman. Datuk Abdullah b. Tahir was Datuk Setia of Johore, and his son Muhammad Eunos had a distinguished career in Singapore public life, as editor of the newspapers *Utusan Melayu* and *Lembaga Melayu* (1907–31), and the first Malay to serve on the Municipal Commission (from 1922) and the Straits Settlement Legislative Council (from 1924). Datuk Abdullah's photograph is between pp. 103–4 in Abdul Majid's *The Malayan Kaleidoscope* (Kuala Lumpur, Selangor Press, 1935).

[5]Manap was senior *bilal* (Ar. *muezzin*, crier to prayer) of the town

Hamid who formed the second group;[6] old Haji Mohamed Sa'id, Pandak Kamal of the Malay Art School and others of the third group.[7] The names I give were those of the people who were more regular in coming and made themselves conspicuous in one thing or another. For example, Haji Mohammad Nur, the Imam, was leader of the party and organiser of the show. Haji Mohamed Tahir, the Kathi, gave us the Malay translation of the Qur'an, whenever the verses were important enough, in his opinion, to be translated for our enlightenment. Haji Abdul Hamid his brother, though quite good in his Qur'an-reading and an able Qur'an translator, was head in the Kitchen or Cooking Department. The food that he produced with all of us as his assistants was universally proclaimed as quite good. This was particularly because as everyone present was in some way/responsible in the preparation of the food, it was not likely that anyone would take to criticising his own actions. Then again, the fact that the food was taken in company during the 'buka puasa'[8] was conducive to its being appreciated. Lastly, if anyone had a particular fancy for any dish or sweetmeats, he was not forbidden to bring it from home and the company was never unwilling to help him to finish such home products, except in one particular case. This was the strong black coffee brought by old Haji Mustafa, the father-in-law of Shaikh Tahir Jalaluddin, who lived near the Railway Station.[9]

---

mosque, and in 1909 became assistant Qur'ān teacher at the Malay College; Din was his deputy as *bilal*. Both were Kuala Kangsar born and bred.

[6] Muhammad Tahir was district *kathi* until 1908 or 1909, when he was succeeded by Haji Muhammad Nur (note 2.) His brother later became Visiting Qur'ān Teacher for the state, with supervisory duties. See below, p. 134 and note 40.

[7] A local man, Pandak Kamal was head of the Malay Art School in Kuala Kangsar, started by the British to encourage Malay arts and crafts. The school was still in existence in 1924 (when some of its products were displayed at the Wembley Empire Exhibition), but closed soon after.

[8] The daily 'breaking of the fast' at sundown.

[9] Muhammad Tahir b. Jalaluddin al-Azahari, from Minangkabau, the leading Malay reformist intellectual in the peninsula during the first decades of this century, had married a daughter of Haji Mustafa b. Datuk Menteri Satu in Kuala Kangsar in 1901.

The party was always a happy one, with plenty of good stories and good jokes. Old Haji Mohamed Sa'id was a good clown, while Pandak Kamal was easily the second. Even old Haji Mustafa could be entertaining and comical whenever he chose to be so.

It is said that a good joke once saved a Sultan from an awkard situation.

It is said that once Sultan Idris had a quarrel with his wife, the Raja Permaisuri. The quarrel developed into such serious proportions that in the royal bedchamber husband and wife slept separately between barricades/of pillows and mattresses. So serious was it that it is said the Raja Permaisuri always moved with a Kris and had even consulted Sir Frank Swettenham, then British Resident of Perak,[10] whether she would be hanged if she murdered anyone! The whole palace was aghast and expected a tragedy any minute. No one dared to speak, much less to suggest a reconciliation between the royal couple.

It was when the situation was at its worst that Haji Mohamed Sa'id appeared on the scene. He was of course warned that the Raja Permaisuri had a Kris with her and meant to use it, but, nothing daunted, Haji Mohamed Sa'id went to the royal bedchamber and saw the seriousness of the situation. He seated himself on a sofa between the royal couple and began relating the story of a Chinese convert repeating his prayers in Arabic. The pronunciation of the words he uttered and the gestures he made were so very awkard and comical that those who saw and heard it would be moved to a good laughter. The story must have been repeated many times but the company did not seem to lose the comic side of the story and laughed every time they heard the story. Perhaps the fact that Haji Mohamed Sa'id repeated it must have added to its comicality. Anyhow, both Sultan Idris and the Raja Permaisuri were moved to laughter when they heard it repeated by Haji Mohamed/Sa'id, perhaps for the tenth time! And once they started to laugh, Haji Mohamed Sa'id kept it up by relating other comical incidents, so much so till at last they unconsciously supported and contradicted each other's statements.

[10]Frank Athelstane Swettenham entered the Straits Settlements Civil Service in 1870, and was Acting British Resident of Perak from 1884 to 1886, and Resident from 1889 to 1895.

In short, they were carefully wheedled into taking an interest of and in each other so that the result was that in the end both saw the wisdom of effecting a reconciliation and the folly of keeping away from each other.

Everyone was of course pleased to see the beloved Ruler and his favourite wife in amicable terms again, and Haji Mohamed Sa'id was regarded henceforth as something of a hero for his useful service.

This incident must have been told to us so many times that most of us began to think the ability to relate a comical or humorous story at the proper critical time would be useful. So, almost everyone of us started telling such stories to the company. I need not record these stories here because some of them are obscene. But they all did excite laughter.

One day, Haji Abdul Hamid, in charge of the cooking for the company in the Mosque came at 5.45 p.m., instead of at 1 p.m., which was his habit. His late arrival was a serious affair indeed,— only half an hour before the 'Buka Puasa'! Everyone had prepared some taunting/words or phrase with which to rebuke or censure him. But when he did come at last no one seemed to be able to find the words or phrase: he walked briskly and was waving his hands to all the crowd asking them to be patient and then listen to his explanation. What he told them was that he had had a big trouble all day with his better half. He explained how a woman could be a nuisance when she chose to be so. In this particular case, even his *serban*[11] was hidden away from him by her. It was in vain that he asked her to get it for him: she was determined to annoy him.

When we heard this, all our feelings against the man for his lateness melted into sympathy.

'But how did you manage to come here at all?' asked one of us.

'By a little piece of wisdom that I learnt during my lifetime; and that is, no woman was ever made to control man and his movements, but vice versa. So, I thought of a humorous incident in our married life and related it to her. Right enough she at once

---

[11]A turban or head cloth wound round a white skull-cap and worn by those who have made the pilgrimage to Mecca.

smiled and laughed. And I got my serban from her: so I came!'

Needless to add, when we heard the story we all had a hearty laugh also, and admired Haji Abdul Hamid for his wit and wisdom!

7   Besides the above, this month of Ramadhan sticks in my mind as the month in which my father died. It was a *malam Jumaat*,[12] the 22nd of the month in the year 1340 A.H. The English year was 1922.[13] I was then stationed at Telok Anson holding the post of Malay Assistant Inspector of Schools, Perak. The news of the death came to me unexpected. On the Thursday 21st of Ramadhan[14] I went to Sabak Bernam to pay the salaries of teachers there. My wife was against my going; but I ignored her advice. When I returned at 5.30 p.m. that day (I had waited and delayed at Hutan Melintang in order to be home shortly before the Buka Puasa) there was a telegram waiting for me with the sad news that my father was seriously ill. The telegram had come early in the morning, after I had left.

I thought of going back home that night after *buka Puasa*; but Kechik, my Chinese driver, told me there was the leaky tank that had to be patched before we could go. So the tank was sent to be patched; and at about 10 p.m. when the tank was patched, I said we should start. But the family and friendly advice was that we should start the next morning. So, I agreed.

Next morning at about 9 a.m., when we were making prepara-
8   tions to go another telegram came/and this time the message said that my father had expired during the night.

So, off we went as soon as we got ready. But the journey of about 120 miles did not take us the usual five to six hours to cover. The patched or repaired tank continued to be leaky all the way. We had to stop very often to fill the tank with water, lest it got burnt. We did not reach our destination till about 9 p.m. that night. I remember having my *buka puasa* somewhere in Bukit Kanching.

[12]Friday's eve, i.e., Thursday evening or night. By Malay/Muslim reckoning, the day runs from sunset to sunset. Friday, being the day of congregational prayer, is regarded as an auspicious day on which to be born or to die.

[13]19 May 1922.

[14]In error for 22 Ramadhan.

When we got to my father's house, he was already buried five or six hours. Haji Mas'ood, a cousin of my father, who was in charge of the whole ceremony told us that the burial took place at 5 p.m., that being the latest time he could keep it waiting.[15]

My sister who was in Kedah had not yet arrived. No telegram was sent to her by Haji Mas'ood; but I sent one from Telok Anson. When she came, she called at Telok Anson first, thinking that father was with me there when he died. She must have felt disgustingly disappointed when she got to my house to find that the death did not take place there. When she came at last, father had already been three days in the grave.

I do not know how she felt when she went to/the grave as I did not go with her. But I know when I went I could not help crying and did not stop till long after I got back to the house.

I remember my sister blaming and scolding Haji Mas'ood for not sending her the telegram. Indeed, if I did not send her one from Telok Anson she would not know of father's death.

Haji Mas'ood was, as I said above, a cousin of my father; and we addressed him as 'Bapa'. It was not right for my sister to scold him. But I think I did not only endorse my sister's conduct towards him but actually used some harsh words to him myself. He was in my opinion quite wrong in not informing my sister by telegram. Indeed, he should have told us of the old man's illness from the very beginning, instead of waiting till he died. In fact, he had acted on behalf of my father as if my sister and I had no right whatsoever in the matter. For example, he had arranged for the marriage of the old man without consulting us.

And what a marriage it was!

I learnt afterwards that the woman actually made my father to pay during his last illness for the chickens she cooked for him. This was because the chickens happened to belong to her.

Anyway, my sister and I never discovered the money/that my wife knew he had with him. Even the roskopf watch bought by my father before his marriage to my mother was there no more. Everything of value had been kept aside by my step-mother.

---

[15]Malay practice is to bury before dusk on the day of death, this being popularly regarded as enjoined by Islam.

What is worse, Haji Mas'ood always backed up the woman's statements in her explanation of the disappearance of any of my father's belongings.

God knows best and will be merciful to us all on the day of judgement!

11   Today I propose to discuss what a dying man thinks of death. I think that no one regards death as a fearful thing. After all, it can only be a transformation from an earthly life into a spiritual life.

Science has proved and declared to the world that nothing in the material world is lost. In the same way, I believe it is definite that nothing in the spiritual world is lost.

I know it is unorthodox to say this; but on the other hand I know also that religious authorities disclose secrets about death to their pupils for a consideration.

When I was in Matang,[16] the local Imam, Haji Musa, once said that there are five things which last for ever. One of these five I remember, is the spirit of man!

Then again, my wife told me when she was in Mecca she heard the mother of Sheikh Yaakub Perak[17] say that when a person dies, his or her spirit returns to the world as the spirit of [a] new-born babe.

These seem to confirm my theory that the spirits are not conveyed, as it were, from our present world to another, which exists somewhere else in the universe. It should be clear, therefore, that the 'next world'—which is so often repeated in religious subjects—really means 'the next age'. In any case, the Arabic word 'akhirat' ...seems to me to support this contention.[18]

In other words, the spirit or soul of man lives in this world

[16] Abdul Majid was appointed Acting Headmaster of the Malay Teachers' Training College at Matang, Perak, on the departure on leave of the incumbent, A. Keir, in March 1919.

[17] Ya'akub b. Ismail, born in Mecca of a Kelantan father who was a *'syaykh haji'* (pilgrimage agent) there, may have been known as Syaykh Ya'akub Perak because he himself (also as *syaykh haji*) looked after mainly Perak pilgrims. (Interview with Haji Idris al-Marbawi, Cairo, 1965).

[18] *'Akhirat'* (from the Arabic *akhirā,*) denotes in Malay 'the hereafter'.

over and over again. I know for a fact that the/Qur'an in the Chapter on 'The Cow'[19] talks of life and death being recurrent two or three times, and not only once, as the popular belief seems to lead us to accept.

Anyhow, I also remember reading in the Islamic Review, edited by Khwaja Kamaluddin,[20] that death opens to the spirit (or soul of man) wonderful opportunities for unlimited progress.

As against this theory, there is the belief that the spirit on being perfected returns to the 'face of its Creator' *Wajhi'llāh* [lit. 'the countenance of Allah']. In Hinduism, this is described as Nirvana!

But here, please do not run away with the idea that I am a Hindu in my belief. The truth is I think that Hinduism is a corrupted form of the old religion of Abraham.

I am sure that Abraham has been deified into Brahma; and the Hindu Trinity or Three Gods are none other than the three Divine qualities described in the 'Fatihah' as (1) *Rabb al-'ālamīn* (2) *ar-Raḥman ar-Raḥīm* (3) *Mālik yaum ad-dīn*.[21]

The digression of man from the pure monotheistic belief and teaching of Abraham must have been very subtle! Anyhow, the well-known miracle of Abraham in being put into the fire and not burnt seems to me to have come down to the Hindu priests who can to this day do the fire-walking!

I cannot presume ever to have lived a perfect life. So I expect after my/death I shall be re-born to this world. And this reminds

---

[19] The second *sura* of the Qur'ān known as 'The Cow' (*al-Baqara*) from the story of a yellow heifer that occurs in it.

[20] Originally from India, Kamāl ud-Dīn, a leading adherent of the Lahore branch of the Ahmadiyya movement, went to England in 1912 as a Muslim missionary, and in 1914 established his headquarters at Woking, Surrey, from whence he published *The Islamic Review*. This journal had something of a following among English-educated Muslims in Malaya, and when Khwāja Kamāl ud-Dīn visited the country in 1921 he was widely welcomed. Cf. below, pp. 133 ff.

[21] *Al-Fātiḥa*, the opening *sura* of the Qur'ān; *Rabbul-'ālamīn*, Lord of the worlds; *ar-Raḥmān ir-Raḥīm*, the merciful, the compassionate; *Māliki yaum id-dīn*, Master of the day of judgement. The *Fātiḥa* is frequently used as an exordium to prayers of many kinds.

me of an incident that happened when Hashim was born.[22]

My mother who died two days after the birth of this boy took the child in her hands and kissed it passionately saying meanwhile: What a nice smell a new arrival from paradise has! (Ah! wangi-nya bau orang baru datang dari shorga!)

Perhaps the soul of the dead after going though a purifying process for the sins that he committed is taken at last to paradise to be reborn to this world!

Only God knows what happens to us beyond the bourne! We can only expect His Mercy.

God's power and authority is absolute! He pardons whomsoever He pleases and He punishes whomsoever He pleases, as it is said in the Qur'an, *Yaghfiru liman yashā'u wayu 'adhdhibu man yashā'u, wa'llāhu 'alā kulli shai'in qadīr* [Sura 2, v. 284: 'He forgives whom He pleases and punishes whom He pleases, for God has power over all things']

As I have said in the previous pages, I am not afraid of Death. No one has ever/escaped and will ever escape Death. It will be unnatural for me to expect to be the only exception in the whole world. No amount of human power, authority or wealth can ever avert that fate. The Qur'an is very explicit on that point, *adhā jā'ā ajaluhum lā yasta' khiruna sā'atan walā yastaqdimūn* [Sura 7, v. 34: 'When their term is reached, not an hour can they cause delay, nor (an hour) can they advance (it in anticipation)']

What I am most anxious about is that I may not have to suffer worse than the present sufferings. As I am now, my eye-sight is nearly gone; and my hands and feet have become numb. My right foot in particular is the worst. Should I go totally blind or become totally numb, then I shudder to think what will happen to me. I cannot expect my wife or any of my two grown-up sons to be able to nurse or look after me in such a helpless condition.

But the Merciful God, I am sure, knows what He is about in my case!

---

[22] Abdul Majid's second son, Hashim, was born early in February 1913.

In a way, I am glad that I am made to suffer for my sins. Perhaps I may be spared further punishment in the next life. *Inna'llaha ghafūrun raḥīm.* [Sura 2, v. 199: 'Indeed God is oft-forgiving, most merciful.']

On the other hand, there is a possibility of recovery particularly if my/complaint is due to the great shock from the bad news about myself, as Latiph[23] seems to think and once told me. But the recovery will be a gradual one and take many years to effect. The only circumstances that support this theory are:– (1) I sleep well as a rule, about 9 to 10 hours at night and 2 to 3 hours in the day-time; (2) I still have strength from the grip in both my hands. (The latter test is one that was told to me by Dr. K.L. Mah, Medical Officer, Kota Bharu, Kelantan.)

Looking back at my past life in my present condition, I am forced to believe/that the world looks upon the success or failure of a man in terms of £. s. d. or $ and cents, plus power and authority. Here I am compelled to confess that such is not the view I have held. Somehow or other, it has never struck me that I should work for money or power. The two appeared to me to be just incidents in a man's life. At least, no one can accuse me of scheming for the possession of any of those two.

For example, as a young man I never tried to find a wife with money, though many such girls were offered to me to be my bride. Neither did I ever attempt to hold any position with power or authority. If I rose at all to any height, it was by sheer merit. Truth to say, all my promotions were forced on me, not applied for, much less schemed.

To me, the useful not the great is the thing that never dies. This is the principle that guided my life. And as a teacher, I am sure I did make myself as useful as I could. Within a few years from the start, I had already produced the 'Vocabulary and Grammer for Beginners'.[24] That this book is very useful,

---

[23] Abdul Majid's elder son, born in May or June 1909.

[24] A primer in English for Malays, first published (in Singapore by the Methodist Publishing House), about 1910, while Abdul Majid was teaching at the Malay College. Cf. below, pp. 60.

there is a lot of evidence to prove it.

I think by this time, it has got to the seventh edition. Besides, there are many Malays today who would not have learnt English but with the use of that/book. It is so very helpful that it explains to them very clearly the difference in the construction of an English sentence from that of a Malay one. Thus, the student using it grasps at once the correct way of stringing the English words.

Similarly, about ten years after that, I prepared the 'Malay Self-Taught'.[25] This book helps Englishmen or English-speaking persons to pick up Malay words and their correct use. On many occasions, I was told that my book helped them in their study of Malay.

I am proud to think that I have been useful to my fellow men during my life.

But, strange to say, it has never bothered my head to see that I am suitably rewarded for the useful books I have written.

Then again, I remember two or three colleagues of mine who never missed writing in for promotion or some such recognition beneficial to them immediately they had done some good work. Whereas with me it was different. I never wrote in or pressed my claim for promotion or recognition immediately after I had done any good work. I must say that I was officially thanked several times for good work.

And on one occasion, the Chief Secretary to the Government, F.M.S., was so pleased with a Report/on some delicate problem that I prepared that he actually offered to give some suitable appointment to my eldest son. But, foolish man that I was, I did not accept the offer.[26]

Some years afterwards, my son was refused the same appointment through a false report of a European officer against his conduct.

However, I have the satisfaction of knowing that this European

---

[25]Published in London in 1920 by E. Marlborough & Co. Ltd., in their 'Self-Taught Series of European and Oriental Languages', this is still in print, the fourteenth impression of the original edition having been published in 1958.

[26]This incident is further referred to below, p. 89.

BOOK ONE 17

officer lost his position through a report made by me. I had
my revenge on the man as a result of a prayer I made at the
Kaabah! I was actually asked to report against this man.
And he deserved what I said against him. He was of the type
that is a disgrace to the fair name of his great nation and a worm
that saps the life of the British Empire!

It was evident to me that I was *fated* to experience this failure
or financial crash. For, apart from my callousness [*sic*] in money
matters, as shown above, there were several other circumstances
that willy-nilly led up to it. Perhaps I should recount them
one by one.

First, there were my sons who did not get employment.[27]

[27]Abdul Majid had two sons, Abdul Latiph (1909–) and Hashim
(1913–43). Both attended Malay schools in Kuala Kangsar and Telok
Anson, and were educated in English at King Edward VII School,
Taiping; Anglo-Chinese School, Telok Anson; Malay College;
Government English School, Kuala Kangsar; and Methodist Boys'
School, Kuala Lumpur. From 1928 Latiph served briefly with the
F.M.S. Police and in 1929 went to Mecca, there marrying Sharifah
Eshah bte Sayyid Othman Abu Sarir of Mecca, by whom he has ten
children. Returning to Malaya in 1931 he went into business with
his father and brother, mainly in Singapore, and took up free-lance
journalism. In 1939 he became editor of the monthly *Modern Light*,
started by his father in Johore Bharu. Having been a member of
the Federated Malay States Volunteer Rifles and of the Singapore
Volunteer Corps, Latiph took part in anti-Japanese activities early
in the occupation, and was imprisoned for nearly a year, later serving
under the Japanese in the Carimon Islands. After the war he became
a founder member of the Malay Nationalist Party (MNP), in Ipoh,
was editor for six months of the party journal *Voice of the People*,
and later went to work for the party in Kelantan. When the MNP
was banned in 1948 he served in various government departments
in Kota Bharu, retiring from the Police Department there in 1968.
In 1932 he published *Sabīl ul-Rashād* (Selangor Press, Kuala Lumpur), a textbook in comparative religion used in Selangor religious
schools. Hashim, on leaving school in the early 1930s, joined the
Straits Settlements Customs Service briefly, and then went into
business. He married Fatimah bte Colonel Muhammad of Batu
Pahat, by whom he had four children. As a member of the Singapore
Royal Naval Volunteer Reserve he was imprisoned for a time early
in the occupation, and died of illness in 1943, shortly before his father.
(Interviews with Haji Abdul Latiph, Kota Bharu and Petaling Jaya,
1960–72.)

Second, there were the pilgrims who borrowed money from me and did not repay.[28] (One case in particular went so far as to suggest that his wife should remain behind with me as security for the loan. But as it turned out not a cent did he pay me.)

Third, business men got out of their obligations to me by dirty tricks. (In one particular instance, a certain Australian miner was shown a piece of rich tin-mining land; but he declared after inspecting the land for over a week that the tin was not in paying quantities. But he got the land eventually, the application was made in the name of his brother-in-law. The agreement with me was made in his own name.)

This land was situated about midway between Haad Yai and Singgora.[29] It was H.E. the Siamese Governor of Singgora who came to know of this rich tin land; and he disclosed it to the Raja Muda of Selangor, Tunku Musaeddin.[30] The Raja Muda, in his turn, took me into his confidence and suggested that I should get in touch with a miner, expecting of course that I should take the precautions to protect his interests. I came to know the Australian miner through Yap Tai Chi, a Chinese merchant in Kuala Lumpur and a son of a former Kapitan China.[31]

H.E. the Governor of Singgora, thinking that the application for the land was made in the name of a friend of the Raja Muda of Selangor, of course saw to it that the application was officially approved.

About a year ago, a friend of mine, Inche Ahmad bin Yahya

[28] This refers to the period during which Abdul Majid was Malay Pilgrimage Officer in Jeddah, 1924–39.
[29] Haad Yai is the rail junction in southern Thailand for the east and west coast peninsular lines, and Singgora (Songkhla) the port town nearby.
[30] Tengku Musa'eddin (b. 1893), eldest son of Sultan Suleiman of Selangor, was Raja Muda (heir apparent) from 1920 to 1934, when he was removed from the succession upon the instigation of the then British Resident, T.S. Adams, and was the Selangor Malay representative on the Federal Council of the F.M.S. from 1927 to 1933.
[31] Presumably of the famous Yap Ah Loy (1837–85), Kapitan China of Selangor from 1868 until his death.

of Johore Bahru,[32] went on business to Patani; and on his return during the conversation he told me that he heard it definitely that the mining land between Haad Yai and Singgora turned out to be very rich one. He did not, of course, say who owned the mines; but I think the brother-in-law of the Australian miner was at the bottom of the whole show. Neither the Raja Muda of Selangor, nor the Governor of Singgora, nor myself benefited by this rich tin-mining land! It certainly proves that we became the tools which helped to enrich the Australian miner and his friends.

Perhaps I should mention here that I was always, or rather *ever,* on the look out for good business propositions. There were other mining areas in which I interested the miners; but none of them proved to be a success to me. There was the land in Ulu Langat which was to have been bought and worked by Selangor Tin, Ltd.[33] Then, there was the land in Setapak in which I helped/a certain European miner from Ipoh—his name starts with a B; but I cannot remember it—to get round H.H. the Sultan of Selangor to agree to its conversion from an agricultural into a mining lease.[34] Then again, there were other areas in Perak and elsewhere.

But mining was not the only business proposition that interested me. Some years ago, I thought of importing goods from the Middle East to this country.

Of these things, the ones that I considered the most suitable for such importation were cigarettes (from Turkey), oranges, grape-fruit, olives, olive oil and preserved fruits (from Syria). In the case of the Turkish cigarettes, I had actually gone beyond

---

[32] A son of Datuk Yahya b. Awaluddin of Johore, known as Datuk Yahya Tinggi, Ahmad served for many years with the Johore Civil Service, but later went into business in Singapore.

[33] This company, which is not mentioned in Yip Yat Hoong, *The Development of the Tin Mining Industry of Malaya* (Kuala Lumpur, University of Malaya Press, 1969), has not been traced.

[34] Expansion of tin mining during the 1920s, especially by dredge, led to the passage of the Mining Enactment (No. 19 of 1928), providing that leases of land alienated for agricultural purposes could not be converted to mining leases without prior approval by the Sultan in Council.

making preliminary enquiries: in fact, I had managed to get the agency for them and brought £10 worth of samples. As Turkish cigarettes are the monopoly of the Turkish Government, I had managed to get the services of the Turkish Minister in Jeddah to help me secure the agency.

From the samples I had obtained, I was sure that there was money to be made from their importation. The only drawback was that these cigarettes were obtainable only in packets. I was promised that they would be packed for me especially in tins; but they wanted me to guarantee the purchase of a certain number of such tins./This meant that I would have to make a deposit of about £1000, and have at my command another £500 to make the purchases. In other words, I required $15,000/- to enable me to start this business.

I thought of a wealthy friend to give me the helping hand. This friend had started to show me that he was willing to have 'friendly' connection with me in business or other profitable work. One year he sent an introduction letter through his brother-in-law who was on pilgrimage. He said that the man was the Raja Muda of a State somewhere in Borneo. And quite willing to be on such friendly terms with such influential people, I entertained the Raja Muda suitable to his position. I thought that the man who introduced his princely brother-in-law to me would at least listen to me if I had a business proposition that would prove profitable to him and to me. But wonder of wonders, when I sent word to him informing him that I would like to see him whenever it was convenient for him, he did not even have the courtesy to reply to my message!

I now understand why most people in position never condescended to entertain or show the ordinary courtesy to others. Or, it goes to prove why there is hardly any understanding among Malays in business. Otherwise, I should not have been born among Malays, as one Chinese clerk who knew me and my ways once remarked. I have said above that I was fated [to] fail; and fail I did in every attempt I made.

It may be that I was a fool. Mr. Thambipillay, a teacher in the Victoria Institution, was once reported to me by a countryman of his to have remarked that he saw in me the *undeveloped soul* of a

man with fertile brains. Mr. Thambipillay was a Hindu.
I know my father once said that I was fated to be remembered only as a writer! One wonders whether human knowledge and wisdom has ever developed to be able to see the Fate of anyone! If it has, I think it can only see very faint glimpses of the future. The Qur'an says only God knows what is in store for us.

To probe into the future and find out what it has for the world has always been an amusement, if not an attraction, to man. And I am no exception to this human tendency. My interest in it, however, is not that of an astrologer, or a money-making professor of the astrological art. What attracts me most is the future of Islam. I do not mean whether Islam will conquer the world and rule it by the force of might. But I mean whether the truths that Islam teaches will be accepted or otherwise. It seems to me that the influences in the world tend rather to reject/than to accept these Islamic truths. The glaring instances of such Islamic truths are:— charity (*zakat* and *fitrah*),[35] usury (*riba*), and polygamy. The general tendency in the world today seems to me to be: grab, grab, grab; so that it is hardly to be expected that man will agree willingly to practise charity and stop usury. There is no end to the greed of man which seems to be curbed only by Law, and not by Religion. While polygamy is destined to become extinct when woman is taught to believe that she is the *equal* of man.

I have seen 'Muslims' take pork without any trace of shame; and I have known 'respectable' Malays committing grievous sins without any signs of regret. The worst part of it is that as long as these sinners have money, the Muslim community do not seem to have anything to say against them. In short, these sinners are not shunned as outlaws; and are thereby encouraged, rather than discouraged, in their evil practices. Money seems to speak with authority, not God and His Law.

One cannot help asking with such circumstances if Islam is a

---

[35]Malay '*fitrah*' is the *zakāt al-fiṭr*, the obligatory gift of provisions (or their equivalent in cash) at the end of the fasting month; *zakāt* proper, levied in Malaya only on the production of *padi*, is ideally applicable to a variety of kinds of property.

Divine religion for the salvation of man.

My religious sentiments are not assumed, but are deep-rooted as the result of the careful upbringing of religious parents.

I remember at the age of seven, I was already taught/many of the essential things that a man should know in religion. I could read the Qur'an,[36] I learnt the articles of Faith *'aqā'id al-imān*,[37] I knew how to say my prayers and I had started fasting. I also remember that my father and mother would prefer to miss a meal rather than to miss saying their prayers, or fasting or any other religious duty. But compare this religious attitude with that of any of his grandchildren! The reverse is the case with any of them!

Then again, take the case of my own grandchildren! My son appears to me to be more anxious about the secular education of his sons than their religious training. He has not even taken steps to get them to read the Qur'an!

This tendency to neglect the religious side of the Malay's life appears to me to be somewhat general. Even in the case of those who are sent for religious studies either in Mecca or in Cairo, I believe they are led to expect remunerative appointments as Qadhis, Chief Qadhis, Muftis or Sheikh-ul-Islam[38] as the reward for their religious zeal. Money is always at the bottom of man's ambitions, religious or otherwise.

Now, with such a tendency, is it unnatural for me to predict that Islamic truths will find it difficult to gain ground in the minds of man. It looks as if Money will rule the world and man's actions will be guided by Law, and not by Religion. Are we to regard

---

[36] That is to say, could read and recite the Arabic text of the Qur'ān, but without necessarily understanding the Arabic language.

[37] Although *al-'aqā'id* implies credal statements of more comprehensive scope, Abdul Majid is probably referring to the standard articles of faith, viz., belief in one God, His Messengers, His revelations, Angels, the Day of Judgement, and God's omnipotence.

[38] The state Mufti, technically 'jurisconsult', was also in many parts of the peninsula the administrative head of the whole religio-legal bureaucracy; the term 'Syaykh ul-Islam' was used in preference to 'Mufti' in some states. Cf. the sarcastic remarks on these dignitaries made by the visiting Minangkabau reformist, Haji Abdul Karim Amrullah, in 1916, quoted in Hamka, *Ajahku: Riwajat Hidup Dr. Abd. Karim Amrullah dan Perdjuangan Kaum Agama* (Djakarta, Widjaja, 1950), p. 19.

religious books as ancient history, and the Prophets of God as mere successful men? Or, is the world being slowly led to accept the principles of Communism where a man may take unto himself any woman as wife as long as he and she agree to live together?

The Qur'an speaks of the ultimate triumph of Islam and Islamic teachings. God promises us this and assures us that He will take the necessary steps to bring about such results.

Are we to expect such a change over night? Or are we expected to take part in effecting the change?

To be sure, nothing ever happened in the past without man as the instrument of God!

Truly, this is a very critical period in the history of the world! Not only are the physical forces of the world pitted against one another, but the spiritual forces are likewise claiming for mastery!

If calm always comes after a tempest, we should have after the present upheaval the long waited for MILLENNIUM!

I would particularly recommend, or rather advise, my sons, relatives and friends/to study physiognomy. The Arabs have a saying: The face is the mirror of the heart. I must say that I was totally ignorant of this science. My choice of friends and servants was particularly a sad failure. My wife often remarked that I trusted everyone as if they all had a good heart like my own. Most of the friends I trusted proved to be my enemies in the end. And most of my servants were cheats. It did not matter how kind I was to them, they would be found them [*sic*] to have cheated me after they had gone. It seems to me that I had befriended ungrateful rogues, in many instances. Ramli bin Haji Ali was one of them.[39] The poor chap died soon after my prayers at the Kaabah to remove him, if he was not true! There were many others whom I need not mention here.

There seems to be no guiding principle among Malays such as

---

[39]Ramli had been 'adopted' by Abdul Majid in the early 1920s, on the death of his father Haji Ali, who had been a close friend. Ramli was a *munsyi* (language teacher, usually to Europeans) by profession, and was well known in Kuala Lumpur. He died around 1927, aged about thirty. The occasion of the difference referred to here is not known. (Interview with Haji Abdul Latiph b. Haji Abdul Majid, Kota Bharu, 1966.)

the one that the Arabs have: 'I have taken salt with that man; so I shall not do him any harm at whatever price.' A people that has no national guiding principles is bound to drown in these days of keen international competition!

27B My wife,—I mean my first wife, the mother of my grown-up children—is a good/old soul. The fact that we have lived together for 33 long years certainly speaks something about my attachment to her and hers to me. When I first came to know her, my impression of her was that of an unrefined diamond. I thought I would be useful in the refining process of her spirit. I did not know then that God says in the Qur'an: You do not guide those whom you love, but God guides those whomsoever He pleases. It appears to me now that we were fated to be the mate of each other, in order to complete God's own scheme. I remember the day—it was a Friday!—I first shook hands with her father, being told inwardly by some unseen spirit that he would be my father-in-law.[40] This was before I knew her. And when I first saw her in the distance walking with her aunt and some other female relatives and friends, something told me that there was my bride in the passing group of females. I did not even see her face as she was covered in the fashion of our Malay ladies. I am sure that she, on her part, did not know who I was then. Within a few days of this incident, I married her without consulting my parents.[41] It was a case of marriage prearranged in the heavens, as it were! It was a shock to the scheming parents who thought they would get a good bargain by securing me as their son-in-law. Some of these people were really rich and influential. And I was known to be a good scholar, both secular and religious (or *dunia* dan *akhirat,* as the Malay phrase has it).[42]

28 I was happy in the thought that I had married for love not for money or worldly/position. In my youthful enthusiasm, I believed that I could earn both with my attainments.

One day, I was in the Istana Negara Kuala Kangsar.[43] There

[40]For further details concerning this family, see below pp. 31-33.
[41]This would appear to have been mid-1908, when Abdul Majid was twenty-one.
[42]Lit., 'in this world and the hereafter', from the Arabic.
[43]*Istana Negara*—'state palace'; the Sultan's principal palace, on the

were many other people present. One of them was a man who was particularly anxious to get me as the husband of one of his many daughters. Seeing me there, he talked particularly on the promotions that his several sons-in-law had obtained in the Government Service. And he ended his talk with the remark that in order to get on in the Government Service one should [use] somebody as a prop.

I did not understand what he meant at first. But I soon found out that his remark was directed towards me and to none other. I was the only one of the Malay College Old Boys at that time who had had no promotion from the time I started work after leaving school. I was still teaching in the College; and he was sure I had been overlooked whenever good positions fell vacant because there was no one with influence to back me. As soon as I grasped his meaning, my spirit at once revolted against the man and his piece of wisdom. In spite of his age, I told him in the presence of the company that in my opinion the man who looked for a prop before he could stand was either suffering from paralysis or from rheumatism. I know he did not like my answer and he left us without saying a word.

9   But that was not the end of the man in his grievance towards me. He had, what he thought, was his revenge against me some years afterwards.

I was then in Telok Anson, having been promoted as Assistant Inspector of Schools, Perak.[44] He was made a Dato by Sultan Abdul Jalil.[45] One Friday I saw him and another Dato in the Telok Anson mosque during the Friday service. I invited both of them

---

hill known as Bukit Chandan.

[44] Abdul Majid was the first Malay Assistant Inspector of Schools, appointed in 1918 as a result of the new education policy brought about by the 'Report of Mr. R.O. Winstedt, Assistant Director of Education, S.S. and F.M.S., on Vernacular and Industrial Education in the Netherlands East Indies and the Philippines' (S.S. *Legislative Council Proceedings,* Council Paper No. 22, 1917).

[45] Sultan Abdul Jalil ibni Almerhum Sultan Idris came to the throne in 1916, on the death of his father, but himself died in 1918. '*Dato*' (the old spelling is retained in Perak, '*Datuk*' being the modern one elsewhere) is a chiefly rank, the degree and title here unspecified.

and a few of the local people to have dinner in my house that evening. I was then in the Government quarters next to the church close by to the Rest House. It was known as 'rumah Tuan Phillips' who was the Asst. Inspector of Schools, Perak, before me; and was a fairly large house.[46]

During dinner, I discovered that the man could not take any meat. So I had to send my servant to the town to get fish curry particularly for him. The dinner was not a grand affair that was meant to impress the guests, but just a suitable one to serve its purpose as the hospitality of one towards his fellow-men 'on a journey'. It did not last long to finish, but the usual conversation among the guests took us to about midnight before the company took their leave.

I went down to send them off as far as the gate. The man being the most highly educated of the crowd naturally was the leader in the conversation. Certain it was that he could discuss on many subjects. Without suspecting/him of anything I mechanically answered to his enquiry as to how many coconut trees there were in the compound. Then he asked me whether I could collect the coconuts from the trees; and as mechanically I told him that I could. His next words were very remarkable as it showed in what spirit he actually accepted my present friendly gesture. He said: 'I am sure you are a very fortunate man,—a favourite of the gods! —(orang bertuah)'.

Fool that I was I again did not catch his meaning then and there. I remember I did not say to him anything in reply. It was not till I got back to the house that I realised he had scored against me at last. I told my wife of what he said and why he did it![47]

I never met him or saw him after that. He died at sea while returning from the pilgrimage. And I was then acting Head Master of the Malay Training College at Matang.

I wonder what he would say if he were alive and saw me in my successes and present failure! He certainly took an interest in my welfare, even though it was in a selfish way indirectly!

---

[46]W.M. Phillips was a younger brother of C.M. Phillips, Assistant Master at Raffles Institution, Singapore, 1894–1906, and Head Master 1906–21.

[47]The point of this anecdote is elusive.

Both Islamic and Western philosophy agree that self should be served first. But like a rebel, I believe that self should be served last! I have said above that I married my first wife for love. But how is it, you will/ask that I married other women? The only explanation I can give is that I was *predestined* to have many wives.

There was a man from Kabul whom my father knew and regarded as a friend. He came to Kuala Kangsar one day when I was still a bachelor. I met him in the mosque and took him to my house as a guest. That evening he asked to be allowed to have a look into my palm. He staggered me by saying that I would marry either seven or nine times. Of the seven or nine women, he said only two would prove to be true wives to me. I told him that I could not believe him as it was my intention to have only one wife. He said that he did not doubt my intention; but must remember that there is such a thing as fate which every one of us follows in the course of our life. The next morning he left me and continued on his journey; and I never saw him again.

It was some years after my marriage that I discovered my financial position to be very unsound. Various circumstances had occurred to bring about this undesirable situation. A cousin whom I employed to take charge of a rubber estate which absorbed all my savings as an investment proved to be dishonest. I was forced by his dishonesty to get into debts more than I could pay. But the fall in the price of rubber immediately after the last Great War brought my position to a climax.[48] I had to sell the land for a mere song, leaving me in debts which took me two or three years/to clear. I got only about $25 every month out of my salary of $100.

It was during this time that I got a proposal for marriage from a woman who had some property which she earned by an evil reputation. I knew all this and could remember that I loathed the

---

[48] The average price of rubber per pound on the London market, which fluctuated between two and three shillings during the war, had fallen to ninepence (with a low of just under sevenpence) by 1922. (J.H. Drabble, 'The Plantation Rubber Industry in Malaya up to 1922', *Journal of the Malayan Branch, Royal Asiatic Society*, XL, 1 (1967), 76.)

sight of that woman. I did not refuse the proposal, however, when it was submitted to me. I told my wife about it and discussed it with her as a weighty matter. The discussion must have been one sided, or rather the mere forcing of my will upon hers, for though she agreed to my taking another wife, I found that at the time when I left the house to go for the marriage, she unconsciously dropped down as if her legs and knees had no more strength in them. It was nearly an hour before she recovered.

With such unhappy preliminaries, it could not be expected that the marriage would be a happy one. I did not go to her house as regularly as I should, so that once she actually served me with a Qadhi's summons for this irregularity.[49] Immediately after the hearing of the case I gave her the divorce, pronouncing the words in the Qadhi's Court!

It was indeed a case of good riddance of bad rubbish. She is remembered as having tried to poison my wife by sending her some poisoned cakes. Luckily for my wife, the woman who was entrusted to take the cakes to her warned her of the poison. The cakes were given to the fowls and those that ate the cakes immediately died! Such is the experience of true lovers in the East!

My other wives were taken more as cooks and household keepers than anything/else for my life in Jedda where I spent seven months in the year as Pilgrimage Officer.[50] It was an arrangement agreed to by my first wife as she herself could not go with me there. I said to her when I consulted her about taking the post in Jedda when it was offered by the Government to me that I would prefer *not* to go if I had to take another wife, she said that I should not be [so] foolish [as] to refuse the offer which would never come again; and added that she would be happier seeing me in my new position which must be regarded as a promotion and 'a feather in

---

[49] It is incumbent upon Muslims with more than one wife (up to the legal maximum of four) to preserve strict equity in treatment. The custom in Malaysia is to provide a separate dwelling for each wife—though in this instance it appears that the lady was able to remain in her own home, and the probability is that she was a *janda* (i.e., widowed or divorced).

[50] This was from 1924. See above, Introduction, pp. xi–xii.

my cap' even with [a] rival or rivals in my *harem* than otherwise. She thought it would be a disgrace to have no promotion in the Service. In short, she was very keen to see me accept the Jedda post. And I must say that I found it very difficult, if not impossible, for a Malay in the position I held to be without a wife. Conditions in Jedda and Mecca were not the same as in other places.

The reason why I married eight times altogether—not seven or nine, according to the prediction of the Afghan palmist—was because my second wives never appeared to me to be satisfied with the position they had, and so took measures to make me divorce my first wife. As soon as I discovered what they were up to, I would marry another one and send her away. In this way, I became to be known soon to be a man who married in order to divorce. This bad reputation was enhanced when in Mecca I married a certain woman one evening and I divorced her the next morning.

The result was that my proposal for marriage was turned down politely two or three times in Mecca so that it looked as if there was to be no more second wife for me in my life in Jedda.

But Sheikh Yaakub Perak,[51] to whom I entrusted my matrimonial arrangement, proved to be more resourceful than the demands of the situation. He stopped proposing for me to divorced women or widows (janda) and started to get a virgin girl (anak dara)! 'Abang Haji' (as he called me) 'has never married virgin girls all his life: let him have one!' he would say to his friends who helped him in the quest. So, after a short time, he was able to inform me that I was to marry the granddaughter of a great *"alim"*.[52]

The girl was an orphan, having lost her grandfather and father who died recently within the short space of fifteen months after each other./After the marriage, I found her to be then about 19 years of age,—a few months younger than my second son and last child by the first wife, Hashim.[53] I often thought that I could never

---

[51]See above, note 17.

[52]One learned in theology.

[53]As Hashim was born in February 1913, it follows that this marriage probably took place during the pilgrimage season of 1932 (*Dzu'l-Hijjah*=April/May), when Abdul Majid was forty-six.

find happiness with her on account of the disparity of our respective age. But she proved to be quite different to my natural expectation. She was as obedient and docile as Muslim upbringing and Arab traditions could make her. As the granddaughter of an *'alim*, she was well-versed in religion. She could discuss with me, and often enlightened me on religious points!

Once she confided to me that she thought she must have been fated to be married by me. She had had proposals of marriage from other men before mine came; and they were men of influence and money. One was a religious scholar, a young man, who became a religious authority in Kedah as I recently discovered. But somehow or other, her father refused those proposals.

A few weeks before my proposal came, she told me that she had a dream one night. She thought she was walking along one of the streets in Mecca with her mother, when she saw a man waving to her from one of the windows. She asked leave of the mother and went up the house to see the man. When she got up, the man told her that the house and all that was in it was hers, if she cared to stay. The man was so very polite to her in all his words and actions that she told her mother from the window to wait for her a few more minutes. She went about the house led by the man. Then she thought she went to the water-tap (a 'hanafiah' as it was called in Arabic) and lo! and behold, the tap suddenly went off its position and the 'hanafiah' became dry!

Once I asked her what she thought the extraordinary incident in the dream meant. She said that according to Sheikh Shafi'ee, the husband of her aunt Fatimah, the drying-up of the water-tap meant the death of our first baby; and this had come to pass!

I had in my mind a different interpretation to that dream; and I wonder if she agrees with me, in the light of recent sad events. I forgot to mention that the man she saw in the dream she found to be exactly like me in his looks, manners and ways!

Anyway, I think my Mecca wife is the second woman, mentioned by the Afghan palmist, who would prove to be my two true wives!

Here, I must mention that her paternal grandfather, the *'alim* above mentioned, originally came from Singgora, and was known as Sheikh Abdullah Singgora./He was well-known to many as he was for fifty years the Sheikh-ul-fuqaha in Mecca; and his pupils came from nearly all parts of the Muslim world.[54] His house in Sha'ab Ali was the favourite rendezvous among the Qaris from Egypt, Syria and other places as they came for the pilgrimage. I went once to that house in 1924 to hear the Qur'an-reading by two Egyptian Qaris.

Her maternal grandmother was an Egyptian lady, the daughter of a well-known Egyptian official, stationed in Mecca. The wife of Ismail Effendi, Oriental Secretary at the British Legation, Jedda, once said that the name was a household word in Egypt, as he in his time had rendered much help to Egyptian pilgrims in their difficulties.

The paternal grandfather and the maternal grandmother of my Mecca wife having lost his wife and she her husband got married and [also got][55] two of his sons and two of her daughters also married. The eldest in both cases were the father and mother of my Mecca wife. His name was Nur, and her name was Zubaidah; while my wife was named Jawahir.

My first wife was Indian on her father's side. Her father, Hassan,—a twin with Hussein—was the grandson of one of the two Indian/soldiers, mentioned by Sir Frank Swettenham in one of his books on Malaya. The two Indian soldiers got into a stockade occupied by Malays and together with a European officer who saw that the enemy were facing the other way they routed the whole crowd.[56] I believe the grandfather was made an officer as Subadar

[54] The meaning of '*Syaykh al-fuqahā*' (from *fiqh*, the term used to denote jurisprudence in Islam) is not altogether clear. Though possibly one who had mastered all four schools of law, and thus considered a final authority (much like the Mufti), it is possible that he was simply the chief jurist of one particular school—in this case undoubtedly the Shāfi'ī. Hurgronje, *Mekka* (1931), mentions neither the office nor the man.

[55] The likely sense of this sentence is clearer with the words in brackets removed. From what follows, it appears that Abdul Majid's wife's parents, Nur and Zubaidah, were respectively father's son and mother's daughter by the earlier marriages of each of their own parents.

[56] This is described, not in Swettenham but in Hugh Clifford's story 'Ram Singh', in his *In a Corner of Asia* (London, 1899), 171–94, concerning an incident during the Pahang rebellion of 1890–1, though

or Jemadar, as I remember seeing a stepmother of my wife in possession of his sword that had become an heirloom in her father's family. I wonder if the sword can be traced now as the stepmother was divorced by my father-in-law and she came to us only for a short time while we were in Kuala Kangsar in order to get employment from us.

On her mother's side, she was from Perak. Her mother's father was one Megat Kassim who getting into 'trouble' in the Sultan's Istana had to flee the country and settle down in Balek Pulau, where he married a daughter of the local Qadhi.[57] I said he got into 'trouble', but the fault was not on his side. In fact, he was not guilty at all.

Once, my wife was introduced to a certain lady, the principal wife of the Sultan, as the granddaughter of Megat Kassim. The lady who was always lying down, being ill and old with age, actually sat up and showed great interest in her. She was very pleased to learn that/my wife's visit and interview with her was to perform the ceremony of giving her our first child.[58] Two days before the birth of Latiph, my wife dreamt that the Sultan came to our house on an elephant with his principal wife and gave her a kris!

It was the same lady who was madly in love with Megat Kassim and caused him to flee from home and thus lose his family title as Bendahara of Perak.[59]

---

details differ somewhat. Cf. Inder Singh, *History of Malay States Guides, 1873–1919* (Penang, n.d. [?1965]), 37–38. Abdul Majid's first wife's given name at birth was Aishah Bee (and she was always called Bee by her husband), but she was renamed Safiah by her father while visiting Mecca, at a date unknown.

[57]'*Megat*' is a hereditary title, usually associated (especially in Perak) with the offspring of morganatic marriages between Malay women of royal blood and commoner husbands, and their descendants indefinitely. Megat Kassim is said to have been a cousin of Megat Osman b. Megat Ali, who played an important role in Kelantan government and politics for many years from 1917, as head of the English division of the school set up by the Majlis Ugama Islam dan Isti'adat Melayu, as Secretary of the Majlis from 1920, and later in the civil service. Balek Pulau is on the outer side of Penang Island.

[58]The 'giving' here referred to is a symbolic act, not as a rule involving surrender of the child. The origin of the 'ceremony' is unknown.

[59]This is a little misleading. Megat Kassim is difficult to trace (he does

My wife, therefore, has many relatives in Balek Pulau and Perak. I remember my mother-in-law saying before her death that even the present Sultan of Perak, who was then Raja Muda, was related or connected with her in some way.[60] Once he actually proposed to marry my sister-in-law, Teh, probably as a means of connecting the fortunes of his family and those of my mother-in-law's![61]

But as Latiph remarked once there was nothing ever discussed in our family, each assuming the responsibility as his or her own whenever any family problem arose. And so I only heard this proposal quite recently. I hope such lapses in the family will not occur again! Even blind men do not lose their sticks twice, they say!

I have said that I married eight wives. My first wife gave me four children,—/two boys and two girls. Of the four, three are alive today. My third child, a daughter, died when she was barely two months old. I believe I would have got many more children by this wife if she had not consulted a lady doctor[62] to stop further

---

not appear, for example, in the genealogy of Megat Teraweh, Bendahara (chief minister) of Perak in the early eighteenth century, given in Abdullah Haji Musa (Lubis), *Sejarah Perak Dahulu dan Sekarang* (Singapore, Qalam, n.d.), p. 110, to which family, however, he certainly belonged). But in any case, the title of Bendahara had not been held by a descendant of Megat Teraweh since the time of Sultan Iskandar Dzu'l-Karnain, who had made his brother (later Sultan Ala'uddin Mansur Shah) Bendahara some time before his own death in 1764. From that time forward the title rotated among segments of the royal lineage according to political circumstance but with the presumption that it carried the right to supply candidates for the throne. (Cf. Sadka, *The Protected Malay States*, op. cit., p. 33, fn. 1, and p. 363; and also the genealogy of the Sultanate given in Abdullah, op. cit., facing p. 16.)

[60]The Sultan at the time of writing (1941) was Sultan Abdul Aziz b. Raja Musa (reg. 1938–48), a nephew of the deposed (1877) Sultan Abdullah.

[61]Teh, sister of Abdul Majid's wife Bee, was still living (in Singapore) in 1967, married to a businessman from Palembang, Ali b. Ahmad. The 'fortunes' referred to presumably relate less to his mother-in-law (daughter of the Penang *kathi*) as such than to the family of her father, Megat Kassim.

[62]Dr. L.S. McLean, wife of John O'May (Assistant Master, Malay College, 1907–18, and Head Master 1918–19), graduate of St. Andrews

child-birth immediately after the arrival of Hashim. She used to suffer a lot during confinement, sometimes so bad that it was thought she would [lose?] her life; and this had induced me to agree to the step she took. I must say that I believe her long illness with one complaint after another was due to this unnatural process. I can well remember that she was well only for seven years after the doctor's 'operation', and ever since then I have not known her to be as healthy as she originally was. When I read the Qur'an in its English translation, it struck me that I had sinned in agreeing to her submitting to the 'operation' for stopping child-birth. The Qur'anic verse referred to reads something like this: 'Do not kill your children for fear of poverty. God provides for them as well as for you'. I am sure to stop their birth is essentially to kill them. However, I think I have been punished enough in this life for that sin. Every time my wife complained of pain in her body seemed to hurt me and my soul. Besides, I had to engage servants where none would be required to help her in her household duties. Perhaps the lady doctor could relieve her; but she is now thousands of miles away from here. Others did not seem to know exactly what her troubles were!

My second wife had no issue with me. My third, an Arab woman divorced by Agoes/Salim[63] and an aunt of Eshah, the wife of my son Abdul Latiph, claimed to have given me a child which, she said, she lost in a miscarriage during the siege of Jedda by the Wahabis.[64] My fourth, fifth and sixth wives had no children with me. My seventh, the Mecca wife, like my first, also gave me four children—two boys and two girls. The first one, a girl, died at

---

University and the London School of Tropical Medicine, who was appointed to the F.M.S. Medical Service in 1913, and transferred to the S.S. in 1921.

[63]Haji Agoes Salim (b. 1884 in West Sumatra, d. 1954), was Netherlands East Indies Pilgrimage Officer in the Dutch Consulate in Jeddah from 1906 to 1911.

[64]This took place during 1925, Jeddah falling to the forces of Ibni Sa'ud in December of that year. The main pilgrimage month, Dzu'l-Hijjah, occurred in June/July 1925, and Abdul Majid presumably left for Malaya with the last pilgrimage ship toward the end of August, as he had done the previous year.

BOOK ONE   35

the age of over a year; and the second and third are alive, two boys, Abbas and Abdullah; the fourth is also a girl who will be three years old in the coming Shawwal.[65] I have not seen these three little children for about thirty months now; and I can only pray in silence to the Almighty to provide for and protect them. Amen! I hope that they will grow to sympathise with their father in his sad and helpless condition. Perhaps some day they may read these lines and judge me for themselves for my apparent neglect of them since November last.[66] I wonder if I can live to see them again. I have the photograph of Abbas and Abdullah, but the photograph of Lotfiah which was sent to me by my wife, according to a letter from her uncle Yahya, never reached me. The person who was said to bring it to me from Mecca had already arrived long ago and had delivered to me through her son all that she was entrusted with to hand over to me. My inquiry about it did not help much. The person is a Malay lady living in Batu Pahat; her son's name is Abdul Aziz.

My eighth wife,—a sister of Mohamed, who became son-in-law of Zainalabidin bin Ahmad of literary fame,[67]—gave me a daughter who was born weak and died during my absence in Arabia. As I divorced this wife on my return, I did not even see my child's grave. It must be somewhere in the Gonggang Cemetry in K.L.

My daughter Maimunah, by my first wife, was buried in the public cemetery at/Kuala Kangsar. My mother was buried next to her at her request. My daughter Hasnah by my Mecca wife was buried in the public cemetery at Jedda. My father was buried at

[65] I.e., October/November 1941. The dates of birth of the two boys are not recorded.
[66] The meaning of this passage is unclear. The progress of the war in Europe may have led to difficulties in remitting money by the end of 1940, but the problem may have been a more personal one, associated with his illness. Abdul Majid himself had last been in Mecca in late March 1939 (see 'Annual Report on the Malayan Pilgrimage for the Season 1938–1939 A.D. or 1357–1358 A.H.', Encl. IB. in Kelantan Setiausaha Kerajaan file No. 489/1939, copy in Kelantan 'K' [British Adviser's Office] file No. 453/1939).
[67] Zainal Abidin b. Ahmad (Za'ba) (1895–1973), later entitled Tan Sri, one of the leading figures of Malay letters, was a near contemporary of Abdul Majid, and their lives crossed at a number of points (see, e.g. below, pp. 106ff, 120ff, 133ff.)

the cemetery, sixth mile (Batu Anam) Gombak. (There is a road branching off at the sixth mile Gombak Road, leading to the Batu Road on the other side and passing the Batu Caves before it ends. Ask the people living within one or two miles from the point where this cross road starts for the locality of this cemetery.)

Of my living children, A. Latiph was born in May or June 1909 or the. . . .? of Jemadi'l-awal 1327 A.H.[68] Aminah was born on 13th Ramadhan 1328 A.H. ([18 Sept.] 1910 A.D.) Hashim was born on 28 (?) Safar 1331 A.H. ([6 (?) Feb.] 1913 A.D.) (I have given A. Latiph and Hashim the proper dates of their respective birthday and asked them to keep).

I have got the proper dates of my Mecca children recorded in official Birth Certificates issued by the British Legation, Jedda. The papers are with my Mecca wife.

My own birthday is Sunday, 3 p.m. on 18th Jemadi'l-akhir 1304 A.H. or 20th (?) March 1887 A.D.[69]

Of my eight wives, or even of the two who still hold my affections to this day,/the first one has been with me the longest. It is natural, therefore, that my thoughts centre round her the most. We have been married for more than 33 years. We have been through thick and thin and seen days of affluence and days of poverty several times. We were just the same in the extreme circumstances. All I can say about us two from our experience during these years is that we are a pair that match but do not agree. We have nothing in common, either education or in upbringing. Seldom a day passes without a quarrel between us. But we evidently care and live for each other.

Honestly speaking, I have never had any complaint against her as a wife, or as my house-keeper or as the mother of my children. She is all that one can expect from a wife in these respects. But the most remarkable thing about her is that she has no wit or sense of humour. I discovered this during the first year of our married life. I remember for a harmless joke I made at her expense, I had

---

[68]The month of Jumada al-Awwal, 1327, ran from 21 May to 20 June 1909.

[69]Assuming the Muslim date to be correct, the corresponding date in the Christian era is in fact 14 March 1887.

the scissors that happened to be in her hand at the time thrown at me and hit and wounded me in the head. Another thing is sometimes she tried to be wise and avoided answering a simple question directly. An example of this happened a few days ago. She was making preparations to go out with her sister. I asked her where she was going. She answered that she had asked Ibrahim to look after me during her absence, and that she would not be away long. This annoyed me and I explained to her the reason why I wanted to know where she was going was that I might send Ibrahim, in case it was found to/be necessary. But the explanation did not produce the required information from her. All she did was to tell her sister that they could not go. This annoyed me more as I did not want to appear to be obstructing my sister-in-law's plan, whatever it might be. She could not understand my line of thinking, and seemed to me to regard her duties towards me as something that must be performed by her as wife. She never looked upon husband and wife as life's partners. She liked to perform her duties in her own way and resented any suggestion from me to do them in any other way. She had an idea that she knew everything that a woman has to do. Anyway if she had to learn anything, she never chose me to teach her. She had amassed a lot of crude knowledge about medicines etc from various sources. She even knew something about spiritualism as the Malays knew it; and took some pride in guiding my movements. Some of these she guided me in proved to be disastrous; but she did not seem to interest herself in results. To be a temporary guide in the situation seemed [to] me to be her sole ambition! Or, perhaps she had no long memory to be able to see 'cause and effects'. Certainly there was no guile in her. This extraordinary trait in her character, I think, is the one that attracted me or amused my teaching spirit. 'But you have not been able to teach her anything all this time', remarked Abdul Latiph once to me.

My second or Mecca wife is, as I have remarked above, very young, even younger/than Hashim. Her father, I found, was (he is dead!) younger than myself; and her mother is again younger than my first wife. Once I said that had I known my mother-in-law to be young, not old, I would have asked Sheikh Yaakub to propose my marriage to her, and not to the daughter! I said this very sincerely, as my idea of having a wife in Arabia was merely to have a cook and housekeeper. My first wife heard this and was angry. She said I should never make such a remark since a mother-in-law must be respected more than a real mother! I remember saying something to her in reply as an explanation to show that my mother-in-law in Mecca was not old; but she would not hear any more from me about her. Perhaps she thought it was a sacrilege for me to discuss about a mother-in-law's age!

I took my Mecca wife back to this country a few months after our marriage.[70] When we landed at Penang, Captain Syed Salleh Alsagoff, M.B.E., took us to his house as his guests.[71] I found out later that it was his house where he had his Kedah wife who was a princess. When I saw my wife again in the train that evening on our way to my home, Kuala Lumpur, I asked her how she managed to converse with the womenfolk in the house of our host as she knew no Malay. She laughingly told me that she had had some/experience in getting over such language difficulties, as there were many Malay women who came to her house as pupils of her grandfather or of her own and knew no Arabic. Then I asked her if she knew the correct use of certain Malay words in addressing the persons she was talking to.

On receiving her reply in the negative, I at once started to explain the various forms of 'I' and 'you', as they are used according to custom. Here I was pleased to find her a very keen student with [a] good memory. I finished up by warning her that among Malays it is considered as an insult to the person or persons you are speaking to if the words used for 'I' and 'you' are incorrect. This piece of information, I think, added to her enthusiasm in the study of Malay, or rather in the first lesson she received from me.

Next morning, we arrived at Kuala Lumpur and saw Latiph waiting for us at the Railway Station. Later in the day, I was told that she had been addressing Latiph as '*abang*'![72] When I asked

[70]This was probably in May/June 1932.
[71]Sayyid Salleh b. Sayyid Ahmad Alsagoff, of Tarim in the Hadramawt, d. circa 1960. His Kedah wife was Tengku Puteri, widow of Tengku Mohd. Jiwa b. Sultan Abdul Hamid, elder brother of Tengku Abdul Rahman, latterly Prime Minister of Malaysia.
[72]Lit., 'elder brother', but often used to address any male somewhat

her why she did that, she simply said: 'Didn't you tell me to address male persons older than myself as *abang?*' For the first time in my life I was beaten as a teacher, despite my reputation. Evidently, she did not grasp the real meaning of my words to her when Latiph came that he was my son. Or perhaps she could not see that my son would be her 'son' also!

Today (2.9.41)[73] something happened which I think is worth recording. I was sitting very/quietly 'to rest my brains' after writing the previous chapter of a few pages and giving Ibrahim some lessons on 'Rukun Islam', 'Rukun Iman' and 'Rukun Sembahyang',[74] when I heard someone giving the *Salaam* to the people next door on the left.[75] As I did not hear him getting the reply to his *Salaam* from the people in the house, I asked Ibrahim who was the person making the *Salaam*. His explanation not being satisfactory, I shouted out to the man that he would not be answered to his *Salaam,* as there were only women in the house. The man came to the front of this house and I continued explaining to him that the males of the other house were not in, having gone to their respective work. That was why there was no answer to his salutation. He could not expect the women to come forward and receive him.

The man was an Indian, about thirty years of age. He said to me that he had made an appointment with the men in the house. There were two of them, one a telephone operator and the other

---

older than oneself. Latiph was some four years older than his stepmother, a situation which might have posed problems of address even for those more familiar with Malay linguistic usage than was Jawahir.

[73]This date cannot be correct if, as the preface indicates, the manuscript was begun on 22 September 1941. Perhaps 29.9.41 was intended.

[74]*Rukun Islam*—the fundamental principles of Islam (i.e., the five 'pillars': the confession of faith, prayer, fasting, poor tax, and the pilgrimage); *rukun iman*—the elements of faith (belief in the One God, in all His Messengers and revelations, in the Day of Judgement, and in God as the source of good or ill in one's life); *rukun sembahyang*— the essentials and rituals of prayer.

[75]*'As-salām 'alaikum',* 'May peace be upon you', a customary greeting on approaching a Malay house, answered (if appropriate, as indicated here by Abdul Majid) by *'Wa'alaikum as-salām'*—'and peace be upon you'.

a dresser. They often consulted him in his profession of astrology. I knew Professor Ilmuddin who was then staying in the Rex Hotel, Bras Basah Road.[76] Once he told me that he had a son who was also in his profession of astrology, but was then working in Deli or Medan in Sumatra. So I asked this young Indian visitor if he was a son of Professor Ilmuddin of the Rex Hotel. He said his father's name was also Ilmuddin, but not Ilmuddin of the Rex Hotel. I asked him what part of India he came from. He said, he came from Punjab in a small village near Lahore.

47 As he came up and sat down, to all appearances prepared to talk or perhaps to secure me as his client, I told him that I did not want to see my fortune, but he could tell me what he knew all about the future of the war. He confessed that he knew nothing about the future of the war, such being the exclusive knowledge of God. But he added that he had heard many old people say that the end of the world was coming. I said I happened to know a lot of people from Punjab. For instance, there is Lieut. (or is he Captain now?) Ehsan Qadir in the Regiment from Punjab. His father is Sir Abdul Qadir a very well-known figure, a Judge, in the Punjab. Then he remarked something about Imam Mahdi,[77] having been born already. I said I once knew a man: he was an Arab who had served as a military officer in Mecca during the time of Sheriff Hussein. When Hussein fled from the Hejaz at the invasion of the Wahabis [in 1925], he also fled from the Hejaz and went to India. There he joined the Arab Irregulars, a regiment in Hyderabad. He told me that in Hyderabad, the astrologers had been telling the Nizam that Imam Mahdi had been born and was biding his time till the Divine Order came for him to act: indeed, he had not been divinely informed as yet that he was Imam Mahdi. So, the Nizam had asked him to look for the man in Mecca. I travelled with this man from Jedda to Mecca in the same car, but did not see him on his return journey. But I added that I did not think he ever came across the man he was looking for.

[76] I.e., Bras Basah Road in Singapore. Abdul Majid was at this time living across the causeway in Johore Bahru.

[77] 'The [Divinely] Guided Leader', whose eventual coming, portending the end of the world, is held by some to have been forecast by the Prophet Muhammad.

8   I also mentioned the incident that happened/a few years before that when on a certain Friday, a man went up the pulpit in the Mecca Mosque just before the Friday service and gave out to the congregation that he was the expected Imam Mahdi of the Muslims. He was greeted with a few volleys from the Police on duty in the mosque and was killed. In any case, he could not be the true Imam Mahdi, I remarked in conclusion.

'There are other false Imam Mahdis also,' said my Indian visitor; 'in India there was Mirza Ghulam Ahmad.[78] His followers are to be found almost everywhere.'

I agreed and told him that you could find Qadianis even in Mecca.

'What did the King of the Hejaz do to him?' he asked.

'Nothing that I know of,' I said.

'In Afghanistan (Kabul)' said my friend, 'four Qadianis were found there and the King had their hands and feet cut off; and then burying them in the sands, they were shot at. It served them right!' opinioned my visitor.

'These Qadianis are really a danger to the Muslim world,' further remarked my Indian friend. 'They mislead and misguide us in our faith.'

'But there are other forces misleading and misguiding the Muslims other than the Qadianis', I remarked. 'I was given the impression,' I said, 'that the Indian Muslims were very staunch in their faith; but today I find their womenfolk going about without *purdah* to show they are *civilised*!'

After this, my Indian friend took his leave and went his way. Noting his anxiety to get clients, I wished him, on leaving, 'God speed' in Islamic fashion.

[78] Mirza Ghulam Ahmad Khan (1839–1908), founder of what became known as the Ahmadiyya movement, claimed himself in 1891 to be the promised Mahdi, and was subsequently declared heretical. After his death the movement split into two, the Qadian party (so named after the Mirza's birthplace) and the Lahore party, the former continuing to regard the Mirza as Mahdi and Prophet, thus rendering itself obnoxious to all true Muslims. The Lahore party, which made lesser claims, became a modernist-reformist group with a marked English-educated bias. Cf. above, note 20, and below, pp. 133ff.

49   No. 2, Treacher Road, Kuala Lumpur, is (it still exists) a house in which I (or rather my first wife and the children) lived for about seven or eight years.[79] It was not a big house, with only two bedrooms with a space which we used as Dining Room, opposite the bedrooms; and another narrow space at one end of the aforesaid bedrooms which we used as Sitting or Drawing room. At the back, there was the kitchen, with two servants rooms on either side and a bath room with latrines facing one of the servants rooms. It was not a house suitable to Muslims as the visitor could see straight to the kitchen or cooking place as he entered the house; and he could see into the bedrooms if he sat down to one of the meals, unless the bedroom doors were closed.[80] Besides, if he had to attend the call of nature, he would have to walk the whole length of the house which meant that he would be disturbing the privacy of the women in the house. But it had a big compound as the land on which the house stood was almost an acre. There were some fruit trees growing on the land, *durian, pomelo, kedondong, jambu, mata-kuching,* and *nangka,* with one or two coconut-trees.[81] During our stay, I planted *rambutan,* (which bore fruit before we left) a date-palm which grew very big but had no fruit and *jering* (believed to be good for diabetes). I must say that we had a lot of the *jambu, pomelo* and *nangka* which were very good. The *mata-*

[79] This was probably from about 1924, when Abdul Majid took up his appointment as Pilgrimage Officer, spending part of the year in the Hejaz and the remainder based in Kuala Lumpur.

[80] It is usual in Malay houses for the women's part of the premises, at the rear, to be kept out of sight of casual male visitors, who are entertained at the front.

[81] The fruits mentioned in this and the next sentence are as follow: *durian* (Durio zibethinus), a large, thorny fruit of inexpressible taste; *pomelo,* a large citrus-type fruit like an oversize orange (prob. from Dutch *pompelmoes,* and also known outside South-East Asia as the *shaddock,* after a Captain Shaddock who introduced it to the West Indies); *kedondong* (Canarium spp.), a fruit resembling the hog-plum; *jambu* (Eugenia spp.), the rose-apple, and a number of similar fruits; *mata kuching* (lit., 'cats' eyes') (Nephelium malaiensa), similar to the Chinese *lychee* (and cf. below, *rambutan*); *nangka* (Artocarpus spp.), the jack-fruit, bread-fruit, and including also the custard apple or soursop; *rambutan* (Nephelium lappaceum), a hairy-skinned fruit similar to the *lychee; jering* (Pithecolobium lobatum), a tree bearing edible pods.

BOOK ONE 43

kuching grew to be very big, but never bore fruit. So I cut it down. We also had flower and vegetable gardens, but on a small/scale. The house, I understood later, was originally built and owned by a Malay woman kept by a European. At the time when I first took it on rent it was owned by a Chinese school-mate of mine. I paid $60 rent per mensem, but the rent was raised to $75 p.m. There was a scarcity of houses in Kuala Lumpur at that time; and I could not get a better one. And there were no Government quarters available for me to occupy. Besides, as I required quarters only during the few months of my stay during my return from Arabia, the Government did not seem to think I had any rights or claim to be given quarters. Then again, if there were any quarters that would fall vacant, the news would be spread among the people of the race or nation who preponderated in the Government Service. There were no Malays in the 'key' positions in the Government Service to help me to get the necessary information.[82]

The best that the Government could do for me was to help me to buy a house of my own. So, when I was told by my wife that the house we were living in was for sale I jumped at the idea of buying it. Somehow I had begun to like the house for its locality, and perhaps the high rent I was paying every month from my own pocket made me to think of buying it. Anyway I was unable to secure another house on rent and I was due to return to Arabia very soon. The thought that my family would be homeless during my absence no doubt helped me to decide to buy the house. The price asked for was $16,000/- and I was told that Ramli[83] could arrange for a loan of $10,000/- on the house, on the cheap interest of 9% per annum. So, I asked for the loan of one year's/salary—$6,000/- from the Government. I remember my application for

[82]The middle and lower echelons of the public services of the F.M.S. were largely Indian and (to a lesser extent) Chinese in composition at this time. While it is true that Malays alone staffed the Malay Administrative Service (M.A.S), and an insignificant number of posts in the prestigious (and otherwise entirely British) Malayan Civil Service (M.C.S) were opened to Malays from 1921, almost all Malays in the M.A.S and M.C.S were posted to the rural areas, not Kuala Lumpur. Cf. William R. Roff, *The Origins of Malay Nationalism* (New Haven, Conn., 1967), pp. 109 & 113 ff.

[83]Ramli b. Haji Ali (see above, note 39).

the loan was treated officially as urgent on account of my impending departure to Arabia. Before I left this country I had the satisfaction of knowing that the Government had approved the loan. I had no doubt that the other $10,000/- loan would be given during my absence. So before I finally departed, I had appointed both my wife and Ramli to be my attorneys for the purpose of signing the papers for the loan.

But on my return from Arabia I discovered that the $10,000/- loan had not been received, not because the moneylender was unwilling to grant it on the security of the house, but because the supposed owner of the house was not, technically speaking, in his rights as the inheritor of the property. The house was still registered in the name of his deceased father. Anyway, the moneylender was the father-in-law of the Chinese lawyer who was responsible in drawing up the Agreement in the transaction. I also discovered that the 'owner' of the house still charged me $75/- per month for the occupation of the house, despite the fact that he had received $6,000/- out of his selling price of $16,000/-. Eventually, the said 'owner' gave the loan of the money required to pay for the house; but the rate of interest I had to pay was 15% (or is it 18%), not 9%. Thus was the origin of my financial difficulties; and I remember to have explained/to the judge in Kuala Lumpur these circumstances in one of the cases brought against me by that 'Chinese friend'; but my version of the case was ignored!

Lastly I was made to sell back the house to that 'Chinese friend' and I still had and have $7,000/- or $8,000/- to pay to him!

I have no doubt from all my experience in this and other transactions between Chinese and Malays that the latter only become *easy prey* to the former.

That 'Chinese friend' is now dead; but if we live again in this world, I hope I shall have my revenge on him and make him my 'easy prey' in money transactions between us!

I think the popular belief is that Chetties[84] are the most hard

---

[84]Chettyars, an Indian Tamil caste of businessmen and financiers. For Chettyars in Malaya, see, e.g., Sinnappah Arasaratnam, *Indians in Malaysia and Singapore* (Kuala Lumpur, 1970), pp. 36–37.

hearted in money-matters; but I find that they will not trouble you as soon as they know that you have nothing to give him, even if you are still, legally speaking indebted to him!

But my Ramadhan yarns cannot be complete unless and until I relate the/following:- It was in the month of Ramadhan, on the day I was in Hutan Melintang on my way [to] or return from Sabak Bernam—the day when I got back to Telok Anson and found the telegram waiting for me telling me that my father was seriously ill. I was in a Chinese shop and the Chinese shopkeeper was smoking with his smoke getting into my nostrils. I told him that I was fasting and therefore did not want the smell of his smoke. He told me he was sorry to be a nuisance to me when I was so hungry with the fast; and he moved away from me. I was touched with his remark and conduct. So in order to keep up his interest I asked him why it was that when every nation in the world was enjoined by their religion to fast, the Chinaman was not. He thought hard and said in reply; God must have forgotten to ask [the] Chinaman to fast!

The idea that God, the All-Knowing and the All-Wise, should for once forget in His commands to Mankind is amusing enough to the man who was taught the All-sufficient qualities of God; but who can improve that remark, in his position as a Chinaman?

I have heard of wicked men being described as the teacher of Satan. But this Chinaman deserves to be described as the teacher of God!

'Know yourself and you know God' is a very well-known Muslim saying. It is to be/in accordance with this saying that I try to know myself and analyse my spirit. I must say that from the very beginning I have been different from other people. At birth I was black, small, sickly, with a head that was longer than the ordinary, and a foot—the right one—that had the heel and the toes in their wrong places. My mother told me that a *pawang*,[85] a Malay from Rembau, then living in Pudu, set this foot right by twisting it

---

[85] A Malay spirit-doctor. Physical deformity at birth used to be seen by many Malays as a common portent of unusual capacities in later life.

into its proper position. I never saw this man in my life. My head got its proper shape by a device that my parents made and that was, they put a cushioned pad above my head as I lay down, and as I often struggled headwards in the manner of all babies, the head was pressed into the cushion and gradually regained its shape. As for my skin, this began to peel off during the first year of my age and continued to do so till I was nine.

As a little child, I remember I was very thoughtful and meditative. Some of the conclusions I arrived at during these early childhood days I found to be real scientific truths that were taught to me when I was in school. Of course my findings proved to be only crude pieces of scientific knowledge about Nature. Anyway, they helped me tremendously in my studies at school.[86] And as a result, every one thought me to be a very bright boy. I was considered to be one who could repeat my lessons in class without studying them the previous night./I remember I did not like such subjects as History and Geography which required a lot of memorising and cramming. I loved Mathematics and Science; and won many prizes in both. In the Cambridge Junior Examination at the Victoria Institution, Kuala Lumpur, in December 1902,[87] I surprised the Presiding Examiner by handing to him my answers in thirty minutes to a Physiology and Hygiene

[86] Abdul Majid attended Malay school at Pudu (Kuala Lumpur) from 1894, and then moved to the English-language Victoria Institution in 1895. The latter school had opened only in July the preceding year, with Bennett Shaw (b. Ireland 1862, educated King's College School and Oxford University) from the Grammar School at Bishop's Stortford, as Head Master. Of the 201 pupils with which V.I. (as it was known) opened, only ten were Malay.

[87] Cambridge University Local Examination Syndicate examinations (local only in the sense that though set in Britain—in London, not Cambridge—they were sat 'locally' throughout the world) were introduced in the Straits Settlements in 1891, and in the Federated Malay States about a decade later. The examinations were at two levels, Junior and Senior, a year apart. After seven years of English education (culminating in the completion of Standard Seven) pupils moved into the Cambridge Junior class (Standard Eight), and were prepared during the year for the Cambridge Junior Certificate examination. If they obtained this certificate they were then eligible to proceed for a further year in the Senior Cambridge class (Standard Nine), and attempt the Cambridge Senior Certificate examination.

paper for which two hours were allowed by the Examiners! When the results came out, it was found that I did pass in Physiology and Hygiene, though I am positive that I gave the wrong answer to the question: 'What is an artesian well?'. I had given the answer and described the functions of the kidney to this question! It is most probable that my answers to the other questions on this subject were so convincing that they satisfied the Examiners who went through these papers of my knowledge on this subject.

I have said that I was considered a very bright pupil at school; but my attendance was very poor. I was caned once for deliberately playing the truant; and this happened when I was in the Seventh Standard. My class teacher was Mr. A.C.J. Towers who became a Chartered Accountant later on and had his office in Ipoh for many years.

I was never serious in my school studies except for two or three months/previous to the time of my leaving the V.I. in December 1902. I was then in the Cambridge Junior class and was asked by my father to leave school at the end of the year. He had understood that I was only in the Seventh Standard. He had never been told of the double promotion that I had in 1901. I think I purposely left him in ignorance of my real progress at school as I had a secret desire of getting into the Senior Cambridge class and competing for the Federal Scholarship.[88] It was a Scholarship that would enable me to study in one of the Universities in Great Britain. I had the ambition of studying medicine and qualifying for a doctor. Some friends and well-wishers recognising my brightness as a student had put this idea into my head; and Mr. B.E. Shaw, the Head Master of the V.I., certainly helped me with a few hints to turn this idea into a conviction that the ambition would be easy of realisation if I only made the effort for it,–or 'put my shoulders to the wheel', as Mr. W. Hargreaves, Head Master of the Malay College, Kuala Kangsar, would say.[89]

---

[88] Comparable to the 'Queen's Scholarships' introduced in the Straits Settlements Colony in 1885, 'Federal Scholarships', of which one was offered annually, were instituted in the F.M.S. in 1901, to be competed for throughout the federation by the best Senior Cambridge pupils.

[89] See below, p. 56, note 8.

In any case, I know I did sound my father to see if he would agree to my going to England for further studies; and he gave it as his opinion that he did not want me to go to England, regardless of the heights that I might rise thereby, but would be satisfied if I only passed my Seventh Standard and became a clerk.

His idea about my future was that I should get a clerical work after leaving school,/save up money and go to Mecca for my religious studies.[90]

Poor, dear father! He must be having smarting pricks in his conscience for not allowing me to go to Mecca with his uncle, Haji Daud, when I was nine and the religious fervour still in me. But in this instance I learned that it was my mother who thought she would not be able to stand the separation from me. Up to that time, I was the only child in the family as *all* my younger brothers had died very young. My sister Haji Eshah, was born when I was eleven.[91] It would have been rather hard on my mother if I had left her. A woman without a child to amuse and occupy her mind is like a man without work!

The line of action adopted by my father in regard to my future was no doubt the most suitable to him and my mother in their circumstances. But the result to me was that I neither qualified as a religious man, nor a medical man nor as a man of any other profession that a University gives the training for.

Such is the course in my life that fate is guiding me to! I wonder whether Occidentals are really serious when they laugh at Orientals in being fatalists. Do they ever realise that there are always limits to the abilities and capabilities of man, no matter what he knows or claims to know. The difference between God and man I believe, starts with these limits! Those who hold their abilities

[90] This pattern was an extremely common one in the Malaya of the time. Cf., for example, the experience of Za'ba, in Zabedah bte Awang Ngah, 'Za'ba: Pandangan dan kritik Za'ba mengenai soal sifat-sifat kemiskinan dan sa-tengah² aspek chara penghidupan serta juga shor²- nya atas jalan keselamatan bagi orang Melayu '[Za'ba: Za'ba's views and criticisms concerning the poverty of the Malays and some aspects of their lives, together with his recommendations for the salvation of the Malays] (Unpublished B.A. thesis, Malay Studies Department, University of Malaya, Kuala Lumpur, 1960), p. 5.

[91] I.e., 1898/99. If this is correct, there was in fact one other child in the family in 1902.

and capabilities are limitless are Pharaohs or disciples of Pharaohs!

58 I often think at this age that the woman who could understand and sympathise with me was never born; or if she was, I never met her. In a large measure, my big total number of wives was no doubt due to this insatiable quest for the *kindred spirit* in the fair sex. And I often wonder if I would find her in my *ninth* wife. But the very thought of having this ninth wife not only at this late age but in my present conditions was somewhat preposterous.

On the other hand, sometimes it struck me if I had missed such a woman among those whom I loved but never married. But I know in such cases, the circumstances were such that the course I took with regard to them was the one approved by everybody who knew me.

It must be said that it is not in women alone that I looked for the *kindred spirit* but also in men. Even my best friends seemed to me to fall short of the ideal. In many instances, it would not be long before I would find out their shallowness; they always turned out to be not the spirit that I had been looking for, they could not understand or sympathise with me.

I must say that I am a very impulsive man: the secret or inner workings of my conscience must be so very extraordinary that no one seemed to be able to follow and understand them. I was never bound by any rule of convention whenever I thought a certain line of action was the right one. Once I brought milk and bread, twice a day for a week, to a sick pilgrim who told me he had no one on board to look after him. I was pleased to learn later that he recovered and got back safely home after this illness. He came to see me in the Kuala Pilah Rest House to show his gratitude. And I had entirely forgotten all about him. 'You must have helped too many people in such circumstances during the pilgrimage seasons to have forgotten this case,' remarked Tunku Kahar who was present.[92] Tunku Kahar is now Tunku

---

[92]Among others testifying to Abdul Majid's personal generosity and kindness in the Hejaz was the Chief Minister of Kelantan, Datuk Nik Mahmud b. Haji Wan Ismail, in a report written following his own pilgrimage in 1930 (Datuk Perdana Menteri to British Adviser, Kelantan, 6 Nov. 1930, Encl. 1 in Kelantan 'K' (BA's Office) Files, No. 1958/30).

Laxamana of Negri Sembilan.

This want of kindred spirit either in any of my wives or my friends seems/to leave a blank in my life. There is no one for me to turn to for approval or censure in my actions. There is no one to guide me. I mean such guidance as is not parental or authoritative. In my case, I believe what is required is a subtle influence from a woman who realises that her own welfare depends on mine!

I have heard some friends telling me that they began to look up to their wives, after years of living together, as their mothers. They must have realised the good influence of their wives on their life.

My eldest son, Latiph, once remarked recently that we never held any family consultation in any step we took in our life. Poor boy! He must be still groping in the dark in his analysis of the causes of my failure. He did not know that there was not a step I took in my life without consultation with my wife. Probably he did not see me doing this recently; but that was because her advice in several instances had proved to be miserable failures. Besides, she had neither the knowledge nor the mentality to talk on many subjects. She did not know even to calculate and check the purchases of the servants. She was good and true as a wife, but she was a failure as my helpmate. As a mother, as Latiph and many others saw it, she was extraordinarily good; if not excellent! In the culinary art, there was none I met who could beat her. And when she was young she could work attending to the household duties like a Trojan! There are many qualities in her which I could admire, despite her weaknesses and shortcomings!

BOOK TWO

[THE second notebook begins here. Pagination continues uninterrupted. Written on the outside of the cover of the notebook is: 'Professor Rajah, the Homeopathic Specialist of North Bridge Road [Singapore] came to see me on 18.10.41. He would try to cure me with his homeopathic treatment [word illegible].'

On the inside of the front cover is:

'I suggest that the title of this work be called 'The Wandering Thoughts of a Dying Man', or 'What I Thought of My Past Life', by Haji Abdul Majid. Please consider if the second title should be *added*, and do write it up accordingly in the relevant places in the writing.']

'There is much wisdom to be learnt from a study of the mistakes of a fool—H.A.M.'

I believe in my dealings with my fellow men no one could say that I was heartless or selfish. I could remember that I was always ready to help where help was needed. I think some people took advantage of this characteristic in me. And in most cases they got what they wanted from or through me; but instead of being grateful these persons became my enemies. If they did not do anything to harm me, they would refuse even to talk to me and avoided my company for no other reason. I am sure I have never done anything to disturb the peace of friends and their wives, so much so that I believe the attitude of such people can only be due to sheer ingratitude. I know they cannot say I was overbearing in my demand for their proof of gratitude, but continued to be friendly to them when ingratitude had been proved. The rejection of a friendly gesture on my part by any such 'old friend' always hurts my heart and gives me more pain than anything can ever do!

61 Perhaps 'Self' is their first consideration as/advocated by that great and well-known English essayist, Samuel Smiles, and taught in Islam; but I am the only one who does not agree with that doctrine; and hold that humanity or a humane outlook should supersede it. At least, neither Samuel Smiles nor Islam preaches that we should be on no speaking terms with those whose interests in life do not agree with our own!

The Malay phrase *terima kaseh* for 'thank you' should be recast and re-modelled in such a way as to be more expressive in its sense of showing one's gratitude for a good turn, already received. It should also lead one to grasp the idea that it is a duty to be grateful. In this I make the following suggestions:-
a) I *thank* you = Saya ber*hutang budi*
b) He asked me to give you this watch *to thank* you = membalas budi.[1]

62 I must record it here that I changed the course of my life after leaving school on two occasions. The first was when I had been two years in the Selangor Government Service. I went back to school when the Malay College, or the Malay Residential School, as it was then called, was first started in Kuala Kangsar, at the instance of Mr. R.J. Wilkinson, who was at that time the Federal Inspector of Schools.[2] The second was when I said good-bye to

---

[1] *Budi* is a portmanteau word implying in general kindness, and qualities of character associated with this. The root *hutang* refers to debt or obligation. Thus *berhutang budi* might be translated as 'owing kindness'. Similarly, the root *balas* refers to repayment or reply. Thus *membalas budi* might be translated as 'repaying kindness'.

[2] R.J. Wilkinson (1867–1941) entered the Straits Settlements Civil Service in 1889, discovered an early enthusiasm for Malay language and literature, and was Federal Inspector of Schools for three years from 1903, exercising a lasting effect on Malay education. It was at his instigation that the Malay Residential School was founded in 1905, as an academy for the training of a new Malay administrative elite. See Khasnor bte Johan, 'The Malay College, Kuala Kangsar, 1905–1941' (Unpublished M.A. thesis, History Department, University of Malaya, Kuala Lumpur, 1969), and William R. Roff, *The Origins of Malay Nationalism,* op. cit., pp. 130 & 100–4.

the work of my profession as a teacher and took up the post of Malay Pilgrimage Officer.³

As a young man I was very ambitious and longed for a position higher than that of a clerk where I could be more useful. I remember when I was still an apprentice clerk in the Selangor Secretariat, I put in my application for the post of Secretary to H.H. The Sultan of Selangor. The post was then newly created; but it was considered so important that a very much senior man to me was selected for it in the person of Inche Abdul Razak, who later became Dato Stia.⁴

This man started life, according to his Record of Service, as a boatman/in Kuala Selangor. Later, he became Malay Writer in the District Office of the district, where it is said that he picked up the work of the other clerks and proved himself capable of acting as the Chief Clerk. Then he became clerk in charge of the Sub-district of Sabak Bernam. From this position, he had been promoted to be an Asst. Conservator of Forests in one of the districts of Pahang when he was made Secretary to H.H. the Sultan of Selangor. And I took this first disappointment in my life with the best grace possible and regarded Inche Abdul Razak as a living example of the heights to which a man could rise by study and work. I saw the man in person for the first time in my life in one of the Government launches as he travelled from Port Swettenham to Kuala Selangor on his return from Pahang where, I was told, he fell ill. I was then a clerk in the Marine Office, Port Swettenham; and as it was a/Sunday I went with him in the same launch to Kuala Selangor, returning home in the same evening. I do not think he knew who I was, though I knew who he was; particularly because none of the crew including the Serang⁵

---

³See below, pp. 145ff., for what led up to this.

⁴Abdul Razak b. Haji Abdul Ghani, son of a Bugis-descended Arabic scholar and *kathi,* was born in Riau and educated at Raffles Institution. His first government appointment was in 1883 as a clerk in the Klang (Selangor) district office, and he was made Secretary to the Sultan of Selangor about 1902. He was created Datuk Setia around 1912. (A. Talaivasingham, *Malayan Notes and Sketches* (Singapore, 1924), p. 56.)

⁵A 'Hindustani' (i.e., Hindi or Urdu patois) term denoting head boatman.

ever knew or learned what it was [*sic*] and how to introduce us to each other.

I remember I got back home very late in the evening—about 10 p.m.—and found my father who had come from Kuala Lumpur already fast asleep in my house!

I was eleven months in Port Swettenham; and soon after my transfer back to Kuala Lumpur I found myself under treatment in the General Hospital. Here I came across an article on 'Education in Egypt'—I forget by whom it was written—in one of the London periodicals found in the Hospital Library. It was an article that made a lasting impression on my soul and spoke of the Egyptians as going in for education for the sake of turning young *felaheens* into quill-drivers, and not for/the sake of the useful knowledge that education imparts to them.

It was this that helped me to decide going back to school. Besides, I discovered that although I [had] passed the Cambridge Junior, I could not express my thoughts well and intelligently.

Another reason that led me to my said decision was my love-affair. I was head over ears in love with a certain girl, the niece of the wife of my adopted father, Haji Mohamed, the Visiting Teacher,[6] and she was very pretty with probably all the young men in the neighbourhood in love with her. I had a suspicion then that she would be my wife and I felt that my friends envied me.

But I must say it was a harmless love-affair. My thoughts of her were only to have her as my life's partner and nothing more.

When I was in Port Swettenham I had written to my father about my intentions toward this girl. The old man had tried to dissuade me/in the most tactful way he could think of from putting

[6]The post of Visiting Teacher, usually held by someone with experience as head teacher in a Malay school, involved inspectorial responsibility for the schools in a defined area. Haji Muhammad, previously Malay teacher at Kinta, Perak, was appointed Visiting Teacher for Selangor, in 1894 (Rex Stevenson, *Cultivators and Administrators: British Educational Policy towards the Malays, 1875–1906* (Oxford University Press, 1975), P. 81, and it would appear that the young Abdul Majid lived with his family after coming out of hospital, thus referring to him as '*bapak angkat*'—'adopted father'.

my intentions into practice and had even suggested other girls to be my bride. At last, he apparently got tired of receiving my letters that must be distasteful to him. He wrote to me saying that if I was bent on marrying the girl, I could do so, when he as father would provide me with the money for the marriage expenses; but I must not expect his presence or my mother's at the marriage ceremony.[7] This was of course very signficant of my father's refusal to agree to my marriage with the girl.

What could I do but submit to my father's decision? The idea of going against his wishes never came to my mind. So I tried my best to forget her; and I was fortunate in this as she was removed from my sight and taken back to her mother's place in Bukit Mertajam.

Nevertheless, she was not to be forgotten until and unless she influenced the course of my life, in some way or other. One day, my adopted mother after washing me in the manner prescribed by the Pawang/who was treating my case, surprised me by opening a discussion on the subject of my proposed marriage to her niece. She told me that her husband had tried to sound my father on the subject, and had received a reply from him that he was leaving the whole question to me to decide. She finished up her talk by telling me she hoped I would soon get well, save up money and take her niece as my wife. She did not know that my father had told me how he would agree to my marriage with her niece; and I never told her of it. In fact, I never said a word to her, but simply smiled. In my heart, however, I thought of the hardheartedness of my father. I believed that if he objected to this marriage, he should not make it appear that I did not want it,

---

[7]It nowhere becomes clear (but cf. below, p. 57) why Abdul Majid's father objected to the proposed marriage. According to Malay custom, it is the responsibility of the male partner to a marriage to find an agreed sum in *belanja kahwin* or 'wedding expenses' (in addition to the largely token amount paid as *mahr*, required by the Muslim contract of marriage), to be given to the family of the bride, going in part towards actual wedding expenses, and sometimes in part towards setting up house. To this degree Abdul Majid's father's offer may appear generous, but his warning that neither he nor his wife would attend the wedding was tantamount to outright repudiation, for it would have occasioned great shame, and might indeed have made the marriage impossible for the bride's family.

especially as he knew I was living with the girl's people. My position appeared to me to be one in which the only solution would be to go away from Kuala Lumpur, the scene of such impossible situations. Hence, my decision to go to Kuala Kangsar.

68   I remember well I took one whole night lying awake and tossing in bed before I came to that decision. At 6 a.m. I got out of bed, took my bath, and by 8 a.m. I had written the letter to the Federal Inspector of Schools asking the Government to allow me to go back to school in the one proposed to be opened in Kuala Kangsar. It was on a Sunday and I posted the letter at 9 a.m. On Tuesday I was asked by the Office Assistant in the State Engineer's Office, Mr. McGregor, to see Mr. Wilkinson in his office. On January 31st, 1905, I took the train and went to Kuala Kangsar. On January 1st 1907, I became an Assistant Master in the same school, on the advice of Mr. R.J. Wilkinson, who with Mr. William Hargreaves, the Head Master,[8] had been watching the progress of the senior boys in the school for the last two years very carefully. I came out No. 1 in the second year examination results.[9] The others, junior to me in class, were given appointments in the Malay Officers Scheme which subsequently became improved![10]

[8]Hargreaves, having obtained an M.A. degree at Trinity, Dublin, taught for a time at Leatherhead (Surrey), and was appointed headmaster of the Penang Free School (founded in 1816, the oldest and, by general reputation in the late century, the best English-language school in Malaya) in 1891. The High Commissioner of the F.M.S., Sir John Anderson, was not an enthusiast for the establishment of the Malay Residential School, and acquiesced only on the urgings of R.J. Wilkinson and the then Resident-General of the F.M.S., W.H. Treacher, and on condition that (among other things) Hargreaves be made headmaster. See Khasnor, op. cit., pp. 51–52, and Roff, op. cit., pp. 100–1. Wilkinson had been moved to a district administrative post from the Federal Inspectorate in 1906, but continued so far as he was permitted to take an interest in the school's progress.

[9]A total of 21 boys passed this examination, described by Wilkinson as the most demanding Standard Seven examination yet set in the F.M.S. (See correspondence quoted in W.H. Treacher, 'British Malay, with More Especial Reference to the Federated Malay States', *Journal of the Royal Society of Arts,* 55 (Mar., 1907), p. 38.) Abdul Majid, of course, had the advantage of having sat the Cambridge Junior Certificate examination two years earlier.

[10]While it is true that graduates of the Malay Residential School were

Some years afterwards, I learnt of the reason why my father could/never agree to my marriage to the pretty girl I first loved, it was a good reason, and with such a reason every father would do the same. And as a son, I know, I was very grateful that my father took the step that he did. Of course I could not appreciate the way he kept the truth from me; but as a father he had relied on my faith in his sincerity as a father to trust him in his judgement. It was a shock to me to hear the truth about her birth; just as it was a shock to me to hear that she came to a bad end! I had been keeping her memory in a soft corner of my heart, as the result of a dream which I had and which happened soon after my marriage to my first wife. I thought I was back in the same old house in Gombak Lane, Kuala Lumpur, where my adopted father entertained me to dinner. When it was over, Pa' Haji Mohamed went in and there she appeared at the door with a pathetic look saying to me: 'How cruel of you not to marry me as you promised.'/Then she disappeared by going inside.

I never made the promise to marry her, but it was understood by everyone who knew us as boy and girl that we were to be married.

When I heard her speaking to me in that accusative tone, I cried. And when I woke up from my sleep, I actually found tears in my eyes, and the sorrowful feeling that brought forth the tears still in my heart. I remember telling my wife why I cried. I thought at that time that it was the night of her own marriage to a man she could not love. But I wonder if she ever loved me.

---

for the most part taken into the government service in one capacity or another, the Malay Administrative Service (M.A.S.), to which the author is here referring, did not come into being until 1910, after the school had been accepted as permanent—under the new name, Malay College—and by way of what was known as the 'Scheme for the Employment of Malays (Higher Subordinate Class)'. Under this scheme, selected College graduates were admitted, after further courses and examinations, to the M.A.S. as 'Malay Assistants' (the term 'Malay Officers' not being adopted until 1917). The M.A.S. was a junior branch of the British Malayan Civil Service (M.C.S.), into which, in due course, it provided a miniscule amount of upward mobility. The M.A.S. itself, however, came to possess considerable prestige, and there are not lacking indications that Abdul Majid felt his worth had been inadequately recognized (see, e.g., below, pp. 92–4).

58 THE WANDERING THOUGHTS OF A DYING MAN

We never spoke to each other on such a subject at any time we were alone together, which seldom happened or never. Respectable Malays were then still very strict in observing such conventional rules about men and woman; and we considered ourselves to belong to [too] respectable families to be loose in that respect. On my part at least I know I wanted her to be my wife. It is most probable that she on her part wanted me as her husband—and no more! Perhaps in the next life, we might meet under better circumstances and get united in marriage!

71   Haji Mohamed was popularly known in Selangor, or in Kuala Lumpur/in particular, as an 'Orang Pulau Pinang' [i.e., a Penang man]. In Perak, however, I learned that he was a descendant of or related to, that famous Inche Long, once the Mentri of Perak.[11] Recently, I learnt from Inche Ahmad bin Yahya of Johore Bharu that he was related to the late Hon. Inche Eunos.[12] It was explained to me that his people originally came from Siak [in South Sumatra]. Some of them settled down in Johore, while others went to Perak. There *is* a sister of Haji Mohamed still in Johore Bharu; and two years ago she was a neighbour of, and known to, Syed Alwi Alhady, then Editor of the now defunct Lembaga Malaya and now Education Officer in the Johore Military Forces.[13]

[11]Long Ja'afar (d. 1857) was the representative of the Sultan of Perak in the district of Larut, which in the late 1850s proved to be rich in tin. Though it is unlikely that he himself ever held the title Orang Kaya Mentri, his son Ngah Ibrahim did, wielding considerable political power in Perak until his banishment in 1875 for alleged complicity in the murder of the first British Resident, J.W.W. Birch. Despite this blot on the family escutcheon, Ngah Ibrahim was succeeded as Mentri by his son on his death in Singapore in 1895.

[12]For Ahmad, see above, Book One, note 32; for Eunos, ibid., note 4. No other evidence of the supposed relationship with Eunos is available.

[13]Sayyid Alwi b. Sayyid Syaykh Alhady (1892–1969) succeeded Onn b. Ja'afar as editor of the weekly *Lembaga Malaya* and the daily *Lembaga* in 1936. *Lembaga Malaya* continued publication at least until the end of December 1941, so the reference to cessation is unclear; possibly *Lembaga* (for which the terminal date is unknown, in the absence of adequate holdings) is intended. Both papers were produced in Johore Bahru, and it is known that sometime late in 1941 Sayyid Alwi was appointed 'Munsyi' (presumably, as Abdul Majid says, Education Officer), then Quartermaster, and finally Captain Adjutant

Haji Nurdin formerly in the Johore Civil Service and now a Government pensioner living near Inche Ahmad bin Yahya in Johore Bharu, is another cousin of Haji Mohamed.[14]

He was a product of the old Malay College of Singapore;[15] and before he became/Chief Visiting Teacher, Selangor, was for some time a teacher in Perak.

I must say that he was a very clever man, always brilliant at repartees and often showed flashes of wisdom during conversation. He was a type of educated men that one met in the old days. Others of his type were Inche Khalid bin Abdullah Munshi, of the Education Department, Johore,[16] Haji Osman, Visiting Teacher, Province Wellesley,[17] Raja Haji Yaakub, Penghulu of Papan[18] and Inche Mohamed Omar, my Malay Teacher in the Victoria Institution. The last two named were Editors of Malay papers at one time.[19] These were the leading lights among Malays I had ever

---

of the Royal Johore Military Forces in Johore Bahru, Kluang and Kota Tinggi successively. The first of these posts may have been held in conjunction with his editorship. (Details encl. in letter to present writer from Sayyid Alwi, January 1969.)

[14] Haji Nurdin b. Abdul Karim's final appointment with the Johore Civil Service was as Magistrate in Mersing in 1926–7, at about which time he retired on pension.

[15] The Malay College at Telok Belanga was opened in 1876, as a central Malay-language 'high school' for Singapore, and became a Training College for teachers in 1882. It was closed in 1893 or 1894, as a result of the then economic recession and the recommendations of a retrenchment committee. The first principal of the college was one Encik Mohamed, then evidently a young man, but it is not known whether this is the Mohamed described by Abdul Majid as a product of the college. Cf. D.D. Chelliah, *A History of the Educational Policy of the Straits Settlements* (Singapore, 2nd. ed. G.H. Kiat & Co., 1960), pp. 65–70.

[16] A son of the famous Munsyi Abdullah b. Abdul Kadir (author of the *Hikayat Abdullah,* etc.,) Khalid was the first superintendent of education in Johore.

[17] Haji Osman cannot now be identified.

[18] Raja Haji Ya'akub b. Raja Bilah is said (interview, Haji Abdullah b. Haji Mohd. Salleh, Ipoh, 1967) to have been editor of the weekly paper *Seri Perak* (the first Malay journal to appear in the peninsular states), published in Taiping in 1893 (printed at *The Perak Pioneer* press, and possibly associated with that English-language bi-weekly, though the latter did not begin publication until 1899).

[19] A Muhammad Omar b. Haji Bakar was editor of the weekly *Jajahan*

met in my life. There might be others besides them; but they never attracted me. To hear them talk was really a treat; and their philosophy was always Islamic! Western ideas and Western ideals had not touched them! They appear now to me as the last links to the old Civilisation that is fast being replaced by a new one!

73 I must say that I am conscious of my singular success as a teacher. Hargreaves and Wilkinson must have detected my aptitude for teaching and directed me to do the work most suitable to my natural inclination. They had the success of the College at heart, of course.

I said my success as a teacher was singular in that no other school, except the Malay College of my time, ever managed to get boys to pass the seventh standard in three or four years. And when it is remembered that English was a foreign language to these boys, you will realise the wonderful progress made.

I claim that this extraordinary achievement was due to a large extent to the simplified form of studying the English language given in my book: 'Vocabulary and Grammar for Beginners' or 'Jalan Belajar Bahasa Inggeris Yang Senang', as I called it in Malay.[20]

The book is a small one, with about 100 pages and 50 gramma-
74 tical rules. It can/be easily gone through two or three times in a school year. At the end of the year, when the contents of the book have been mastered, the boys would be found to be equal in their knowledge of English to Fifth Standard or Fourth Standard boys.

In two or three years after leaving my class, the boys would find themselves under Mr. R.C.W. Rowlands[21] and Mr. W. Har-

---

Melayu (Taiping, 1896–7, under the direct auspices of *The Perak Pioneer*), from its inception in November 1896 until the issue of 3 July 1897.

[20]See above, Book One, note 24.

[21]A Ceylon burgher (Eurasian) by origin, and one of the three initial appointments to the Malay Residential School, Rowlands had been acting headmaster of the King Edward VII School (known as the Central School from its founding in 1883 to 1901), Taiping, then the leading English-language school in Perak. He remained at Malay College until his retirement in 1926, and died in Ceylon in 1945. For a brief memory of him by a pupil, see *Malay College, 1905–1965* (no place or date of publication [? 1966]), pp. 8–9.

greaves respectively who, keen teachers that they were, saw to it that they got through the Final Examination, the Seventh Standard.

It must not be imagined that the then Seventh Standard was a poor qualification compared to the present Junior or Senior Cambridge. When it is recognised that capable men like Raja Musa,[22] Raja Uda,[23] H.H. The Yang di-Pertuan Besar of Negri Sembilan,[24] Inche Abdul Malek[25] and many others in the Civil Service were 'boys' who passed the Seventh Standard in the Malay College, you will realise what a Seventh Standard qualification really means.

It must not be supposed that the students in the Malay College were hurriedly gone through the Examinations without any regard

[22] Raja Musa b. Raja Haji Bot (1897–194?), son of a leading Selangor chief, graduated from Malay College and joined the M.A.S. in 1910. In the early 1920s he was the first Malay to be sent by the government to study law in Britain, and on his return was promoted in January 1924 (with Raja Uda, see note 23 below) to the M.C.S.—the second Malay to be so forwarded. By 1940 he was a judge in the F.M.S. supreme court. He died during the Japanese Occupation.

[23] Raja Uda b. Raja Muhammad (1894–1967), a close connection of the Selangor royal house, graduated from the College in the same year as Raja Musa (above), and like the latter was promoted to the M.C.S. in 1924. In 1933 he became the Selangor Malay representative on the Federal Council, and by 1940 was Secretary to the British Resident of Selangor. After the war he was Menteri Besar of Selangor between 1949 and 1955, and crowned a distinguished public career with his appointment as Governor of Penang in 1957, a post he held until his death.

[24] Tunku Abdul Rahman b. Tunku Muhammad (1895–1960), son of the Yang di-Pertuan Besar (Ruler) of Negri Sembilan, graduated from the College in 1914, and joined the M.A.S. in 1921, being promoted in March 1930 (with Abdul Malek, see note 25 below) to the M.C.S. On the death of his father in 1933 he succeeded to the throne, and in August 1957 was chosen by his fellow Rulers to be the first Yang di-Pertuan Agong (King) of the newly independent Federation of Malaya. He died in office.

[25] Abdul Malek b. Yusof (1899–   ), now Tun Haji Abdul Malek, graduated from the College and joined the M.A.S. in 1917, being promoted to the M.C.S. in March 1930, together with Tunku Abdul Rahman (above). After the war he was Menteri Besar of Negeri Sembilan (his home state) from 1948 to 1953, and in 1959 became Governor of Malacca, a post he held until 1971.

to the building up of their character. Mr. Hargreaves, who came with the reputation of a successful teacher as Head Master of the Penang Free School, winning the Queen Scholarships for his boys eleven times in thirteen years, was of course responsible for this side of the boys' up-bringing. I can vouch for it that he took great pains in this and assiduously kept in touch with the boys years after they had left school. There was always the advice and guidance from old Hargreaves to those who wrote to him in their troubles. It is a pity that the Government never recognised his valuable services as an educationalist with any of the ordinary honours so often bestowed on such men; but his pupils honoured and honour him to a man. His name as a great teacher/will long be remembered by many.

In the height of my enthusiasm as 'a builder of the nation', as Hargreaves often fondly called his profession, I translated a book on teaching by Professor Garlick (?) into Malay.[26] I discovered as I went through the English version of the book that Hargreaves' methods of teaching agreed with those advocated in the book. I called my Malay translation: Rahsia Mengajar—or the Secrets of Teaching—and confined myself to the chapter on Discipline which had among other things many useful 'tips' on character-building. The work was printed in Muar and in a few months the whole edition was sold out. It was never re-printed!

This book was dedicated to:

'W. Hargreaves Esq. M.A.
My Teacher'

and was introduced to the Malay School teachers by the Education Department of nearly all the Malay States.

I am proud to bring it to the notice of the reader that in religious education of the College I was instrumental in bringing about a standard to be adopted that was really required for Muslim students. When the College was first started, the Government of

---

[26] Abdul Majid has the name right. Alfred Hezekiah Garlick published *A New Manual of Method* in 1896 (reprinted Longmans, London, 1897; 6th ed., New York and Bombay, 1904) and *A Primer of School Method* in 1905 (place and publisher unknown). Either may have been the source for *Rahsia Mengajar*.

course appointed a Qur'an teacher. And after the manner of those days this man taught the boys Qur'an-reading only. The result was when the boys left school after the first two years of the College existence,—some of the students on joining the College in January 1905 had passed the Seventh Standard in other schools all over the country while others did not even know the alphabet—they did not know even the rudiments of religion; or if they knew these, they were not acquired in the College. It stands to reason that if religious lessons imparted to the boys were to be confined to Qur'an-reading only, these boys would grow up to be men ignorant of religion. Indeed, in those days it was not an uncommon practice for Qadhis before performing the '*akad*[27] in marriage ceremonies to teach bridegrooms the five pillars of Islam[28]/so as to be sure that the bridegrooms were Muslims and knew the first lesson in Islam! Many young men, I knew, did not even know how to wash themselves.[29]

The reason for this religious ignorance to be prevailing certainly could not be traced to a deliberate scheme on the part of the British to suppress religious knowledge from the Malays. They had undertaken in their Treaty with the Malay Rulers in protecting the country *not to interfere with the Religion of the people*,[30] and they were not going to break their word. It appeared to me, therefore, that the real trouble was due to their belief that the

[27]The *akad nikah* (Ar. *'aqd an-nikāḥ*) is the contract entered into in marriage. Though it is not required in Islam that the *kathi* (religious magistrate) record the contract, this was habitually done in much of Malaya by the early twentieth century.

[28]See above, Book One, note 74, *Rukun Islam*.

[29]Given the context, the reference is probably to the *ghusl wājib* (Malay, *mandi wajib*), the mandatory bath required of Muslim males after sexual intercourse or emission. This is preceded by a *niat* (Ar. *niyya*) or expression of intent that one is cleansing oneself in the name of God, following which all parts of the body have to be wetted at least three times.

[30]Clause VI of the Pangkor Engagement between the British and the Malay rulers of Perak signed in 1874, which became the model (with minor variations) for all subsequent treaties of the sort, explicitly excluded from the competence of Residential advice questions touching upon 'Malay religion and custom'. In theory this constituted a prohibition upon British interference in Islam in the peninsular states.

Qur'an classes they had established were exactly like the Bible classes they had in their schools.[31] They did not know that the Malays had understood their Qur'an classes to be classes for Qur'an reading only. For religious knowledge, the Malays should have a *Kitab* class.[32] But religious knowledge is such a vast subject that it should be explained the religious knowledge that is essential for every Muslim to have is known as the *fardhu 'ain*.[33]

I had to explain all this in detail to Mr. Hargreaves and convince him of the necessity for a Kitab class before he agreed to dismiss Haji Kassim, the College Qur'an teacher and engage Haji Mohamed Noor, the Imam, to be the teacher for the Kitab class and Abdul Manap, the Bilal, to be the teacher for the Qur'an class.[34]

I for one was very happy at the removal of Haji Kassim who went back with his wife to his village, Bukit Tengah in Province Wellesley. Both husband and wife in spite of their position had been making small sums of money as additions to their small salary by teaching some of the big boys of the College—some of them were young men—'ilmu muda'.[35]

A few years after, Haji Kassim came and stayed in my house for one night. I could not refuse putting him up for the night as he arrived about sunset. At 5 a.m. of the next night, after he had gone, the drum of my right ear burst like a pistol shot; and I have been deaf in that ear ever since. Some said it was his work

---

[31] This is further testified to by the fact that in the early days of the school, at least, the Qur'ān classes were held not on Fridays, as might have been expected, but on Sundays.

[32] The literal meaning of *kitab* (Ar. *kitāb*) is simply 'book', but '*kitab* literature' in Malay is understood to denote religious literature in general, and in particular (for educational purposes) standard Qur'ānic exegeses, collections of and commentaries upon *ḥadīth*, introduction to the foundations of Islamic jurisprudence, and the like.

[33] Ar. *farḍ al'ain,* individual duty (in Islamic law), as distinct from *farḍ al-kifāya,* collective duty. From the root *faraḍa,* to decide, determine, decree or make incumbent; and *al-'ain,* eye (by analogy, central, personal).

[34] These changes took place in 1909. See *The Malay College Magazine,* I, 3 (1947), p. 53.

[35] Lit., 'knowledge of youth', the phrase refers to instruction in sexual matters.

as his revenge on me. There was a hole in the ground under the house exactly below the place where my bed stood with/something buried in it, which my wife found a few days after he had gone!³⁶ Some of the 'devil's works' resorted to by some Malays in order to get even with their enemies are very uncanny.

I was told later that Haji Kassim was not a Haji at all.³⁷ He assumed the title of 'Haji' on becoming Qur'an teacher of the Malay College to give him the air of sanctity and piety in the eyes of the European responsible for his engagement. To his credit, however, his Qur'an-reading was not bad; but everyone I met who knew him before said that he was known to be a man of doubtful character. Mr. Hargreaves' 'boy' told me that once he tried to give chicken curry to Mr. Hargreaves; but it was refused. It was his attempt to 'influence' the mind of Mr. Hargreaves to look to him with favour.³⁸

Poor Haji Kassim! He had trusted too much on his knowledge of the magician's science!

As I look back to my past life, I find that that period is the busiest of all. Not only was I engaged in simplifying methods for the study of English by Malay boys and the study of Malay by Englishmen—I also gave lessons in Malay to young Cadets (the Hon. Mr. W. Linehan, now Director of Education, S.S. and F.M.S. was one of these),³⁹ Police Officers, doctors and teachers. Besides this work as teacher and Munshi, I also had the work of writing and translating books; occasionally I wrote articles to the Malay

---

³⁶Belief in the efficacy of working harm by means of planting some article or substance, made malignant by magic, in the ground below a Malay house was, and occasionally still is, very prevalent.

³⁷One who has made the *haj*, the pilgrimage to Mecca.

³⁸The implication here may not be ingratiation, but that some magical substance had been introduced into the curry, to work the desired effect.

³⁹Born in Ireland in 1892, Linehan graduated with high honours from University College, Cork, in 1916, and joined the Malayan Civil Service as a cadet in the same year. After holding numerous district and general administrative posts, he was appointed Director of Education, S.S., and Adviser on Education, F.M.S., in 1939. All entrants to the cadet (i.e., junior or probationary) ranks of the M.C.S. had to study and pass examinations in a local language. Most, like Linehan, chose Malay

papers and for some time was the K.K. Correspondent to the now defunct *Straits Echo* of Penang and the *Times of Malaya* of Ipoh.[40] In short, both educational work and current events engaged my interest. I must say I derived much pleasure in writing as I felt that not only did I enlighten my fellowmen in things they should know but also helped to guide Malay public opinion in what I believed to be the right direction.

My first article to the *Utusan Melayu*,[41] then run by Inche Eunos (afterwards the Hon. Inche/Eunos) as Editor was on the subject of smoking which I suggested should not be allowed to be enjoyed by those under 16. I was pleased to find that the article had editorial support.

Other articles I wrote were chiefly on the subject of religious education for Malay boys in which I stressed over and over again, under various nom-de-plumes,[42] the necessity of having the knowledge of fardhu 'ain taught in the Qur'ān classes of the Malay schools.

[40] The latter were both English-language papers. The *Straits Echo*, owned by the Chinese-owned Criterion Press, began publication daily in 1903; the British-owned *Times of Malaya* began publication daily in 1904. The *Straits Echo* lost its separate identity and was amalgamated with the *Times* in 1939.

[41] The first *Utusan Melayu* began publication in Singapore thrice-weekly in November 1907, edited by Muhammad Eunos b. Abdullah. There is some confusion about the term of the latter's editorship, Muhammad b. Datuk Muda, *Tarikh Surat^2 Khabar* (Bukit Mertajam, Matba'ah al-Zainiah, 1940), p. 132, saying that he left only in 1914; Nik Ahmad b. Haji Nik Hassan, 'The Malay Press', *Journal of the Malayan Branch Royal Asiatic Society*, XXXVI, 1 (1963), p. 46, giving the end of 1909. The article referred to here by Abdul Majid has not been traced, and thus cannot be dated.

[42] The practice of writing long letters and articles (the two were frequently indistinguishable) under pseudonyms was exceedingly common in the Malay press of this time, prompted in part by the disapproval likely to be visited upon the writer by official or other superiors. Different pseudonyms were sometimes used quite systematically by the same writer for different kinds of letters or articles. Thus Abdul Majid's contemporary Zainal Abidin b. Ahmad wrote simultaneously under three pseudonyms: 'Zai Penjelmaan' (Zai the Incarnate) for literary disputation; 'Patriot' for comments on Malay society; and 'Za'ba' for language and letters (see Zabedah bte Awang Ngah, op. cit., p. 11). Whether Abdul Majid's pseudonym's were as systematized is not known, and he informs us of only one (see below, p. 135).

BOOK TWO 67

I had the satisfaction of knowing in 1918 that the Education Department under Mr. (afterwards Dr.; then Sir) Richard O. Winstedt,[43] handed over the Qur'an classes to the various Religious Committees in the different States; as it was felt that religious education should be under their supervision and guidance.[44] But I regret to say that this religious education, as directed by the various States Religious Committees, is still far from being satisfactory, except in two or three States. When I took charge of the Malay Training College, Matang, in 1919, as acting Head Master,[45] I was/surprised to find that during the *Kitab*-lessons, the boys had *maulud* and *berzanji* recited and sung.[46] I learned that Mr. A. Keir,[47] my predecessor, was pleased with

[43]See below, p. 99 and note 116.

[44]For the most part these committees took the form of Malay sub-committees of the State Councils of the individual federated states, though often with a preponderance of non-*ulama* members. The unfederated states were not affected, religious education having all along been matters for the Malay establishment.

[45]The Matang (Perak) Training College for Malay teachers had been started in 1913, in part as a result of dissatisfaction by the Perak state authorities (including Sultan Idris) concerning the limited number of teachers (thirty) produced annually by the Malacca training college (founded in 1900 to serve all three Straits Settlements and the four federated states). Matang was designed to produce fifteen teachers annually, for Perak alone. In 1922, the Malacca and Matang colleges were discontinued, with the opening of the new Sultan Idris Training College at Tanjong Malim. (Cf. Roff, *The Origins of Malay Nationalism*, pp. 132, 136 and 142 ff.)

[46]*Maulud* refers to readings from biographical works about the Prophet Muhammad, the term deriving from *Mawlid an-Nabi* (Ar. Prophet's birthday), though such readings take place on many other sorts of occasion; *berzanji*, the Malayanized name given to certain popular songs in Arabic glorifying the Prophet Muhammad, the term thought to be derived from originals composed by an Indian (?) whose name ended in al-Barazanjī or Barazanjī (cf. *Encyclopedia Islam*, art. 'Barazanjī').

[47]Alexander Keir (1884–?), born in Scotland, graduated from Aberdeen University in 1905 and joined the Department of Education, S.S. and F.M.S., in 1906. He was appointed headmaster at Matang when the college opened in 1913, and promoted to the post of Inspector of Schools, Perak, in 1920, on return from the home leave, begun in March 1919, during which Abdul Majid replaced him. He retired as Acting Chief Inspector of English Schools, S.S. and F.M.S., in 1938.

this *Kitab* class only when the students made a lot of noise. Needless to add, I re-organised this class and told old Haji Ali, the Qur'an teacher, what I expected him to teach. I do not think the old man was pleased. Anyway, he retired shortly after that; and his place was filled by a youngish man, named Ja'afar.

Somehow [or] other, I suspected that the Malay public did not quite grasp what the religious education of schoolboys should be. I also believed that some of the Malay Qadhis and Imams were 'square pegs in round holes'. This led me to suggest that the Government should establish a Religious College, for the training of religious teachers and religious officials.[48] But my request was like the 'voice in the desert'.

When I said that this was the busiest period of my past life, I did not mean that I had no time for sports and games and other pleasures: I could boast of being a good centre half at football and of playing for the district of Kuala Kangsar in the Walker Cup Football matches.[49] Once in a match between Kuala Kangsar and Ipoh, Mr. (afterwards the Hon. Mr.) A.N. Kenion was the referee.[50] He saw that I played so very good a game that day that he offered

---

For some Malay comments on his career, see *Warta Malaya*, 28 November 1938.

[48] The date of this proposal is not, of course, clear from the text. It may be remarked, however, that from the mid-1920s, at least, there was frequent discussion in the Malay press and elsewhere (for example, at the first Durbar of Rulers in 1927, Sultan of Selangor speaking) concerning the need for a central college of higher Islamic education. It was not until well after the war, however, in 1955, that the present Kolej Islam was set up in Kelang, Selangor.

[49] The cup, which was competed for among association football teams throughout Perak, appears to have been presented by Lieut. Colonel R.S.F. Walker. Born in 1850, Walker joined the 28th Foot from Sandhurst in 1871, saw service in Perak in 1876, and from 1879 served with the Perak Armed Police (from 1884 known as the 1st Perak Sikhs). In 1896 he became Commandant of the Malay States Guides, a force he himself organized. He retired in 1910.

[50] A.N. Kenion, senior partner in the law firm Maxwell and Kenion, of Ipoh, was an Unofficial (i.e., not *ex-officio*) member of the Federal Council from 1915 to 1923. It is clear that the incident described here occurred before Kenion was appointed to the Council and acquired his honorific.

to engage me as Head Boy on $25/- p.m. with special duties to play football only. It was a generous offer, of course intended to secure my services as a footballer for the most important town in the States. But before I could thank Mr. Kenion for the offer Mr. Hargreaves who had overheard it in the distance told Mr. Kenion that I was not the ordinary type of Malays who looked for cheap jobs like house-boys and the like. There was a loud laugh following the explanation who I really was at the expense of Mr. Kenion who I noticed tried to hide/away from the gathering crowd. It was the first time that Mr. Kenion came in touch with an educated Malay and mistook him for an uneducated man. The mistake was perhaps natural as I had been playing without boots; and the centre forward playing for Ipoh that day was the centre forward for the State. And the Ipoh team had expected to have a walk-over against Kuala Kangsar; but the result proved that they were beaten by 3 to 2! It was indeed a great day for me as everyone of the spectators believed that in my important position on the field I had turned the table in favour of the Kuala Kangsar team!

Many years after this, the Hon. Mr. Kenion and I happened to be travelling together in the same train. I went up to him and told him that I would accept his offer as Head Boy on $500/- per month, instead of the $25/- p.m., he had agreed to pay. I was then getting $400/- p.m. He looked at me and said that he would not pay me even $5/- p.m. for playing football. I must say he was right as I had already put on a paunch by that time and would be useless at football!

In the clubs (I joined the Kastan Zarian Club—now the Iskandar Polo Club[51]—and the Ellerton Club)[52] I was/perhaps the

---

[51]Kastan Zarian (Wilkinson's *Malay-English Dictionary* has Kastanzarian) is an ancient or traditional name for Perak, the origin of which is not known. The club appears to have been exclusively Malay, its members were largely of the Malay aristocracy and government servants above the clerical level, and its interests were mainly recreational. The president in 1915 was Raja Chulan b. Sultan Abdullah (see below, note 71). Abdul Majid was honorary secretary. The club is to be distinguished from the multi-racial Idris Club (also in Kuala Kangsar), of which Sultan Iskandar himself was president in 1920, but whose date of foundation is not known.

[52]The Ellerton Club, for Asian clerks and subordinate officials, was

most talkative, the most boisterous and the most lively of all members. I enjoyed holding the others spellbound listening to my yarns or my views on current topics. I got the yarns from Mr. Rowlands who seemed to have an endless stock of them and improved upon them or adapted them to suit my audience. As for current events there was practically nothing that I had none [*sic*] to suggest for their improvement. I strongly objected and openly criticised the old custom of sitting on the floor with Europeans, Chinese, Indians and others sitting on chairs in the same room. I maintained that Malays should be made to sit on chairs like the other guests. Once I was told in the Istana Negara that the chairs were meant only for the Anak Rajas;[53] but I thought that Kanagapathi Pillay or Chan Kim Loon could not be regarded as Anak Rajas by any stretch of the imagination:[54] anyway, I could not agree to place myself at the feet of some of those on the chairs by/sitting on the floor. I felt strongly that I was in the honourable position of being *guru* to the Anak Rajas. So, if the Istana was no place for me and my position, I had better go away. And go away did I do, without seeing the ceremony to which I was invited to the end.

On another occasion, a farewell dinner was to be given in the Kastan Zarian Club to a certain European Officer who was leaving the district on long leave. He was a good man, very much liked by the Malays; and a grand occasion was made to entertain him with many people in the district invited to take part in honouring him and wishing him 'Good-bye'. I was asked, as usual, to prepare the address and have it printed and framed. I was to read the address after the dinner. I discovered in the evening before the dinner that I was to sit on the floor during the dinner while the Chinese, Indian and Eurasian guests would be on chairs. This

---

named after H.B. Ellerton, District Officer Kuala Kangsar from 1911 to 1919 (see below, note 81).

[53] The Istana Negara, was the principal formal residence of the Sultan. The term '*anak raja*', lit., 'children of royal birth', is used to denote royalty at large.

[54] Kanagapathi Pillay is thought to have been the leading member of the Chettyar community in Kuala Kangsar. Chan Kim Loon has not been identified, but was doubtless a prominent Chinese merchant in the town, or possibly a tin-mining magnate.

was too much for me; so I did not attend the/dinner. At about 7.30, one of the Committee members of the Club came to my house and asked me excitedly why I did not dress myself up to go to the dinner. I told him that at the last minute I remembered the *sambal blachan*[55] we had for tiffin that day was so very tasty that I could not afford to miss it at dinner. He asked me if I knew I had to read the address in the Club. I said I did and assured him that I would be in the Club in good time for the address. He was satisfied with my assurance and went back to the Club. And I did keep my word to him about reading the address. After all, like many others, this man only cared to get the best service out of me without ever wishing to know what my feelings were.

Of all the people I spoke to about my feelings on such occasions, I found that the only man in Perak who understood and sympathised with me in this respect was the Dato Panglima Kinta, Che Wan.[56]

Sultan Idris was a great man; and at the time of which I now write/he was well-advanced in age and had won the reputation he deserved.[57] Sir Frank Swettenham and other able writers had given glimpses into his life in their books.[58]

I believe his greatness was due not so much to his ability as a ruler, though it was said that he was wise in Council and quickly

---

[55] A condiment made from fermented shrimps and red peppers.

[56] A son of the previous Dato' Panglima Kinta, Muhammad Yusof, and one of the eight senior Perak chiefs of the second rank, Cik Wan lived in Ipoh and is said (interview, Raja Razman b. Raja Abdul Hamid, Kuala Kangsar, 1967) to have been 'very Westernized', a great sportsman, the only Malay member (possibly the only Asian member) of the exclusive Ipoh Club, and a favourite of Sultan Iskandar (reg. 1918–1938). He died about 1947. For a brief biography, see A. Talib b. Haji Ahmad, *Riwayat Kinta* (Kuala Lumpur, Pustaka Rusna, [? 1959]), pp. 81–86.

[57] See above, Book One, note 3. Sultan Idris ruled Perak for nearly thirty years, and having been born in 1849 was 67 at the time of his death in January 1916. He was widely recognized as the leading Sultan in the F.M.S., and was frequently spokesman for them collectively.

[58] Stray references only occur in Swettenham's writings, but see, e.g., his *Footprints in Malaya* (London, Hutchinson, 1942), pp. 97 and 99.

understood as well as whole-heartedly supported every measure advanced by his Adviser, the British Resident, for the progress of his State and the advancement of his people, but to his good understanding of the mentality of his people with whom he really sympathised and for whose welfare he was ever solicitous. He appeared to me to be always studying the history and progress of every intelligent and ambitious Malay in his State; and was ever ready to help such men with his advice and guidance, as unobtrusively as circumstances would permit.

90   It must be pointed out here that the intellectual/Malays of the old school were real masters in the art of giving *indirect* hits in their speech. In fact, *direct* speech was considered to be boorish and a sign of bad breeding. Sultan Idris was of course an expert in this art; and once, I was told, a certain Malay who was a graduate of the Al-Azhar University and was then in danger of suffering from a swollen-head was mercilessly criticised for the good of his own soul by the old Sultan; but the man took everything in the light of a good yarn, when he was in the presence of the good old Ruler and only understood the real purport of what was said to him when he got home and was lying in bed that evening. He was, however, good enough to admit being severely criticised in a way that he would not forget all his life the next morning.

I should add that I have not come across anyone of the younger generations with this type of wisdom and old-world form of indirect hits in their speech. It would appear that the art was
91   buried with the old generations!/As an ambitious and intelligent young man, it was not long before I received my share of the old Sultan's attentions

The way he took to introduce me to that circle of his Court suitable to my position was characteristic of his time and the old-world ways which are now fast being forgotten in the limbo of things unknown and replaced by modern Western ones. It was in the mosque after the Friday service was over that the Sultan began the initiation ceremony of my introduction by asking the Imam and a few other leading men present who I was. He did this not because he had not seen me before, particularly as I had been very conspicuous in his presence on Prize-giving days and on Sports days in the College several times previous to that; but that was the correct way for His Highness to do. Then came his enquiries on personal matters to everyone he knew, which was understood and taken to mean that those he did not address or did not refer to could leave, no need to wait. Once or twice I noticed some men who had prepared to go taking their/seats again on being spoken to by His Highness. I remember making an attempt to go but was told by some kind friend that it would be rude on my part to do so.

At last when the unwanted ones had left, His Highness asked old Haji Abdullah, the Visiting Teacher of Kuala Kangsar, when it would be convenient for him to prepare a feast and how many goats would he require for the number of people then remaining present. Haji Abdullah, though not a cook by profession, was responsible for the preparation of the food at some of the Sultan's feasts; and he did it half Arabic, half Indian fashion. He had learned cooking when he was in Mecca.[59]

As soon as the arrangements for the dinner had been made, the Sultan stood up to return to the house of his third wife in Talang, saying to everyone present in the meantime: 'Please do not forget tomorrow night! Haji Nat Noor! Do bring To' Majid along!' while he nodded and smiled at me.

'Tuanku!' replied Haji Mohamed Noor, the Imam, signifying that he would obey His Highness's command.

As he and I discussed when and where we would meet so as to go to the Talang Istana together, he told me confidentially that the Sultan got up the feast especially for the purpose of meeting me. He explained that the Sultan took a great liking to me and was pleased whenever he read any of my articles in the *Utusan Melayu*. He appreciated my idea of displaying one's knowledge with the object of enlightening the others. Anyway, he added, knowledge is not like bananas that get ripe more quickly if they are wrapped up and hidden away from sight in some corner!

To say that I was pleased would not correctly describe my

---

[59]Haji Abdullah cannot be further identified. For district Visiting Teachers see above, note 6.

feelings. I felt as if I was moving with wings in the seventh heavens! It was indeed a great man who could make you feel great like that!

94 The feast itself, I discovered, was not a grand affair for an Istana of a great Sultan to boast of and the company was not an exclusive one: at least there was not a single person present whom I did not know personally and intimately before. I cannot say that I enjoyed it very much; and what I did not like about it most was that at the end there was Qur'an reading in which I did not particularly shine as there were many brilliant Qaris.[60] I asked Haji Mat Noor what the Qur'an-reading was intended for. Haji Mat Noor told me that it was meant for nothing in particular, but the whole show was got up by the Sultan for the purpose of publishing the fact that he was taking me into his own personal care. Being a novice in the ways of the Sultan's Court, I asked again what that meant. I think I noticed signs of annoyance on his face as he said that I could consider myself henceforth as one of the Sultan's men and ask for relief whenever I got into trouble. I did not ask for further detail as that would show my ignorance

95 in the eyes of Haji Mat Noor who was I was sure would/retail it to the others as was his wont; so I left him at that, feeling somewhat elated all the time with the information that I was one of the Sultan's own favourite men.

The Malay College, by this time, had made a good reputation, thanks to the good work of the able Head Master, Mr. W. Hargreaves. His first assistant, Mr. F.A. Vanrenen, who had been found to be below standard as a teacher in such an important school for high class Malays was conveniently removed with a promotion as Inspector of Schools, Selangor. Before he came to the College, he was Assistant Inspector of Schools, Perak, with headquarters at Batu Gajah.[61] The man who took Mr. Vanrenen's place in

[60] After a *kenduri*, or feast, it is frequently the custom for those present to read in turn from the Qur'ān, a copy of which is passed among the company.

[61] Frank Adrian Vanrenen, son of General D.C. Vanrenen, was born at Southampton and educated at Charterhouse and Cambridge,

the college was Mr. J. O'May.[62] It was understood by the boys in the College that Mr. Hargreaves himself who was home on leave immediately before Mr. O'May's appointment made the selection. It was expected that Mr. O'May would be very good at football, cricket and other games in which he would be the College coach./When he came, everyone was surprised to find that he was not at all good at any of the athletic games. Mr. Hargreaves was, I think, the most disappointed with Mr. O'May. He took immediate steps to rectify the mistake, as it were; and within a year, another man in the person of Mr. E.A.G. Stuart, came out as 2nd Assistant Master of the College.[63]

Mr. O'May was found to be good and useful in the College for teaching Mathematics and Surveying, two subjects that were considered then to be indispensable in the qualification of a Malay Officer. Mr. Stuart was found to be a very good sportsman, having been a Captain in the Cambridge University Football

---

graduating from the latter in 1891. After a period of school teaching in England he farmed in Australia for six years. He was appointed Assistant Inspector of Schools, Perak, in 1900, and in 1905 became one of the first three members of staff (with Hargreaves and Rowlands) to be appointed to the Malay Residential School, leaving in 1907 to become Inspector of Schools in Selangor. (Khasnor, 'The Malay College', op. cit., p. 70, fn. 20).

[62]John O'May, Irish by birth and a graduate of Oxford University, was the first person brought out from England specifically to join the Kuala Kangsar staff, in 1908. Despite the implications of Abdul Majid's remarks in the passage that follows, O'May was Hargreaves' choice as headmaster when the latter retired in 1918. This occasioned much controversy (he was disapproved of by the Board of Governors, seemingly on the grounds that he was a socialist and—somewhat improbably, not to say contradictorily—had engaged in trade by opening in 1915 an agency for Scottish cod), and though he spent a year acting in the post he was eventually passed over in favour of a new appointee from England, L.S. Jermyn. O'May's later career is mentioned briefly below, p. 76. (For details of the controversy over the headmastership, see Khasnor, 'The Malay College', pp. 101-5.)

[63]Educated at Rugby and Cambridge (where he just failed to get his soccer Blue), Stuart joined the College staff in 1909, and in 1913 was put in charge of the newly opened preparatory school. He is said to have left Kuala Kangsar in 1914 to become Director (or Superintendant) of Education in Kedah (Ismail b. Saleh, 'Persekolahan Melayu di-Kedah hingga Pechah Perang Dunia II', *Kedah dari Segi Sejarah*, IV, 1, Apr. 1970, p. 59). He died in office in October 1927.

Eleven in his day. His real place was as a goalkeeper; but he could play a good game in any position, either as a Forward or as a Back. Above all he was a loveable man in many respects; and everybody was pleased with him. I understand he was a descendant of the Scottish king with that name; and I know when H.E. Sir John Anderson, a Scotsman, who was then/Governor of the Straits Settlements and High Commissioner for the Malay States,[64] came on an official visit to the Malay College, he kissed Mr. Stuart on meeting him and did not shake his hands as usual. Perhaps that was the Scottish custom of saluting a person of the royal blood, regardless of his actual position in life![65]

As I was their Malay Munshi and therefore their confidant to a certain extent to their private feelings, I got some insight to the differences on the opinions and views on life in general held by these two men of different birth and upbringing! But the worst part of it all was, to my mind, due to the fact that they had to live in the same house for some years.

I believe in the end Mr. Stuart showed nobility of action by going to Alor Star and taking up the post of Superintendent of Education Kedah,—an appointment which, I understood later, was created to tempt away Mr. O'May and leave Mr. Stuart to succeed Mr. Hargreaves when he retired on pension. As it happened Mr. O'May was left with the door/open to him to become Head Master of the Malay College on the retirement of Mr. Hargreaves, which he eventually did in 1918. He did not, however, hold that position very long owing to his incapability; and I believe he was actually asked to leave the place. He became Secretary in Messrs. Harrison & Barker Co. Ltd., Kuala Lumpur;[66] and the last I heard of him was that he got transferred to the Company's London office.

[64]Anderson was Governor and High Commissioner from 1904 to 1911.
[65]This improbable incident may have been mis-observed, but if not cannot be explained by the editor.
[66]Strictly, Harisons, Barker & Co. Ltd., a firm of import and export merchants, managing agents, and secretaries of estates, registered in London and with offices in Singapore, Penang, Kuala Lumpur, Kelang, Port Swettenham and Telok Anson.

Mr. Stuart did very well in Kedah, liked and loved by everybody who came in contact with him. But he died young, about 40 years of age, in the hospital at Penang whither he had been sent for treatment. I believe there is a Library in the Government English School, Alor Star, founded to commemorate his name, with his own books forming the nucleus of the collection.[67] Mr. J.E. Kempe, A.D.O. Kuala Kangsar who became later the British Adviser, Tringganu, was the principal mourner at his funeral, and attended to his affairs on his death.[68]

We all believed that Mr. E.A.G. Stuart would make [a] very good Head Master for the Malay College; but God in His own scheme had thought it otherwise. He was very popular with the boys as well as with the leading men in the place; but neither his popularity, nor his superiority in birth, manners and work could alter that Will. He would long be remembered as the Head of the School Cadet Corps where many of us got our first military training. Mr. O'May, on the other hand, was nicknamed by some of the boys as 'Orang Malacca', not for his free and frequent use of abusive words when he was annoyed with their want of intelligence in class, but for his perpetual rush through all his works.[69]

Much of my spare time about this period I spent in the two clubs mentioned above; but as the Kastan Zarian Club was a purely Malay Club I went there more often than to the Ellerton Club which was a Club for the clerks and other subordinates of all nationalities. Once in a Billiard Tournament of the Kastan Zarian Club, I got to the Semi Final, but did not play the/Final game as the other man died a few days before the match was to be played. This man was a schoolmate of mine, named Raja Abdu-

[67] The library was opened by the Sultan of Kedah in 1349 (1930/31).
[68] John Erskine Kempe, b. 1888, entered the cadet service of the M.C.S. in 1911. He was Assistant District Officer, Kuala Kangsar, from October 1912 to February 1915, and served subsequently in many other parts of the peninsula before retiring as British Adviser, Trengganu, in 1937. His personal diaries, several covering his years in Kuala Kangsar, are in Rhodes House Library, Oxford (Mss. Ind. Ocn. S. 94.+1).
[69] '*Orang Malacca*', Malacca man—the Malacca people having a reputation for impetuosity and impatience.

llah, and was a Penghulu, or Assistant Penghulu in Kota Lama Kanan when he died.[70] There was an epidemic of cholera or something of the sort at that time; and Raja Abdullah was only one victim out of many. We were all sorry in the Club when we heard of his death at such an early age. At the Club Prize-giving function,—there were other tournaments as well, Tennis, Croquet and Chess,—I consented to receive the second prize of the Billiard Tournament on condition that the first prize, a very valuable billiard cue, presented by the President of the Club, Raja (afterwards Raja Sir) Chulan, the Raja di-Hilir of Perak,[71] would be kept for and given to the only son of Raja Abdullah, a child who was born a few weeks after his father's death. After all, there was very little chance of my winning the match against Raja Abdullah as he was really a very good billiard player!

When the tournament was over, I was mildly rebuked for not getting some outstation members to compete/in the Tournament. I discovered that some of these players were really experts in the game. I remember that the Dato Panglima Kinta, Che Wan, was one of these; and I saw him play an exhibition game in the Club with Raja Chulan. I must say that he was the best billiard player among Malays that I have seen. I was told that once he played in Ipoh against a well-known World Billiard Champion when this man came to that town in one of his tours. Later, I travelled with him in the same train on his return from Hong Kong whither he had gone to play a Billiard Match against the champion of Hong

[70]Raja Abdullah cannot be further identified. The *mukim* (parish) of Kota Lama Kanan was about two miles upstream from Kuala Kangsar, directly opposite Kota Lama Kiri, '*kanan*' and '*kiri*' meaning 'right' and 'left' respectively, though—in relation to rivers—employed in a manner contrary to that customary in the West.

[71]Raja Chulan, the second son of the exiled Sultan Abdullah, was born in 1869, and had entered the civil service in 1886, after studying at Raffles Institution, Singapore, and the High School, Malacca. He retired from government in 1910, was appointed Raja di-Hilir in 1921, and became the first Malay to be appointed an Unofficial (i.e., not *ex officio*) member of the Federal Council, in 1924, remaining there for three terms until January 1933. He died in April 1933. He was created an Honorary Knight Commander of the Order of the British Empire (K.C.B.E.) in 1930, entitling him to the honorific 'Sir' in addition to his Malay rank.

Kong, a Chinaman. It was at this time that the Dato told me how delicious lyechees [*sic*] are, if they are eaten ripe and fresh from the trees. Tinned lyechees that one gets in this country do not have the same taste and flavour as those ripe and fresh ones, because for one thing they are packed in those tins before they are actually ripe. The Dato said he preferred lyechees to any other fruits he had ever tasted!

It was during the year I was Hon. Secretary of the Kastan Zarian/Club that the Silver Jubilee of Sultan Idris on the Perak Throne was celebrated.[72] I was told that Kastan Zarian was the old name for the State of Perak. Sultan Idris was the twenty eighth Sultan from the first one in the Perak Dynasty, popularly known as *Marhum Tanah Abang*.[73] Perak flourished most during the reign of Sultan Idris; so, it was only fitting that this Silver Jubilee should be celebrated on a grand scale so as to make the event as memorable in the public mind as possible. But the old Sultan had a different view. He wanted it in the form of a Thanksgiving Day more than anything else, to show the public gratitude to the Almighty for sparing their beloved Ruler and Overlord on the throne for such a long period. Only one or two other Sultans of the twenty-eight ever lived to reign in Perak for twenty-five years or more.[74]

It was decided to hold feasts followed with the usual prayers (doa') for the Sultan as well as the reading of congratulatory addresses from the/various communities of the public.

---

[72] I.e., 1912.

[73] Sultan Mudzaffar Shah b. Sultan Mahmud Shah (reg. 1528–1549), second son of the last Malay ruler of Malacca. Sultan Mudzaffar was buried at Tanah Abang (some four miles from Kuala Kangsar), and by Malay custom was thus styled '*Marhum* Tanah Abang' (from the Arabic *al-marḥūm,* one residing in God's grace, esp. as the dead know it; the term being used in Malay to signify 'the late'). Cf. Wilkinson, *Malay Dictionary*, art. *marhum*, for a discussion of the practice in general of supplying post-mortem names or epithets to rulers.

[74] Sultan Mansur Shah reigned for twenty-eight years (1549–1577), and Sultan Mahmud Iskandar Shah for forty-seven (1653–1720). Sultan Mudzaffar Shah III may be said to have reigned for some twenty-six years (1728–1754), but for part of this period the throne was disputed with his brother Sultan Muhammad Shah (1744–1750).

The Kastan Zarian Club held a feast (khenduri)[75] in the Club House on the evening of the Jubilee Day, according to the Malay reckoning. Here it must be noted that from sunset on Saturday evening, it is called in Malay Sunday night.[76] The *Khenduri* at the Club passed off very quietly. The addresses were to be read on the next day. I learned at the eleventh hour that the Club address had been written on an ordinary foolscap, whereas those from the European community, the Chinese community and the Indian community were printed on silk enclosed in silver caskets. As Hon. Secretary of the Club, I felt annoyed that I had not been consulted in getting up the address. I said so and was told that the address was written by a very able man. None seemed to understand that what I felt was amiss was that it was not printed like the others. I thought it would be remarkable for the Club address to be just on plain paper when it was known that Club was one for princes (*anak rajas*) and/chiefs (*orang besar-besar*). At least, it would show bad taste and reflect very seriously on the poor way in which the royal and aristocratic classes esteemed their own Sultan at such an important event in his life.

However, I was regarded as an 'anak dagang' more than as an 'Orang Perak' in such matter;[77] and no matter what I did in the interests of the Perak Malays the people would look upon me as a rank outsider and not fit to put in any word in the counsel of their affairs.

Sheikh Tahir Jalaluddin, who had been much longer in Kuala Kangsar than I evidently realised this attitude; so, he was going to read an address to the Sultan from the 'anak dagang' as a community. He asked me to be with him before the Sultan when he read the 'Anak Dagang' address.[78]

[75] Here written in the *jawi* (Arabic) script, in parentheses.
[76] See above, Book One, note 12. From the passage that follows it is clear that the eve of Jubilee Day is intended, not the evening.
[77] '*Anak dagang*', foreigner (in this case from Selangor and of Minangkabau (Sumatran) parentage) as opposed to '*orang Perak*', a Perak man. For some useful remarks on the concept of foreigness among Malays, see J.M. Gullick, *Indigenous Political Systems of Western Malaya* (London, University of London, Athlone Press, 1958), pp. 135–6. But cf. also below, note 91.
[78] For Syaykh Tahir, originally from Minangkabau, see above, Book One, note 9.

BOOK TWO 81

The Malay Football Association of Singapore which was anxious to have as many/Malay Sultans [as possible] as their Patrons took the opportunity to make this event as a means of introducing themselves to the notice of Sultan Idris by submitting through me their desire to give a congratulatory address on the happy occasion. I thought that Capt. N.M. Hashim, as Hon. Secretary of the Association, would come to Kuala Kangsar for the purpose.[79] I was told by letter later that the Association would depute me to read their address for them and that the address itself would reach me in time for the function.

I must say I was disappointed at this since I had been counting on Capt. Hashim's coming to my town in order that I may return to him the hospitality he extended to me during my visit to Singapore in 1911.[80]

As it turned out, I could only expect the Association address, not Capt. Hashim. And this arrived by post at 6 p.m. on the eve of the/Jubilee Day.

I remember I would not have been able to read the address at the function if I had not gone to the Post Office to receive it and hand it over in time to Mr. H. Ellerton, District Officer, Kuala Kangsar, for him to go through it before he, as Master of

[79]The Association had been formed in 1910, and had a membership of forty clubs (*Neracha*, Singapore, 2 July 1913). Nur Muhammad Hashim b. Muhammad Dali was born in Penang in August 1880 and educated in Malay and English. He joined the government service as a Malay Student Interpreter, attached to the Police Courts Penang, in 1898, and in 1899 was transferred as a Malay Interpreter to Singapore. There he rapidly made a reputation in public life, being active especially in the founding of the Malay Football Association and the Malay Company of the Singapore Volunteer Infantry in 1910, and on the Singapore Muhammadan Advisory Board, of which he was for many years secretary. In 1919 he became the first Malay in the S.S. Civil Service to be promoted to a post ordinarily reserved for Europeans, becoming Acting District Officer, Balek Pulau, Penang. In 1922 he was transferred to the Federated States' M.C.S., and held appointments in the Co-Operative Societies Department until his retirement. He was appointed the Malay member on the Straits Settlements Legislative Council in 1936, and served in that capacity until the war. For a brief biography and appreciation, see *The Muslim Messenger* (Singapore), April 1936, pp. 15–16.

[80]Abdul Majid had gone to Singapore to take part in the welcome to a visiting member of the British royal family.

the Ceremonies, could allow me to read it before the Sultan.[81] It was in the Istana on the next day that the address was given back to me with the necessary permission to read it.

Those who took part in the function at the Istana went there in a Motor Car Procession, section by section, or community by community. The Club had the loan of the Hon. Towkey Eu Tong Seng's big car, the most beautiful and the biggest car in the whole State.[82] Those who represented the Club and therefore went by this big car were Inche Mohamed Talkah,[83] Haji Mohamed Noor, Dr. S. Cassim[84] and myself. As we were moving along slowly towards the Istana, Haji Mohamed Noor remarked/to me slowly: 'Think of the irony of Fate! The Perak Malays always look down upon the *anak dagang*; and yet here we are as the representatives of their most exclusive Club—all four are *anak dagang*'.

Later on, he said that the man who felt most at this selection

[81]H.B. Ellerton, born in 1862, joined the Pahang Civil Service in 1892 as Acting Treasurer. In 1911 he was appointed District Officer, Larut, and Assistant D.O. Kuala Kangsar, being confirmed D.O. there in 1912. He remained in Kuala Kangsar, apart from a brief period between November 1915 and May 1916, until his retirement in 1919. Before coming to Malaya he had done lay missionary work in China, and was said by a colleague to have been 'deeply religious'. He found considerable affection among the Malays, and was created a *Dato'* (Chief) on his retirement. (See T.P. Coe, 'Recollections of Kuala Kangsar (July 1911 to February 1912)', Ms. in Royal Commonwealth Society Library, London).

[82]The Hon. Eu Tong Seng, an extremely rich Perak tin magnate and Singapore financier (chairman, Lee Wah Bank), the telegraphic address of whose family interests was 'HUGE', was also a member of the Federal Council until 1921 (see speeches in appreciation of his services, *Federal Council Proceedings,* 1921, pp. B50 and 52.)

[83]Muhammad Talkah b. Mohd. Arif was from Penang, had entered the civil service before the formation of the M.A.S. in 1910, and served in numerous posts throughout Perak.

[84]Dr. Shamsuddin b. Kassim, son of a Ceylon Malay (known familiarly as Kerani Kassim, or Kassim the Clerk) and a Telok Anson Malay woman related to Raja Abdul Aziz b. Raja Muda Musa (Sultan of Perak, 1938–1948), was a graduate of Madras University and joined the Malayan government medical service as an Assistant Surgeon in Kuala Kangsar, later moving to the mental hospital at Tanjong Rambutan. On his retirement he opened a clinic in Ipoh and practised privately. (Interview, Raja Razman b. Raja Abdul Hamid, Kuala Kangsar, July 1967.)

BOOK TWO 83

of *anak dagang* was Penghulu Mohamed Yatim. He was a son of a Perak Dato who had been exiled with Sultan Yusof in Johore.[85] There he learned his Malay under the tuition of the able writer and well known Munshi Abdullah.[86] Before my time in Kuala Kangsar, Penghulu Mohamed Yatim was the literary man most in demand by Rajas and Datos. I could feel for him in his position of being outshone by another star.

In the Istana, I came before His Highness three times. The first was with the party reading and presenting the Club address; the second was when the address of the *anak dagang* was read and handed over; and the third was when the address of the Singapore Malay Football Association/was read.

I cannot remember now who read the first one, as I can the second one; it was Sheikh Tahir Jalaluddin. And of course I read the third one. In all cases, the man reading the addresses was supported by a few friends, when he approached the Sultan on the Throne; but I was alone when I went up to read the Football Association address, which came last on the programme.

I remember my admiration for the Sultan increased every time he uttered a few words in reply to the various addresses. Not only were the replies very sensible, but in many instances they were also humourous, so much so that every one was happy and pleased. The Chetty community, for example, was told that with their money they helped the Malays to develop the country in a way undreamt of in their history in the past; but Chetties must remember that they should not charge high rates of/interest and so oppress the people in whose country they live,—a country

[85]Muhammad Yatim had been *penghulu* (district headman, the basis of the government administrative establishment in the rural areas) at Chenderiong before being appointed to Kuala Kangsar. His father has not been identified. Raja Yusof b. Sultan Abdullah Muhammad Shah, appointed 'Chief Native Authority' (Regent) of Perak from March 1877 to October 1886 and Sultan until his death in July 1887, was never exiled. Presumably Sultan Ismail b. Sayyid Syaykh al-Khairat of Siak (reg. 1871–1874) is intended, who was exiled to Johore for complicity in the assassination in November 1875 of the first British Resident of Perak, J.W.W. Birch.

[86]This could not have been Abdullah b. Abdul Kadir (who died in Jeddah in 1854), but was probably his son Khalid, first superintendent of education in Johore (see above, note 16).

that does not make any revenue from the Chetty's trade of money-lending!

The 'Anak Dagang' were told that they might consider themselves as such, but in his (the Sultan's) eyes, such men like Sheikh Tahir Jalaluddin, Haji Mat Noor and To' Majid (these were the only three before him representing that community) are not *anak dagang* but his own men.

Thus did this memorable day pass, full of good sentiments expressed by a great man for the peace and happiness of his people and country.

His great wisdom was only equalled by his generosity; for I discovered later that the *Khenduri* in the Club was given at his expense!

I heard afterwards that Sultan Abu Bakar of Johore was the only other Malay Ruler who was anywhere as wise and generous as Sultan Idris of Perak. But I did not know the latter personally as I did the former; so my knowledge about him was only from hearsay.[87]

110   I can safely claim to have had my fair share of 'youth's excitement' in love affairs. I was not bad looking as a young man, and I was always neatly, if not expensively, dressed. All this, with my position as a College teacher, had attracted the attention of the fair sex with doubtful morals towards me. Quite a number of them seriously thought of securing me as their lover and if possible of turning me to be their husband, in place of their own, whenever these had proved to them to be faithless. But it was characteristic of me as a young man to look with disfavour on those women who, I knew, showed their interest in me or made any advances towards me. I had a feeling that such women could never be true. Only those who would not look at me but were pretty in their looks ever took my fancy. Under such extraordinary conditions,

[87] Abu Bakar b. Temenggong Ibrahim (1834–1895), eldest son of the *de facto* ruler of Johore from the mid-century, succeeded his father in 1862, assumed the title of Maharaja in 1868 (with British approval), and became Sultan in 1885. During his thirty-three year reign (1862–1895) he did much to modernize Johore and was in many respects very pro-British, but resisted incorporation and retained for the state much of its Malay character.

it was only natural that my 'love affair' never came to anything. Besides, the thought of disturbing the peace between husband and wife was always repulsive to me as I had been taught if I took the wife of somebody, some day somebody would take my wife from me. This idea of God's revenge seemed to grow in me as I became older in age.

Sheikh Yaakub Perak in Mecca[88] told me of a very remarkable incident that happened within his knowledge to support this idea. He said there was a goldsmith, quite a respectable family man, to whom one day a woman came, shewing him a pair of bangles with the request to name his price for certain repairs to be made. The man had a look at the bangles, gave her a figure for the work to be done, and pinched the woman's hand as if to tell her it was so pretty that he could not see it without getting infatuated with its owner. The woman was sensible enough not to create any unpleasant scene for this unexpected conduct of the goldsmith but went away as quietly as she came. When the goldsmith got home that evening, he was greatly surprised to find his wife keep asking him what mischief he had done during the day; and he could find no peace with her until he told her what he had done on condition that she told him what/happened to her. When she had heard his story, she said to him: 'Now I understand why our water-carrier was rude to me today! He had brought the usual number of *qirbas*[89] of water for the house requirements and was standing as usual on the stairs for me to hand out the money to him. When I put out my hand, he pinched it and went away. He had never behaved to me like that all these years that he had been our water-carrier'.

'How swift is God in His reckoning!' both husband and wife ejaculated.

'And I am glad that nothing worse had happened to you!' said the man thoughtfully.

Thus, I can assert at this age without fear of contradiction that as a young man I led my life with certain principles; though, I must confess that I cannot call it a saintly life.

[88] See above, Book One, note 17.
[89] Ar., *qirba,* a waterskin.

After being disabled at football with a nasty kick in my right shin, at an early age, I went in for billiards and skittles; I believe I was then pretty good at/the latter game of which I was very fond. I remember I often played skittles all night and won as much as $100/- during the night. But I never lost that sum at any time. And once when my son, Abdul Latiph, was ill and had to be fed at the doctor's orders with chicken soup, quaker oats[90] and other expensive luxuries which we never had as our daily food, my winnings at skittles came in very handy. My wife confessed to me afterwards that she took a few dollars of these winnings every morning and bought a certain piece of jewellery with the money for herself when the total amount thus collected reached the necessary figure!

There was a craze in the Club for a long time for the game of poker and other card games. I know hundreds of dollars changed hands at every sitting; but never did I join, nor could anyone tempt me to join in such card games. The only explanation I could give as to why I did not play in those card games was that I did not have the money with which to indulge in them. The stakes for any of the card games were too big for my pockets to stand.

It must not be imagined that my life outside my teaching profession/was all absorbed in sports and games or any other amusements, though I would admit that my friends could always see me in either of the two Clubs mentioned above. I regarded my regular goings to the clubs more than [sic] as a mere relaxation to my brains from my writing work. Raja Chulan once took the place of the Sultan to give away the prizes at the College annual prize-distribution function; and in the end he gave his speech in English. It was the first time I heard a Malay giving his speech in English. One particular remark he made at the end of his speech made a lasting memory in my mind, and this was: 'All work and no play, makes Jack a dull boy'. I regarded 'play', henceforth, as the best 'pick me up' after a spell of hard writing work.

[90]Quaker Oats is an (originally American) brand of breakfast cereal, prepared from oatmeal.

BOOK TWO 87

The eventful Jubilee Celebration Day gave me food for thought and action in one or two things which I considered to be important. I could not agree to the term 'anak dagang' being applied to persons born in this country, particularly/when such persons, like myself, had lost all connection and all interest in the country of their parents' origin. It would not be correct to consider the English king, Edward VIII, as a German; or President Wilson of the United States as a Britisher. I felt the mistake of looking upon me as a Sumatran (Minangkabau) Malay all the more when some one told me that the reason why I was not taken as a Malay Officer was because I was not a Malay of this country, that is to say an *Anak Dagang*.[91] This, to my mind, was a gross injustice[91] as I was not born in Minangkabau, nor had any thought for Minangkabau in all my activities. When I saw more of the country during my official rounds as Asst. Inspector of Schools, Perak, I discovered that there were more of the *Anak Dagang* than real Perak Malays in the State.[92] This gave me the idea that if the

[91] Aside from the fact that when Abdul Majid graduated from the Malay Residential School (1907) no formal scheme existed for Malay recruitment to the administrative ranks of government, there is no evidence that at any time before or after the creation of the M.A.S. in 1910, possessing parents who were peninsular-born was a pre-requisite for entry—though rank and connection certainly were. It is clear from this passage that the question of who was or was not '*anak dagang*' was itself laden with emotion and fraught with confusion (Abdul Majid's own continued concern with it is referred to in the Introduction, p. xiv). Depending upon context and intent, the term might signify (within the limits of those generally regarded as ethnically Malay or 'Malaysian'), 'foreigner of non-peninsular birth', 'foreigner of peninsular birth but non-peninsular parentage', or 'foreigner from any state in the peninsula other than my own' (with the possibility of combination of the last two categories). It may be noted that of the four '*anak dagang*' representing the Kastan Zarian Club at the Jubilee ceremonies, only one was actually born outside Malaya (Syaykh Tahir), one was born in Malaya but outside Perak and of non-peninsular parents (Abdul Majid), a third was born in Perak of non-peninsular parents (Dr. Kassim), and the fourth was born in a peninsular state other than Perak (Penang) of parents whose place of birth is not specified but may well also have been Penang. The whole question of Malay identity came to be of great moment, politically and in other ways, in the course of the 1930s (see, e.g., Roff, *The Origins of Malay Nationalism,* op. cit., pp. 242-5).

[92] A perhaps pardonable but nonetheless real exaggeration. In 1921,

Malay public in Perak continued to insist on/making the distinction between 'Anak Dagang' and a Perak Malay especially for official appointments where merit should be the deciding factor, I would send in a petition to the Government praying for them to look upon the 'anak dagang' as a separate community with rights and privileges that were enjoyed by the Chinese, Indian and other communities, such as seats on the State and Federal Councils.[93] The 'anak dagang' whom I saw and to whom I explained their disadvantageous position in the official eye all agreed to sign the petition. One and all these people saw clearly that they did not get a fair chance, like the others, to rise as Government officials or as public-spirited men. 'If we are to be treated for ever as 'anak dagang', I usually would sum up my arguments, 'then let one of us be installed as *Dato Dagang*![94] As it is, we are a community without a leader recognised by the Government.'

I do not know whether the Authorities ever got wind of my activities to set right this very unsatisfactory condition; but I was not allowed to be stationed in Telok Anson long/enough to be able to see the work of sending the petition through. I was ordered to go to Matang to be the acting Head Master of the Malay

---

185,592 'Malays' resident in Perak recorded themselves as born in the peninsula, 161,337 of them in Perak itself—though this does not, of course, preclude birth to one or more immigrant parent. In addition nearly 24,800 persons were enumerated as Banjarese, nearly 14,800 as Javanese, 1,356 as Mandailing or Korinci (Sumatra) and nearly a thousand as Bawean or Bugis. (*Census of British Malaya*, 1921, pp. 180-1 and 404.)

[93] Prior to 1923, the Federal Council (founded in 1909) had in addition to its European official and Malay ruler members, one Chinese member and three (from 1913, four; from 1920, five) European 'Unofficials'. In 1923, a second Chinese was added, and in 1928 an Indian. The State Councils (founded at various dates) differed in composition from one state to another, but for the F.M.S., before the major reorganization that took effect in 1932, non-Malay 'communal' representation was as follows: Perak, two Chinese and (from 1929) one Indian; Selangor, two Chinese; Negri Sembilan, one Chinese; Pahang, none. The general notion of communal representation had become somewhat more pressing by the time Abdul Majid came to write his autobiography.

[94] Chief of Foreigners. The title was conferred in the western states (especially Perak and Selangor) during the nineteenth century, upon leading Sumatran, Javanese and other 'Malaysian' immigrants, as 'headmen' of their communities.

Training College, there, before I was one year in Telok Anson as Assistant Inspector of Schools.[95]

Later on, when I was doing intelligence work in the F.M.S. Police, Kuala Lumpur,[96] I wrote a report on the unfavourable position and general dissatisfaction of the 'anak dagang' in their official treatment on the lines detailed here; and this report received the serious attention of the then Chief Secretary, F.M.S., Sir William Peel,[97] who gave me an official interview and discussed with me the merits and demerits of the report. He assured me that the Government never had a different eye for an 'anak dagang' from a local Malay for purposes of appointments. I think I mumbled out something that that principle existed in theory but not in practice. So, he asked me if I was an 'Anak Dagang'. When I told him I was, he said to me that he was ready to help me if I found any difficulty in getting work for my sons. Then he asked me if my sons had left school, and what standard they passed.

I thanked Sir William Peel for his offer to help me, but asked nothing for my sons. I felt I had come in the interests of the 'anak dagang' and so thought it would be out of place to speak on my family matters. Anyway, I know I was pleased to hear that there was no difference between the 'anak dagang' and the local Malays in the official eye. It was just what I struggled and fought for; and it was just what I got!

Another thing that interested me as the result of my association with people during the Jubilee Celebration Day of Sultan Idris

[95] Abdul Majid was appointed to Telok Anson about the middle of 1918, and to Matang in March 1919.

[96] See below, pp. 145 ff. Abdul Majid was formally appointed Malay Pilgrimage Officer for the 1924 season (having in 1923 made the *haj* at government request), and on his return was confirmed in the post. When not out of Malaya on the pilgrimage, he served as a liaison officer with the Political Intelligence Bureau of the F.M.S. Police. For further discussion, see William R. Roff, 'The Conduct of the Haj from Malaya, and the first Malay Pilgrimage Officer', in Amin Sweeney (ed.) *Sari Terbitan Tak Berkala* [*Occasional Papers*] No. 1, Institute of Malay Language, Literature and Culture (National University of Malaya Press, Kuala Lumpur, 1975), pp. 81–112.

[97] Born in 1875 and educated at Cambridge, Peel joined the M.C.S. in 1897, and was appointed Chief Secretary of the F.M.S. in June 1926. He became Governor of Hongkong in 1930, and retired in 1935.

was volunteering for the military training of the Malays. The Hon. Secretary of the Malay Football Association, Singapore, was Captain N.M. Hashim, a very keen Malay Volunteer. I came to know his name in the *Utusan Melayu* when he was Colour Sergeant of the Malay Company, Singapore, Volunteer Force.[98]/He had risen to be a second lieutenant when he wrote to me asking me to represent the Malay Football Association at the reading of the congratulatory address on the Jubilee Celebration Day of Sultan Idris. Then he asked me to go to Sri Menanti to pay our respects to H.H. the Yang di-Pertuan Besar of Negri Sembilan. We met in Seremban and stayed in the Rest House together before we proceeded to Sri Menanti.

His Highness Tunku Mohamed, the Yang di-Pertuan Besar, was then in the prime of manhood; and as everyone then knew he had the fine bearing and good build of a soldier.[99] And about this time, he had just made the suggestion at the Federal Council meeting to have a standing army of at least 20,000 Malays.[100] He pointed out that the Malays as a race were a military people. Capt. Hashim's mission was therefore to promote the scheme to a success and discuss matters with H.H. the Yang di-Pertuan Besar. In the conversation at which I was present, Capt. Hashim hinted/that a Militia would be most suitable, rather than an army, for the Malays who were peasants by a large majority. I do not know exactly how the proposed Militia never came into existence. I have a suspicion that the movement was not supported by Sultan Idris of Perak.[101]

[98]The Malay Company of the Singapore Volunteer Infantry, a section of the Singapore Volunteer Corps, had been formed in 1910, largely as a result of the efforts of N.M. Hashim (T.M. Winsley, *A History of the Singapore Volunteer Corps, 1854–1937, being also an historical outline of volunteering in Malaya* (Singapore, Government Printer, 1938) pp. 56–7.) For N.M. Hashim, see above, note 79.

[99]Tunku Muhammad Shah b. Yam Tuan Antah (1865–1933) succeeded his father as Yang di-Pertuan Besar (Ruler) of Sri Menanti on the latter's death in 1887, and was installed as Yang di-Pertuan Besar of Negri Sembilan in 1898, three years after the creation of that confederation.

[100]See *Federal Council Proceedings, 1914,* pp. B34–5, meeting of 4 November.

[101]The Malay States Guides, which had garrisoned the F.M.S. since their

'What can you expect from my people in the way of fighting?' the Sultan was quoted to have remarked by Haji Mohamed Noor to me, when he was approached with the subject by the British Resident, 'The Malays are no longer the men that they were; they have been turned into women'. Thus did Sultan Idris disapprove all attempts to have Malay soldiers.

Whether this was true I have no means of verifying the Sultan's attitude. But I know for a fact that we did not have the Malays in the F.M.S. as volunteers till after he had died. I cannot understand what moved him to have such a strong objection to any military work done by Malays. I always believed that he was a loyal/and staunch supporter of the British Empire.

Indeed, I had come to regard Sultan Idris as an extraordinarily wise man under the new conditions of British Protection and to model my life after his ideals. But in this instance, evidently, it was not to be as I had intended. We were poles apart in our views on the subject. I was all for keeping up the Malay tradition as a fighting race.

'There are four things [on ?] which the world stands', says the

formation from Colonel Walker's Perak Sikhs in 1896 (see above, note 49), were disbanded after overseas service during the First World War, seemingly against the desires of the Malay rulers, and especially that of the Sultan of Perak (Inder Singh, *History of the Malay States Guides*, op. cit., pp. 81-9; by late 1918, the Sultan of Perak was, of course, Iskandar). They were replaced in 1919 by an Indian Army unit, the 70th Burmese Rifles (it being arguable that under Section 5 of the Treaty of Federation of 1895, the F.M.S. was obliged to hold in readiness 'a body of armed and equipped Indian troops'—text in W.G. Maxwell & W.S. Gibson, *Treaties and Engagements Affecting the Malay States and Borneo*, London, James Truscott, 1924, p. 70), and it was not until 1932 that the decision was taken to raise a permanent Malay Regiment which might, in time, replace the Indian Army garrison. The first battalion of the Regiment was recruited and commissioned in 1933-4, a second battalion coming into service a week before the Japanese invasion in 1941. A force of (European) Malay States Volunteer Rifles had been formed (in Selangor) in 1902, but it was not until June 1915 that the first Malay volunteer unit was formed, in Perak, as a platoon of the newly conceived Malayan Volunteer Infantry, and with the active leadership of Raja Alang Iskandar, second son of Sultan Idris (and himself Sultan from 1918). Cf. T.P. Coe, 'The Federation Volunteers, 1902-1958', *Malaya in History*, V, 1 (1959), pp. 22-23.

Prophet of Islam, 'the first is the prayers of the good, the second is the justice of kings, the third is the liberality of the rich, and the fourth is the valour of the brave'. Unless we have fighting men in the Malay race, how can we ever have the fourth of these four things, I said to myself. And these sentiments often found expression in the articles I wrote to the papers. The last of these articles appeared in the 'Malay Mail', and was reproduced in my book 'The Malayan Kaleidoscope' with the heading: 'Malays and Empire Service'.[102]

122   I have referred to myself somewhere in the previous pages as a successful teacher. By this I meant that I was successful in my work of teaching. I would add that I evolved a system whereby the boys could learn English much quicker as well as maintained the discipline of my class exceedingly well. But I was not successful in getting a good salary. Although I was made to understand by Mr. R.J. Wilkinson who chose the profession for me that I would be on the same scheme of salary as the Malay officers, I found some years afterwards that the only scheme of salary I was entitled to belong to was a very poor one with only $100/- p.m. as the maximum, which was far below that for the Clerical Scheme to which I had belonged before coming to the College, to study further. I also found that this particular scheme for teachers was drawn up and published by the Government in 1908,—one year after I had worked as a teacher.[103]

[102] *The Malayan Kaleidoscope* (Kuala Lumpur, Selangor Press, 1935), pp. 93-6. The piece, which is in verse form, first appeared in the *Malay Mail* on 28 December 1914, contains a reference to the Federal Council remarks of the Yang di-Pertuan Besar of Negri Sembilan in November, and was presumably written close to the time of the Sri Menanti visit.

[103] Comparative figures for the general clerical service in Selangor, of which Abdul Majid had been a member, are not available for the first decade of the century. Malay Assistants (not then styled Officers) under the 1910 'Scheme for Employment of Malays (Higher Subordinate Class)', however, were given a starting salary of $50 p.m. in Grade III, rising to a maximum of $160 at the top of Grade I—a process adjudged to take some seventeen years except for some of the thirty-four Malays already employed at administrative levels (mainly as '[Land] Settlement Officers') prior to 1910 and admitted to the

BOOK TWO 93

3 There was another Scheme for Teachers, which/appeared in the same official publication; and this other Scheme gave $200/- as the maximum salary for teachers. The only difference in the qualifications of the two classes of teachers was that in the one he must hold a Cambridge Senior Certificate, while in the other, he must hold a Cambridge Junior Certificate. Unfortunately in my case I only had a Cambridge Junior Certificate which I obtained on leaving the Victoria Institution. My two years' study at the Malay College had not been considered to be worth anything, much less as equal to having passed the Cambridge Senior.

I was at a loss to understand why instead of improving my prospects by going back to school I found myself worse off than in my previous position. My contemporaries in the Selangor Clerical Services in the meantime had got into the Malay Officers'
4 Scheme, in one or two instances,/and were getting better salaries than mine, on the grounds that they happened to be the educated Malays available for promotion to that Scheme when the demand for their services was made.[104] As time went on, the situation became more annoying to me when the very boys I taught and helped to pass their School-leaving Examination in much quicker

---

scheme subsequently (see Khasnor, 'The Malay College', op. cit., pp. 197–202). Though the 1910 scheme was improved after 1917 (giving a maximum of $200 p.m. at the top of Grade I), it seems likely that Abdul Majid, who, despite the lack of Senior Cambridge qualifications, appears to have been getting $200 p.m. in 1916 (F.M.S., *Federal List of Establishments, 1916,* p. 48), was in fact better off than most of his Malay Administrative Service contemporaries, as indicated in note 104. But cf. also his remarks on p. 121 below.

[104]*The Malay Administrative Service List, 1932* (the first known to have been published) gives details of eleven officers from various states who were admitted to the 1910 Scheme after an initial career in state clerical services or their equivalent. Those most directly comparable with Abdul Majid (b. 1887, joined Selangor Clerical Service 1903) are Abdul Hamid b. Baduk (b. 1880) and Daud b. Mohd. Shah (b. 1885), both of whom also joined the Selangor Clerical Service in 1903. By 1916 (before salaries rose somewhat under the new M.A.S. Scheme of 1917), the latter was earning $90 a month, and the former certainly no more. Abdul Majid's salary at this date, as noted above (note 103) seems to have been more than double this. Only with the 1921 revision, which gave major salary increases to the M.A.S. (Khasnor, op. cit., p. 210), did this position perhaps alter, but Abdul Majid was by this time, in any case, an Assistant Inspector of Malay Schools.

time than in any other school were known to be getting more income than the salary I was drawing. Truth to say, I did not grumble much as I loved my work and felt happy every time I produced a book for the educational improvement of the Malays or whenever any of my articles appeared in the papers to enlighten my fellow countrymen. As might be expected, I was always as poor as the proverbial church mouse; but I always managed to make some money from my book-writing to supplement my income whenever necessary.

125 I remember on one occasion, Hari Raya was fast approaching; and there was no fund with which to provide my children with the new clothes, so much beloved by the little ones on such occasions. I went about feeling as sad as sad could be. But I was not depressed, as my ideas always seemed to come to me best during such moments. One day, I sat down and thought and thought. The result of this thinking was that I could not sleep the whole night. Early the next morning, the whole of the book: 'Anak Kunchi Pengetahuan'[105] in MSS was prepared. By eight o'clock, it was already posted to my publishers, the Methodist (now Malaya) Publishing House, Singapore. In three days' time, I received a cheque for $100/-. I cannot say whether the children were happier with their new clothes than their father, as he sat on Hari Raya morning to enjoy his breakfast of *roti chanai* and chicken korma![106]

126 Good was the reason I had, as I thought, for being dissatisfied at the treatment I received in the College; but I believed the other man in my time, Mr. Rowlands, had better. He was a man, much longer than myself in the profession, with a reputation of being an able teacher. I understood he had acted as the Head Master of the Central (later called the King Edward VII) School, Taiping, on one or two occasions, with good results, before he was asked

[105] *Anak Kunchi Pengetahuan* (Key to Knowledge), (Singapore, Methodist Publishing House, 19?).
[106] *Roti canai* and chicken *kurma,* hot puff-pastry dipped in a chicken curry, both Indian in origin but much favoured by Malays.

BOOK TWO   95

to come to Kuala Kangsar.[107]
 'I thought when Mr. H.B. Collinge, the Inspector of Schools, Perak,[108] spoke to me about my being selected for this high-class school I was assured of my future' Mr. Rowlands told me one day confidentially. 'But I found I was better off in Taiping than here. I made money by giving night classes to the sons of wealthy Chinese parents; and on Christmas or Chinese New Year's day as well as on Race day, I would receive from them their presents of whisky and money. I had only to tell them what I wanted and they would give them to me.'
 I believed every word Mr. Rowlands said to me as/I knew the generous nature of the Chinese and the esteem they had, as an Oriental custom, for the teacher.
 In Kuala Kangsar, Mr. Rowlands had no increment to his salary for seven years; and that salary was only $105/- per mensem. How could Mr. Rowlands keep a wife of his own *bangsa*[109] (he was a Ceylon burgher who as a class in many instances held responsible Government positions and was generally looked upon as *tuan* in their expensive ways)[110] with such a small salary, I argued things out to myself when I heard that there was a black

---

[107]See above, note 21.
[108]Collinge, 'a trained teacher of good standing' from Malacca, as he was described by the Governor of the Straits Settlements, had been appointed Superintendent of Education, Perak, in 1890. Governor to Resident of Selangor, 3 Feb. 1890, in Selangor Secretariat file No. 75 of 1890, cited in Rex Stevenson, 'British Educational Policy towards the Malays', op. cit., p. 56.
[109]Race, ethnic group, or community.
[110]Of the 402 Ceylonese enumerated in Perak in 1891 (340 male, 62 female), only 62 were Burghers, and within Perak, of the six males in the Larut district (chief town Taiping) two were 'Government civil servants' (possibly including teachers), one a clerk, and three of no occupation while in Kuala Kangsar district all three males were civil servants (*Census of the State of Perak, 1891,* cited in S. Durai Raja Singham, *A Hundred Years of Ceylonese in Malaysia and Singapore (1867–1967)*, Petaling Jaya, Published by the Author, n.d., p. 165). Of the approximately 25,000 Ceylonese in 'British Malaya' in 1931, only 500 were Burghers, most employed in mercantile establishments and as managerial staff on rubber estates (see V. Coomaraswamy, *Report on the General and Economic Conditions of the Ceylonese in Malaya, June 1946.* Sessional Paper of the Ceylon Parliament, No. IX of 1946).

mark against his name in the official records, for keeping a girl of the *sharifah* class.[111] 'She was offered to me by her grandmother', explained Mr. Rowlands when he and I opened our hearts to each other for mutual sympathy and self consolation, 'and I had no heart to leave her to go to the streets, especially as her father did not want to help her in any way'./Poor Mr. Rowlands! He suffered for helping a girl to live and saving her from the worries of the uncertainties of the existence of an immoral life.

However, the girl herself soon proved that she was not worthy of the man's attention and kindness. She soon went to the streets and there died a miserable death, leaving Mr. Rowlands to marry one of his own cousins who was asked particularly by her people to come out from Colombo to look after Mr. Rowlands as his wife.

Mr. Rowlands and I became very friendly for some time and exchanged opinions and confidences on many occasions. As a man, he seemed to me to be able to advise me on many questions of life. Above all, he had a friend in the Federal Secretariat, one Mr. Colomb who was Office Assistant and therefore could tell us exactly what was written by Mr. Hargreaves about us in his official reports on the progress of the school. I discovered from this source that Mr. Hargreaves seldom wrote to the Government about/us as he told us he did.

'You cannot expect a man like Hargreaves to be doing all he could for us' said Mr. Rowlands to me as his explanation for the difference in Mr. Hargreaves' actual action from what he said to us he did. 'People in his position always saw to it that they got the best men to assist them, but on the cheapest salaries. Good work with the lowest possible expenditure speaks very well for pension purposes.'

I changed this view when I heard Mr. Hargreaves himself say that Lord Kitchener felt sorry for being responsible in bringing Zaghlul into the official limelight, thus helping him on to succeed in his work as the Egyptian Nationalist leader.[112]

---

[111]Daughter of a *sayyid*, one tracing his descent back to the Prophet Muhammad.

[112]Sa'd Zaghlul Pasha (c. 1860–1927). It was Cromer rather than Kitchener who, by appointing Zaghlul Minister of Education in 1906, brought him into official prominence, though the new (but short-lived)

BOOK TWO 97

Are the interests of the British people always to go against those of other people who come under their rule? I have always maintained and will always maintain that unless the various nations adopt the principle/of: 'Live and let live', and act upon it, there will be no peace and progress in the world. Or, in any case, when those in power in a cosmopolitan country like Malaya act in their official capacity according to the dictates of their own Nationalist Spirit, they are bound to create serious trouble, sooner or later. Real love for each other cannot be fostered among the nations under such conditions. And 'God is Love', preaches the Christian propagandist!

By this time, I had already to my credit the authorship of (a) the *Vocabulary and Grammar for Beginners*, (b) *Rahsia Mengajar* and (c) *Anak Kunchi Pengetahuan*. I believed I had the official recognition of my ability as a writer of educational books when the Director of Education, S.S. & F.M.S., Mr. J.B. Elcum,[113] commissioned me to translate into Malay, for use in the Malay schools, Phillips' 'Geography and History of the Malay Peninsula'. Mr. Phillips was then/Head Master of Raffles Institution; and a younger brother of his was Assistant Inspector of Schools Perak.[114]

Although I eventually went through this work as best as I could; but I know I did not write it with my spirit. All my thoughts were centred on producing a new series of Reading books for the Malay Schools as I had formed the opinion that the series of Malay Readers then in use were already out of date. This opinion,

Legislative Assembly set up in 1913 under Kitchener's auspices may have played some part in giving him a platform. In 1918 he was responsible for founding, and became leader of, the nationalist Wafd organization. During a subsequent stormy career, Zaghlul was briefly Prime Minister of Egypt under the 1923 constitution.

[113] John Bowen Elcum, educated at Highgate School, London, and at Oxford, joined the Straits Settlements Civil Service in 1884, and after serving in a number of district and educational posts succeeded R.J. Wilkinson as Director of Education, S.S. and F.M.S. (the title was new, and the office in some respects also) in 1906. He died in 1916 (see below).

[114] See above, Book One, p. 26 and note 46. C.M. Phillips, *A Text-book of the Malay Peninsula* (Singapore, Kelly & Walsh, 1904), is the title given in Cheeseman's *Bibliography of Malaya*, p. 61. The date of the commission is unclear, but appears to have been prior to 1914.

I found, was supported by practically all the leading Malays interested in the education of the growing generations of their own people. Everyone agreed that these books for the schoolboys should not only enlighten them on the principal workings and chief uses of the latest discoveries and inventions that happened to be popular but also give them a fair idea of the moral principles to guide them in the conduct of their daily life.

132 I was convinced that education is the only step towards civilisation, in its best sense. And I was also convinced that coming as I did from a life having associations with people of the 'Old World' straight into the life under the changed conditions of the 'New World', I would be the best person to advise the educational authorities how or in what form that education should be to give the best results to the Malays in their condition of being transformed from their ideals of the old into those of the new world.

The idea grew in me as I worked and saw the process of transformation in the boys as they passed through my hands. I noted with great pride the progress of the various changes in their mentality and outlook and inwardly told myself that I was the potter who gave these earthenware vessels their new pleasing forms and admirable shapes. And what was more satisfying to my soul, the work of moulding the clay into the new patterns required no special effort on my part. I could find my way to the goal of satisfaction in the work of teaching with my eyes closed, so to speak.

133 By the year 1914, I had already collected, classified and arranged the headings for the essays and stories in the Reading Books I proposed to write for the Malay Schools, according to the existing standards, namely, Standard O to Standard V.

When this was ready, I began to write the stories and essays in right earnest. It was not long before I finished the work for Standard 0, 1 and 2. I sent the MSS to the Director of Education, S.S. & F.M.S., for his opinion and advice as to whether I should continue and finish the work, Mr. Elcum favoured me with a reply saying that it certainly was advisable for me to finish the work since the part that I had sent to him was in his opinion quite good. Above all, he agreed with me that new Readers were required to replace those in use. In short, I received a very encouraging answer.

This made me to write for terms of publication to the Methodist Publishing House; but this firm would not agree to my suggestion of a 20% royalty on the sales of the books, so I wrote to Messrs. Kelly & Walsh, who in reply said that they would agree to pay me the 20% royalty, provided I got the approval of the Education Department for my work.

I remember 'building castles in the air' on the bases of such promises for the success of my work. Never once did it occur to me that the gods had other plans in the scheme for actual events.

Mr. J.B. Elcum died before he retired. I was told later by Abdul Rahman (son of Haji Osman, Qadhi and Imam of Kuala Lumpur) who was then Malay Writer in the Education Office, Singapore, that Mr. Elcum took his own life with a revolver to save himself from the entanglements he had with a school mistress. She had trusted his words in the youthful ardour of her ambitions and paid for the mistake with her own life. The disclosure of the whole affair which must happen when her correspondence would be gone through was no doubt regarded too much of an ordeal for/Mr. Elcum in his position and at his age to stand. He took the best course to extricate himself from the unpleasant situation, according to the light of the non-Muslim Europeans.[115]

Shortly before his death, I received an official letter from Mr. Elcum requesting me to forward my MSS for the Malay Readers to Mr. R.O. Winstedt, District Officer, Kuala Pilah, who would be made Assistant Director of Education S.S. & F.M.S. to take charge of the Malay Schools.[116]

[115] The circumstances of Elcum's death in 1916 are unknown. Early in that year he had been 'declared of unsound mind' and admitted to mental hospital (Governor, S.S., to Colonial Office, Desp. 33 of 28 Jan. 1916, CO 273/440).

[116] Winstedt, after graduating from Oxford University, joined the cadet service of the M.C.S. in 1902, and under the tutelage of R.J. Wilkinson early acquired a reputation as a Malay scholar. He was District Officer, Kuala Pilah (Negri Sembilan) from 1912 until 1916, when he was appointed Assistant Director of Education (Malay). For some account of his career, see the Introduction to J. Bastin and R. Roolvink (eds.), *Malayan and Indonesian Studies: Essays presented to Sir Richard*

The new appointment was publicly announced soon afterwards; but when I wrote to Mr. Winstedt about my new books all I could get from him was that he would give me his decision in the matter on his return from Java and the Philippines whither, he said, he would go to study the system of education in those places.

It was nearly one year before I heard from Mr. Winstedt again. He had come back from his study trip for some time, but I did not write to him as I thought he would be busy writing/his Report on the educational systems in Java and the Philippines which would include, I knew, his own personal observations and recommendations.[117]

When I did hear at last from Mr. Winstedt, I was officially informed through Mr. Hargreaves, the Head Master of the Malay College, that I was to report myself for a short training in Mr. Winstedt's office, Kuala Lumpur, before assuming the duties of a Malay Assistant Inspector of Schools. But this important event in my life was to take place only after Mr. Hargreaves' retirement that year.[118]

The School was all excitement with the news that two teachers, Hargreaves and myself, were to leave them at the same time.

The School held a meeting and decided that the Old Boys of the College should subscribe and pay for the Farewell Dinner to Mr. Hargreaves together with the presents as a token of the School appreciation of his work, and that the Present Boys should subscribe and pay for the presents to be given to me. As the man on the spot among the Old Boys I was selected/and asked to do

---

Winstedt on his eighty-fifth birthday (Oxford, Clarendon Press, 1964), pp. 1–9.

[117]'Report by Mr. R.O. Winstedt, Assistant Director of Education, S.S. and F.M.S., on Vernacular and Industrial Education in the Netherlands East Indies and the Philippines', *S.S. Legislative Council Proceedings*, Council Paper No. 22, 1917. Among the recommendations in the report (which set the pattern for Malay vernacular education for decades to come; for discussion, see, e.g., Roff, *The Origins of Malay Nationalism,* op. cit., pp. 139–42) was one concerning the establishment of a separate, Malay-staffed, school inspectorate for vernacular schools, of which Abdul Majid became one of the first members.

[118]I.e., in June 1918.

everything in connection with the work of entertaining Mr. Hargreaves. There was the Farewell Dinner, the Address, the Group Photograph of the Old Boys, and the Football Match between the Past and the Present of the College boys. And more in the sense that I would be doing the work of paying my last tribute to my teacher and immediate superior in my profession, I agreed to do everything that was asked of me as I could see nothing in any of those things that would be difficult, much less impossible, to arrange. It could only be the work of writing or seeing the various professional or expert people for everything required.

But when the Rest House boy in Kuala Kangsar, then the Rest House boy in Taiping informed me that they could not undertake to give the Dinner as they either had no crockery or no men sufficient to cope with the number of diners, I began to feel anxious about/the success of the College function. Nor did my enquiry to the Station Hotel, Kuala Lumpur, relieve me of this anxiety when in their reply to me I was informed that they would want $9/- each person for the dinner.

This was too high a rate for us to pay; and all that the Entertainment Committee, under the Presidentship of Raja Abdul Rashid, now Raja di-Hilir of Perak,[119] could suggest to me was that I should prepare the dinner on contract at $3/- per person and that I could get all the crockery etc. for the purpose from the three Istanas of the Sultan. Now, as Raja Abdul Rashid was then A.D.C. to, as well as a son of H.H. the Sultan of Perak, I thought there would be no difficulty at all in getting the loan of the Istana's crockery; but in this I was disappointed. I discovered later that the Istanas and all that there was in them were under the direct supervision of the District Officer, Kuala Kangsar; and so to him I must write/officially for the loan of the Istana's crockery, and not to Raja Abdul Rashid.

As my bad luck would have it, this Officer would not even condescend to reply to my request, either 'yes' or 'no'; so three

---

[119]On the evidence, Raja Abdul Rashid must have been a son of Sultan Abdul Aziz (d. October 1918). He continued as A.D.C. to the latter's successor, Sultan Iskandar. It seems likely that he was created Raja di-Hilir in 1933, after the death of the then title-holder, Raja Chulan b. Sultan Abdullah, in April of that year.

days before the dinner, I sent a long telegram to the British Resident of Perak asking him to give me his official permission to use crockery etc. in the Government House, Kuala Kangsar, the official residence of H.E. the High Commissioner for the Malay States, on loan for the dinner to the retiring Head Master of the Malay College. The telegram was so long that it read more like a letter of appeal. It cost me more than $2/- at the old rate of 3 cents per word.

I do not know if the wording of the telegram did it or if Mr. Oliver Marks[120] was better disposed towards the College and its popular Head Master than Mr. H.B. Ellerton; but in due course I received a reply to my telegram telling me/that I could use the Government House crockery etc. for the dinner to Mr. Hargreaves on loan. This was indeed a great relief to me on that score.

The dinner itself consisted of European and Malay food. There was the soup, followed by fish, then mutton prepared after the European way by Chinese cooks in the employ of Europeans then living in Kuala Kangsar; after that came the rice and curry prepared in my own house; and it ended up with pudding, coffee and fruits. Ah Teng, the Sultan's head Boy or Major Domo, came with his assistants in the Istana to serve the food and supervise the whole show. But at the last moment he asked me to write to all the *Tuans* asking them to allow their boys to come and help at the dinner as he at the last moment discovered that he and his men would be insufficient in number to do the work expected of him at the dinner. Well! it had to be done; and so I had to sit up another whole night writing all the letters. But that was/not the end of my worries over the dinner, by any means; although for one whole week, I was working at it for twelve to fifteen hours a day. I found at the last moment that my men could not get a rickshaw to take the rice and curry from my house, where they were prepared, to the school, where the dinner was to be held. I had just returned from the school watching the Football Match

---

[120]Born in 1866, Marks was employed on public works in Perak from 1891, transferring to the civil service proper in 1894. He acted as British Resident, Perak, on several occasions from 1910, including the period April to August 1918, referred to here. He retired as British Resident, Selangor, in 1922, and died in 1940.

between the Past and Present, expecting to find the rice and curry sent over according to my instruction. It looked as if the rickshaw community was in league with everyone to put obstacles in my way to spoil the function of my life. I at once wrote to a few people informing them that the dinner would be ready at 8.30 p.m., instead of at 8 p.m. and requesting them to inform the others. At the same time, I also wrote to the Inspector of Police who was living next door asking him to help me by sending some of his policemen to get me the rickshaw.[121]

When my messenger arrived with the note, Mr. and Mrs. Colgan were dressing up for the dinner; and both had a good laugh over my difficulty as conveyed in the note. However, in fifteen minutes one rickshaw came to my house with a policeman who asked me if I wanted his help in getting anything else.

No less than three hundred people sat down to the dinner that evening,—200 Old Boys of the College, and 100 guests. I noticed that a number of Old Boys who did not care to pay up their subscription came and attended the function with their friends. I told them point blank that I would not expect them at the dinner, particularly their friends who were not the College guests at all; and although I know they did not come to the dinner, but I believe they still owe me a grudge for it even to this day![122]

I must remark here that I am no expert at making other people realise their own faults or admit that they had no rights where they had/none: it seems to me that I always annoyed such people even if I thought I said the right thing to them in principle.

Probably, principles do not come into play in the estimation of certain people; and I am at a loss to say where [sic] such type exists. I am definite that it is not a 'class' weakness, for the people about whom I mentioned above were of the highest class in Malay Society and gazetted officers in the Government Service.

[121]The small scale of Kuala Kangsar in 1918, at which time the majority of the Malay and official European elite lived in close proximity on the hill known as Bukit Chandan, is well suggested by the despatch by hand of these last-minute notes.
[122]The meaning of this sentence, given here exactly as in the manuscript, is not altogether clear.

In my life, I came across one very clever man in this respect; and he was Dato Abdullah bin Jaafar, Prime Minister of Johore.[123] I know from my association with him that he always said the right thing to everybody under any circumstance. His severest criticism of anyone's misconduct in anything would be so expressed that the guilty person he addressed would take it not in the light of censure to disgrace him but in the light of brotherly advice to improve his ways./I liked and respected the Dato for his wisdom in this respect; and I think he liked and respected me for my wisdom in a certain respect.

That he had his own weakness and I had mine was another story!

When the dinner was over, the address was read not by me but by Raja Mohamed Tahir, much to the disappointment of everyone who knew it was written not by Raja Mohamed Tahir, but by me.[124] Mr. Hargreaves had told me earlier in the day— that is to say, after the group photograph of the Old Boys was taken—that it would not be proper if I read the address to him as it was well-known to the public that he and I were together in the College for a long time. So I relegated the work to be performed by the man who was second to me in class when we were schoolboys again [sic] at the College in its early days. I confess I did not hear much of Mr. Hargreaves' reply to the College address, nor to the other speeches of some of the important guests. I remember I was deeply absorbed in trying to know what the guests thought of the dinner. I know that was the first question I asked Mr. Vanrenen and Mr. Rowlands/as soon as I saw that they were free to talk to me. They assured me that the guests

---

[123]Born in Johore in 1876, Abdullah became a Lieutenant in the Johore Military Forces in 1897, was Probationer Commissioner of Police, Johore Bahru, 1900; the same in Muar, 1902; and Commissioner of Police there from 1903. He was appointed State Commissioner and President of the Town Board, Muar, in 1907, and became Mentri Besar (Chief Minister) of Johore in 1922, until a dispute with the Sultan led to his dismissal in 1928.

[124]Raja Muhammad Tahir, who was from Selangor, has not been further identified. As appears below (Book Three, p. 125), he died during the influenza epidemic of 1918, while Assistant District Office of Kajang, Selangor, not long after the occasion described.

were very pleased and considered it to be excellent. Mr. O'May, however, when asked, went a step further by asking me to have a drink and instructing his 'boy' to give me whatever I asked for.

This was unusual for Mr. O'May to do as he was known to be a teetotaller, neither accepting any drink from, nor offering it to, anyone. Needless to add, I accepted the drink offered by Mr. O'May and took a few more from the bar at the *ronggeng* show.[125] The result was that within one hour I was so drunk that I actually danced with one of the *ronggeng* girls and made a fool of myself, much to the merriment of those present.

Writing as I do now, nearly twenty-five years after the event, I am inclined to believe that the *ronggeng* was organized by some Old Boy/or a clique of Old Boys, determined to make some fun out of me. I must say that they succeeded very well; at least, to get Mr. O'May to stand all the drinks given at the *ronggeng* bar was in itself a success!

Mr. O'May was Honorary Secretary of the Sultan Idris Club; and as such he could get as many bottles of whisky, brandy or any other kind of drink he wanted by simply signing the chit for them. Payment would be made at the end of the month.

Next day, the School assembled in the Library Room to give their address and hand over their presents to me. The former was not printed on silk, illuminated and framed, like the address to Mr. Hargreaves, but written out on a foolscap paper; while the latter took the form of a watch and a gold chain. I did not know what these presents were till I saw them; they kept the whole thing a secret from me till the last moment.

I was moved not by the address assuring me/of the boys' appreciation of my work, nor by the liberality of the boys' presents

---

[125] *Ronggeng*—Malay dancing girl, and thus the popular form of public dance associated with these girls, who danced either by themselves or opposite members of the audience who were venturesome enough to join them. The more puritanical sections of Malay society professed to disapprove of *ronggeng*, and in addition the consumption of alcohol is forbidden to Muslims. It follows that the character of the evening, though proper and traditional in its way, was somewhat daring and certainly Westernized or 'modern', as befitted an institution which did much to Westernize an important section of the Malay ruling class.

to me, but by the thought that I would be missed by the boys as some of them had begun to look up to me 'as their own father for advice and guidance', as they told my wife who repeated it to me when I was about to go and meet them in the Library Room.

'Poor boys!' I had said to myself, 'they would indeed be *like chickens without the mother-hen*' (*seperti anak ayam kehilangan ibu,*) (as they themselves described it) when both of us were gone.

In my reply to the address of the boys, I told them that I was as much sorry as they were to leave the College as I had begun to look to the boys as my own children. But it is God's Will that I should work elsewhere; and we poor creatures of God must submit to that Will of His. However, I told them, I would not be as far away as in England like Mr. Hargreaves, but/only in this country. So I would continue to watch the progress of the School and do all I can in their interests. In short, I said to them, I might not be in the College in person any longer, but I would be in spirit.

Now, that would not, and could not, be an empty boast. In my great anxiety for the progress and reputation of the school, I had recommended one who I believed would prove as successful as I was to succeed me in the College. I knew that steps had been taken to secure his services, and I wrote him privately asking him to accept the offer when it came. I knew that he was a man with a Senior Cambridge certificate; so he would not experience the same difficulty as I did, over the question of salary. Anyhow I warned him not to come over to the College, unless he was sure that he could improve his prospects thereby. To start with, I told him that there was provision in the Estimates for the salary of/ $100/- p.m. to be paid to the man taking my place; and he said he was getting only $75/- p.m. as a teacher in the Government English College, Johore Bahru.

This man was Inche Zainalabidin bin Ahmad (more popularly known as Za'ba)[126] who became famous as the Head Translator in the Translation Bureau at the Sultan Idris Training College, Tanjong Malim where he translated many books into Malay for

---

[126]This pen-name, or familiar name, given in the text in the Arabic script, is compounded of the initials Z[ainal] a[bidin] 'b[in] a[hmad].

use in the Malay Schools.[127]

I had not met Inche Zainalabidin in person up to this time but formed my opinion of him from his articles that appeared in the Malay papers. Later when I saw some Johore friends I was told that the articles of Zainalabidin which had struck me to be very sensible were really the views and opinions of many Johore leaders of thought in whose company he moved. Inche Mohamed bin Haji Ilyas, Head Official Translator of the Johore Government[128] told me that he knew Inche Zainalabidin when/he first came to Johore as teacher. He certainly did not know as much Malay as when he had associated himself in the Johore Malay Literary Society where he learned much that there was to know about the

[127]Zainal Abidin b. Ahmad (later Tan Sri Haji), was born in Negri Sembilan in 1895, and educated in Malay and English, in 1916 being appointed to teach English at the Johore Bahru English School. In 1918 he succeeded Abdul Majid as Malay teacher at the College, but also taught English to the lower forms. Transferred in 1923 to the Translation Section of the Education Department, he moved to Sultan Idris Training College, Tanjong Malim, Perak, when the Translation Bureau was started there the following year, remaining there as a senior translator until 1939. From his early twenties he was an active contributor to Malay intellectual life, and wrote frequently for the press on religious and social matters. A strong sense of rivalry developed between the two men, as is evidenced in some degree in Book Three, below. For some account of Za'ba's life, see Zabedah bte Awang Ngah, 'Pandangan dan Kritik Za'ba Mengenai Soal Sifat^2 Kemiskinan dan Sa-tengah^2 Aspek Chara penghidupan serta juga Shor^2-nya atas Jalan Keselamatan bagi Orang Melayu' (Za'ba's Views and Criticisms concerning the Poverty of the Malays and Several Aspects of their Life, together with His Recommendations for the Salvation of the Malays), (unpublished academic exercise, Malay Studies Department, University of Malaya, Kuala Lumpur, 1960); and for the Translation Bureau, see Abdullah Sanusi b. Ahmad *Peranan Pejabat Karang Mengarang dalam Bidang^2 Pelajaran Sekolah^2 Melayu dan Kesusasteraan di-kalangan orang ramai* (Role of the Translation Bureau in the Field of Malay School Education, and general Literature), (Kuala Lumpur, Dewan Bahasa & Pustaka, 1966). Za'ba died in 1973.

[128]Eldest of a trio of well known brothers in Johore, Javanese by origin (though not necessarily by birth), Muhammad was also a writer, and edited for publication the first part of the autobiography and diaries of the Datuk Bentara Luar of Johore (Muhammad Salleh b. Perang), *Tarikh Dato' Bentara Luar* (Johore Bahru, 1928), suppressed after publication because critical of Sultan Ibrahim.

108   THE WANDERING THOUGHTS OF A DYING MAN

Malay Language.[129] I am only sorry that in all his writings he never acknowledged even once his indebtedness to his Johore friends for his knowledge of Malay. But that was not all: he entirely severed his connection or friendly relation with us as if he never lived and moved among us all his life!

Before taking the gentle reader with me to Kuala Lumpur in my new appointment, I would dwell on two or three important events in my life that had a direct or indirect bearing on my future. First, there was the proposal to have a Malay as the Superintendent of Education for the Malay Schools, Pahang, in 1912;[130] and I sent in my application to the Government for this post. I failed to get this appointment simply because Mr./J. Watson, Inspector of Schools, Pahang, refused to go to Singapore as Chief Inspector of English Schools, S.S. & F.M.S. which post was to be created as a promotion for him, since he thought that the proposed promotion would not benefit him financially on account of the higher cost of living in Singapore than in Pahang. He told me this some years later when he was stationed in Kuala Lumpur and there met me at a certain school function.[131]

Second, I was offered by H.H. Tunku Mahmud, the Regent of Kedah,[132] to be the Head Master of the English School, Alor

[129]The original title of this society, founded in 1888, was Pakatan Belajar Mengajar Pengetahuan Bahasa (PBMPB, Society for the Learning and Teaching of Linguistic Knowledge). According to Za'ba, 'Modern Developments', in R.O. Winstedt, 'A History of Malay Literature', *Journal of the Malayan Branch, Royal Asiatic Society*, XVII, 3 (1939), p. 144, the society died some years after its inception, was revived briefly in 1904, and then again in 1934, under the same initials but with a new name and a royal charter, the Pakatan Bahasa Melayu Persuratan Buku Di-Raja (officially translated as Royal Society of Malay Language and Literature).

[130]Nothing is known to the editor concerning this supposed proposal, which appears in any case to be wrongly dated (see following note).

[131]James Watson, b. 1883, graduated from Edinburgh University (M.A. 1902, B.Sc. 1904), and taught at Raffles Institution, Singapore, from 1906. He became Inspector of Schools, Pahang, only in 1915 (see, e.g. *The Dominions Office and Colonial Office List, 1931*), and remained there until appointed headmaster of Anderson School, Ipoh, in 1920. Abdul Majid's dating therefore appears incorrect. Later, in 1923, Watson did become Chief Inspector of English Schools, S.S. and F.M.S., the post he is said to have turned down some years earlier.

[132]Tunku Mahmud b. Sultan Ahmad Tajuddin (1876–1937), a younger

Star, when that post fell vacant and I found myself under his roof as his guest.[133] Before Ramadhan one year, Mr. Hargreaves, Head Master of the Malay College, Kuala Kangsar, received a telegram asking him to keep back with him Tunku Abdullah, son of Tunku Mahmud during the Puasa holidays. Tunku Abdullah was not allowed to return home for a certain misbehaviour in his conduct which displeased his father. Mr. Hargreaves sent the boy to stay in my house as there was no one else in the school for him to live with./A few days before Hari Raya, I was asked to take back Tunku Abdullah to Alor Star. As my luck would have it, the boy changed his conduct entirely when he got back home. And this so pleased the father that he made the above offer to me. But I was so prejudiced by my friends in Kuala Kangsar against the drinking habits of high class Malays in Kedah, a prejudice that was confirmed on my arrival at Alor Star when I saw parties of high class Malays come to the Rest House and take their drinks, in spite of the month being Ramadhan, that I refused the offer then and there. I could not help noticing further the evil effects of drinks on Sheikh Omar who took to drinking only in Kedah to please his royal patrons. Sheikh Omar was an Arab who came from Mecca with the reputation of being a *Qari* and knowing the Qur'an by heart.[134] I thought that a life in Kedah would soon make me change my condition into something like that of poor Sheikh Omar. Never did I feel sorry for not taking the Kedah appointment./The vacancy was eventually filled by Mr. Ismail Merican,[135] an Old Boy of Mr. Hargreaves in the Penang Free

---

brother of Sultan Abdul Hamid of Kedah (reg. 1882–1943), was at no time Regent during his brother's incapacitating illness (Abdul Hamid's eldest son, Tunku Ibrahim, was declared Regent in 1913) but was President of the State Council from 1907, and Vice-President from 1915. Abdul Majid's error is understandable, as Tunku Mahmud was unquestionably the most powerful man in the state during this period.

[133] The date is uncertain, but may have been August 1914, in which year E.A.G. Stuart, who had taught at Malay College with Abdul Majid, became Superintendant of Education, Kedah (see above, note 63).

[134] One who has committed the Qur'an to memory is described in Arabic (and Malay) as *ḥāfiẓ*.

[135] Member of a well-known Jawi Peranakan (Malayan-born Muslim of mixed South Indian and Malay descent, culturally Malay) family in

School and a teacher of some years' experience. Later, he became the official translator of the Kedah Government and was responsible for giving the Malay version of the Penal Code and other Government Enactments, in use in Kedah. He told me he got into the Kedah Civil Service by taking up this translator's work, as the post was intended to give him a 'lift' in life for his high qualifications. It happened during the time when Mr. (afterwards Sir) George E. Maxwell [sic] was the British Adviser, Kedah.[136] Tuan Haji Mohamed Sheriff, C.B.E.,[137] the present State Secretary of Kedah, also an Old Boy of Mr. Hargreaves at the Penang Free School, was then a clerk in the office of the British Adviser; and I met him when I made my official call to the British Adviser and enquired unofficially when I could return to Kuala Kangsar. He appeared to me to be ever on the alert to satisfy everyone; and he had a red *tarbush* on his head!

154　Third, there was a lady in Kuala Kangsar whose love-advances towards me created such a condition that it was impossible for me to go on living where I was without doing one of two things either of which was disagreeable to me. She was one of three wives of a certain man of position and influence, very charming and pretty, with the reputation of being a good and faithful wife.

Penang, Ismail Merican was by 1920 Registrar of the Kedah Supreme Court.

[136] William George Maxwell (generally known as George, to distinguish him from his father Sir William Edward Maxwell), was born in 1871, and joined the civil service in Perak in 1891. He was appointed first British Adviser to Kedah in July 1909, and remained in this post until late 1914.

[137] Muhammad Sheriff b. Awang Osman, born Alor Star 15 Nov. 1890, educated at Penang Free School, graduated from Std. VII in 1909 to enter the Kedah government service as a translator in the British Adviser's office. In a long, distinguished, and powerful official career, he became Under Secretary to Government in 1916, Director of Lands in 1923, and Secretary to Government (Abdul Majid's State Secretary) in 1931. After the war he was appointed Kedah's first Mentri Besar, until his retirement in 1957. He was awarded the C.B.E. in 1937, and later became in turn C.M.G. and K.B.E. He died on 27 September, 1962. For the foregoing and certain other Kedah information, I am indebted to Professor Sharom Ahmat.

I met her first in the house of Dr. McLean who was married by [i.e. to] Mr. O'May and who was then the Lady Medical Officer, Kuala Kangsar. I went there one afternoon at 5 p.m. as usual, to give the Lady doctor lessons in Malay, and found her just arrived. She was invited to tea at 4 p.m.; but was late. She said she found her car to be out of order at the last moment; and she had to come by rickshaw; hence the delay. When I got into the house, I found the tea-things being just placed on the table and the party just taking their seats. I made preparations to go away from a place where I was not wanted; but Dr. McLean insisted that I should join the party. I found myself seated in front of the lady with the doctor on my right and/another Malay lady who accompanied her on my left. I remember feeling very shy as I sat down to that tea; I could not help being embarrassed as the two Malay ladies were strangers to me. I did not eat much, nor did I speak much.

When the two ladies had gone half an hour later, I asked Dr. McLean who they were; but she smilingly said: 'I thought you knew the lady sitting in front of you. She told me she knew you'. And I reminded Dr. McLean that there was nothing strange in that: Malay ladies could always see the men from behind curtains; but it is different with men. They cannot see the ladies as they like, according to the Malay custom.

Anyhow Dr. McLean never enlightened me as to who the ladies were. I had to be left guessing; and I did not press my enquiry as it might appear rude. Anyhow, I told myself that they were the wives of respectable people: I had no right to know them, unless introduced to me by their husbands or with their approval. So I dismissed them from my mind. But I was destined to know more about the lady who sat in front of me, as the following events would show.

[The following is written on the inside of the back cover of the second notebook]

N.B.
On the 23rd Ramadhan 1360 A.H. or on 14.10.1941, Tuesday

at about 4 p.m. as I was reading the *Fatihah* and *Qulhu Allah*,[138] as usual for the souls of the eight patron saints I suddenly got the smell of *minyak attar*[139] on my left. It lasted for *one minute* and then was no more. I believe I was reading for the *Kramat in Cheras* at that particular time. I will watch and see the significance of this. The eight patron saints in their order as I named them are as follows:–

1) Kramat Pulau Besar, Malacca;
2) Kramat Batu 8, Johore Road, Syed Ismail Wali;
3) Kramat To' Pusu—on an islet;
4) *Kramat Cheras;*
5) Kramat Syed Noh Alhabshi;
6) Kramat Sharifah Maimunah;
7) Kramat Syed Abdullah bin Idrus Ba-Rum;
8) Kramat Sheikh Abdullah Minangkabau.

(No. 8 came to be known in a dream of my wife)

[138] *Al-Fātiḥah* is the first *sura* or chapter of the Qur'ān; *'Qul huwa'llāhu aḥad'* ('Say: He is God, the One and Only') is the first verse of the 112th *sura* (*Al-Ikhlāṣ*).

[139] *Minyak attar* (lit. 'perfumed oil, from Ar. *'iṭr,* perfume or scent), often, though not necessarily, attar of roses.

Saints and others of exalted spiritual status are popularly believed to exude or be surrounded, when present, by certain fragrances. It is a common practice among Muslims, especially during the holy month of Ramadhan, to read certain *sura* of the Qur'ān a number of times with the intention of dedicating the merit of doing so to the souls of the departed. *Al-Fātiḥah* and *al-Ikhlāṣ* are especially favoured as they are held by many to possess particular virtue. Where saints, or *keramat,* are concerned, popular belief (frowned upon by strict orthodoxy) is often that such readings bring specific blessings, though general reverence is also implied. The eight 'patron' saints referred to by Abdul Majid in the passage that follows are clearly particular to himself and his family, though several are well and widely known (e.g., No. 5, Keramat Sayyid [more usually, Habib] Noh, whose shrine is in Singapore).

BOOK THREE

[The third notebook begins at this point. Pagination continues uninterrupted. On the inside of the front cover is written:

'Title: Probably the title: My Wandering Thoughts is better than the title given in the other two books—the Red Writing Pad and the Exercise Book.'

On the first page is written:

'My Wandering Thoughts or What I think of my Past Life by Haji Abdul Majid.']

On the next day, I met an elderly woman whom we called in the house as/'Kak Bedah'. This is not the 'Kak Bedah', sister of Yazid, son of Haji Said, a Rawa Malay merchant of Kuala Kangsar. She was the wife of an old Malay from Palembang with whom she evidently was not happy. She often visited us; and it was understood that she had her love-affair with my cousin Din (short for Maadin) who, she hoped, would marry her. She was eventually divorced by her old husband and married by a Minangkabau Malay who had a shop in Kuala Kangsar as a tailor. A cousin of Dato Rakna,[1] she found happiness at last with her new husband [and] became exemplary as a good and faithful wife.

I was rather surprised when she beckoned to me asking me to talk to her away from where we could be seen by anyone in her

[1] To' Rakna was said by Raja Razman b. Raja Abdul Hamid (interview, 1967) to have been a *bentara* (minor chief) to Sultan Idris (reg. 1887–1916). An office of *To' Rakta* [sic] *Pahlawan* is referred to in Wan Abdul Karim b. Wan Abdul Majid, *Tawarikh Raja-Raja dan Adat-Istiadat Zaman Purbakala Negeri Perak Dar-ul Ridzwan* (Penang, Persama Press, n.d.), p. 19. Other persons in this paragraph have not been identified.

house. I suspected that after her affair with my cousin she was going to try and have me. But her first words to me removed this suspicion; and I felt more at ease.

'So, you had a good time yesterday' she began. I was at a loss 157 to understand/what she was referring to, and candidly told her so.

'Did you have tea together with Inche........² yesterday?' she asked.

I was thunderstruck,—dumbfounded!

'So, that was Inche........ who sat in front of me at tea in the lady doctor's house yesterday', I said more to myself than to Kak Bedah.

'Believe me, Inche........ was very glad she had tea with you,' continued Kak Bedah.

'What else did she say?' was all that I could remark.

'She said that if you were her husband, she would not agree to your sitting for hours alone with the Lady doctor', Kak Bedah then said.

I laughed at this and asked Kak Bedah to tell Inche........ that fortunately for her and for me I was not her husband, so that I could not and would not be stopped from giving the Malay lessons to the Lady doctor.

It was Kak Bedah's turn to laugh; and she said: 'You are a fool!'

'Why am I a fool?' I asked her to explain.

158 'You should know that she loves you', she said hurriedly as she prepared to go and resume her household work.

That night I could not sleep till I had solved this new life's problem. The beautiful and virtuous Inche........ in love with me! Could this be true? I repeatedly asked myself. Is Kak Bedah merely pulling my legs as a revenge for my cousin's breach of promise to her? There is no end to a woman's scheme to satisfy her vanity, I thought. But I would expose her in her own trick, I said to myself. So, with this object in my mind I determined to ask Kak Bedah to get one or two things from her. So, when I saw her again, I told her that I could not believe Inche........

²The name is omitted in the original.

loved me unless and until she gave me her photograph.

But Kak Bedah was not to be dismayed with such a request. In fact, she said Inche........ had foreseen this request and had taken her photograph especially for me a few days ago. When it was ready she would certainly give it to me. Right enough, in two days I got the photograph in a handkerchief that was heavily scented.

But I told Kak Bedah that I was still dissatisfied with her story of the lady's love for me: I asked her for further proofs.

So, I received from Inche........ through Kak Bedah first a silk sarong, then a pair of slippers. After that, I was told to wait at certain places and there I saw Inche........ pass by in a motor-car. I could not say I appreciated the idea of seeing my lady-love passing in a motor-car. So, one day as I was teaching in my class in the preparatory school, I saw a closed rickshaw stop and the hand of a woman beckoning me to come. There were two women in the rickshaw, and I thought one of them was my wife. No other woman had ever come like that before or since. I was conscious that there might be trouble in my house which sent my wife to come to me at such an awkward time. So, I went to the closed rickshaw and to my surprise, the other woman in the rickshaw said/to me: 'This is Inche........ come to see you'.

I must say I did not know what I thought of the visit from her at such an hour. I can only remember telling her that it was my working time and asking her if she had any ring to give to me.

As it happened, she had no ring to give me; but at the same time she had no word to say to me. So, she went away as she came, leaving me wondering what was the purpose of her visit. When she had gone, I also wondered if she really was Inche........ because the woman who was shewn to me as Inche........ appeared to me to be darker and less pretty. I tried to look at her photograph; but to my great surprise the photograph was no longer in my pocket. I rushed home and asked my wife if she had seen and taken it. She said she had; but added she would keep it for me as she feared the photograph might be seen in my pocket by someone who would interpret it in a bad sense, detrimental to my character. I thanked her for her forethought to protect my fair name and asked her to keep the photograph for me.

It is surprising but nevertheless true that I always told my
161 wife about my/love-affairs and often discussed with her about the
character of the women who came to my notice. I found that she
was candid in her opinion about them according to the information
she received. In fact, it was from her that I learned Inche........
was a good and faithful wife who never cared how many other
wives her husband took unto himself. She was ever patient and
obedient.

Of course, I had to be equally candid to my wife and so I told
her that I was not at all charmed by the beauty of Inche........
On the other hand, as she had shewn so many signs of her love
towards me, I thought it unwise to reject her advances point
blank. She might resent my refusal and take steps to cover her
shame while at the same time have her revenge on me by simply
telling her husband that I made my love-advances towards her!
That would indeed put me in trouble and disgrace. So, I thought
it advisable to make her believe that I cared for her. I explained
162 to my wife the reason why I behaved towards/her as I did. 'You
are right', said my wife. 'But now, since you have admitted you
do not care for her, I will tell you what I heard about her. She
is not the true woman and faithful wife that we have thought her
to be. There is a man who came to her whenever her husband
went to his other wives.'

This information not only convinced me of the absurdity of
expecting faithfulness in the woman towards the man who had
many wives but also confirmed me in my opinion that Inche
.... was not worthy of my affection. I believed I had made
a reputation up to that time of being a faithful husband. I could
not think of any other attraction in me that would make Inche
.... to give up her husband for me.

Anyway, [at] once I asked Kak Bedah to get an explanation
from Inche........ for her preference of me to her husband
who was superior to me in every respect. She replied through
the same messenger to me that she had thought [over] that point
very carefully and come to the conclusion that she would not
163 consider it/a disgrace to come down from the back of an elephant
and mount on the back of a horse. After all, her position is like
that of a bird in a cage. The cage might be made of gold; but it

is a cage all the same. I thought this was a very clever reply,—at least, I could not say anything to contradict it. But it also showed how serious she was. She was prepared to give up her husband and his position and come to me. Did she want me to give up my wife before taking her, I wonder. The idea would be ridiculous and preposterous! She should know that I had just refused to marry a rich and beautiful widow just because she made it a condition of the marriage that she should not have a rival in my harem.

But she did not know my thoughts. So, as if to follow up the course of love between her and me, she sent Kak Bedah to my house with some presents and a message to say that she herself would come to the house on the coming Sunday.

The student of the feminine mind would detect a good reason for this move of hers./But I was not afforded the opportunity to find out the reason; for my wife scolded Kak Bedah as soon as she delivered the message and the presents to her. 'Tell her', my wife had said, 'that I am not a fool. I want none of her presents, nor her presence.'[3]

Still, Inche........ was not to be easily changed from the object her mind had determined to win. She asked Kak Bedah to tell me to come to her house at certain hours on a certain night.

This was indeed her greatest test on me. Should I disappoint her and give some sort of explanation later? Kak Bedah had of course warned me that she expected me to prove to her that I was a man, and not a coward. In short, she appealed to me in that feminine art whereby I should act with daring and bravado to meet my lady-love. 'There is nothing more hateful to a woman than to find a woman in a man', she said to me as a last piece of advice.

The night of the opening ceremony of the 'Ubudiah Mosque at Bukit Chandan was/a memorable one.[4] The mosque was built by the Government to commemorate the reign of the great Sultan

---

[3]This pun can be made in Malay as well as English: Saya ta' mahu hadiahnya atau hadhirnya'.

[4]The 'Ubudiah Mosque, one of the most striking in appearance in Malaya, was begun in 1914 and formally opened by Sultan Idris's successor, Sultan Abdul Jalil, in 1917.

Idris. It was understood that the Government agreed to build this mosque as an appreciation of the service rendered by the Sultan in moving the Federal Council to vote for and approve the gift of H.M.S. Malaya to the British Navy.[5] Great Britain was then at war with Germany, and the gift was received with great joy as a token of Malayan loyalty to the British Empire. Sultan Idris always got something when he gave anything remarked the Malays.

I heard from Raja Abdul Rashid (Raja di-Hilir) then A.D.C. to the Sultan that it was the ambition of Sultan Idris to see a new Railway Station built in Kuala Kangsar with a waiting room suitable for His Highness and other visitors of importance to occupy. Kuala Kangsar had no end of royal personages and important dignitaries visiting it. The station as it was (and is) was far too small on such/occasions. But one thing at a time was His Highness' policy.

The actual function at the 'Ubudiah Mosque took place in the day-time. That night, there was the feast (*khenduri*) followed by the usual recitation of the Qur'an and *do'a* [prayers].

People who were invited assembled there at 8 p.m. And by 9 p.m. those who could not join in the Qur'an-reading had already gone; while those who remained sat wherever they pleased waiting for their turn to read. It was about this time that I remembered my promise to visit Inche .... in her house. So, I quietly slipped out and saw in the distance a light in her house where her bedroom was. I turned to my right and to my left and found that I was alone. I was sure that no one was following me. So in a twinkling I left the road and got to the path leading to her house. I walked straight ahead of me as if I was going to my own house./I must not show any signs of fear lest she would see it.

[5]See *Federal Council Proceedings,* 1912, pp. B57–62 and 87, meeting of 12 November. The proposal, as is evident, preceded the First World War. There is no reason to suppose that the *idea* of the gift emanated from Sultan Idris, though he undoubtedly moved the resolution in Council. Cf., also, the London *Times,* 17 Dec. 1912 (which gives the text of Despatch MS No. 555, Governor to Secretary of State, 14 Nov., describing the circumstances of the Council's resolution) and 30 Jan. 1913 (which estimates the cost of the vessel, to be called H.M.S. *Malaya,* at £2,250,000).

But [when] I got within ten yards of her house, I heard a man coughing two or three times in the unlighted porch of the house. I remember I had a white *baju* and *seluar* on.⁶ If there was a man in the dark, he must have seen me. My white clothes must be clear for anyone to see. What could I do? To proceed would be impossible. And so would it be to turn back. I was in a compound where I had no right to be. I could not give an excuse for being there. There was only one meaning to my presence there. I could not be accused as a thief. No magistrate, I am sure, would believe that. But I could be charged for trespassing with intent to molest the womenfolk, I told myself. So, the best thing to do was to avoid meeting the man in the dark, whoever he was. And the only way to do this was to disappear from his sight as best as I could.

Like a flash, it occurred to me that I had a black sarong; And like a flash/I covered myself with it, taking care to roll up the sleeves of my *baju* and the legs of my *seluar* so that no part of my white clothes could be seen. Then I got into the drain by the side of the path and followed it right to the road.

I gave a sigh of relief when I again stood on the road and looked as if I was on my way home from the mosque. There was not a soul anywhere to say where I came from. I certainly did not show by my looks what had happened to me. But inwardly I was cursing Inche .... of luring me to a trap, as I thought. Did she not tell me that there would be no one in her house? And how was it that the man waited for me in the dark? And who was the man? Her husband or her lover? Isn't it foolishness to trust in a woman's word? Surely, a woman puts no value in a man's fair name and will trample on it to please her vanity!

When I saw Kak Bedah after this incident, I told her what I thought of Inche......../ But she only laughed saying: 'So, you are the ghost that suddenly disappeared that night. The man who saw you was a cousin of Inche .... He came from Kampong ....⁷ that evening. He got so frightened when

---

⁶*Baju*, tunic or long blouse; *seluar*, trousers; worn in formal Malay style in this instance, as appears, with a sarong doubled over in such a way as to form an 'apron' draped from waist to knee.

⁷The name of the *kampung* is omitted in the original.

he saw the white figure disappear that he went into the house and got a lamp with which he went to see what it was that he saw. The whole house was astir and talked about the ghost.

'So, they thought I was a ghost, did they', I said.

'No!' answered Kak Bedah. 'I think Inche .... knew it was you.'

This satisfied me as I had proved to her that I was not a coward.

But nothing could tempt me after that to see Inche .... in her house again. Anyway, the prospect of being transferred from Kuala Kangsar made me to forget all about her. Once, she sent Kak Bedah to persuade me not to go anywhere, but to remain in Kuala Kangsar. 'You are here known to everybody; whereas in your new place, you will be a stranger to everybody. It will take you some years before you know/the people and the people know you', she pleaded. In my heart of hearts, I said to myself: 'It will take you some years to know Inche. .... ; but I am already known to my wife'.

So, the reader can imagine how glad I was to get out of Kuala Kangsar. I could only see trouble as the result of any development in the love-affair with Inche .... After all, I had a wife and by her I had children. And I was sure, as any man could be sure, that my wife was faithful to me.

I never met Inche. ...., as lovers meet, all my life. But she and I travelled once in the same carriage of a train between Taiping and Kuala Kangsar. I was then living in Matang.[8] When I entered the carriage, there was a European sitting in the seat opposite hers; and he was holding the little boy by her side in such a way that I thought she was his Malay keep. Only when we reached Kuala Kangsar did I realise the woman was Inche .... I learned that she died a few years afterwards!

Very soon after the College dinner to the retiring Head Master, Inche Zainalabidin/arrived to interview the new Head Master, Mr. J. O'May. He came straight to my house and became my guest till he returned to Johore after the interview. That was the first time I met Inche Zainalabidin in person. He did not even

---

[8]This must have been sometime between early 1919 and early 1922; see below, note 45.

write to me to say he was coming. Probably he thought the cost of the postage would be a big waste to him. Anyhow he did not strike me to be a very intelligent person when I first saw him. But Mr. O'May was evidently satisfied with his qualifications as I learned afterwards that he was appointed to take my place. That evening I told Inche Zainalabidin all about the scheme of salaries for teachers which was very unfavourable to me and warned him to study in the Normal classes and pass the Normal Examinations so as not to find himself without prospect of getting the benefit of the Scheme, like me. In short, I did all I could to remove all causes for dissatisfaction to him. I felt the double duty of getting a good man to work in the College and of/shewing this man the way to success.

Unfortunately, I only realise now that he was not interested in what was meant to be friendly 'tips' for his guidance. At that time, he neither asked me any question nor thanked me.

Several years later, I met my friend, Inche Pandak Kamal of the Malay Art School; during the conversation we had, he said to me: 'Your friend Inche Zainalabidin seems to me to have an unfriendly attitude towards you. Once someone remarked that you were a clever man and could do many things to help the public; but your friend said why should you get only $100/- as a teacher in the College after so many years; whereas he was given the $100/- on joining the College?'

On hearing this, I kept quiet. I knew his remark was true. I felt that Inche Zainalabidin was not a friend to me to have said that. But did I treat him as an enemy? No! I accepted him and his wife as my guests for some days in Matang. I only regarded his unfriendly remark about me as the words/of an unrefined man. I believed he would get out of that unrefined mentality as he grew older and studied the lives of great men. In short, being the elder man I thought I should have the patience to wait and see the development of my friend's mind into perfection.

To put this idea of developing the mind into operation, I thought of starting a Literary Society among my literary friends. Instead of sending their articles for publication to the Malay newspapers where they usually got lost eventually, the proposed Society would have an official organ wherein would be published the articles containing all the considered thoughts of the best Malay writers. In this way, not only would those thoughts be preserved for posterity, but they would also act as the landmarks of the national progress so as to remind the coming generations not to tread over covered grounds and thus waste time.

174 During his stay in my house, I told Inche Zainalabidin about my proposed Society, and he listened to me very attentively to the end. I thought he would give me his support ungrudgingly as he appeared to be very deeply interested as I spoke. At last, he said: 'I do not want to join in any Movement started by you whereby you expect to rise'.

I was thunderstruck! I never expected that reply from my friend, Inche Zainalabidin. The idea as to who would be the Head in the Show never bothered me. I thought that was a question for the public to decide. Anyway, an ordinary member of the Society could make himself more useful than the President. Everything would depend on the *truth* of the remarks he wrote.

Shortly afterwards when for political reasons he was removed from the Malay College, Kuala Kangsar, to Kuala Lumpur,[9] I learned that Inche Zainalabidin formed and established a Malay
175 Literary Society with Inche Abdul/Razak, the Dato Stia of Selangor, as its President.[10] But this Society had [as] its 'aims and

[9] Za'ba ('Zainalabidin') was transferred to Kuala Lumpur as Malay Translator for the Education Department in 1923. In January of that year the *Malayan Bulletin of Political Intelligence* had reported that Za'ba regularly received two proscribed newspapers (*The Muslim Standard*, London, and *Light*; both seemingly pro-Khilafat); was in the habit of expressing anti-British views; and was 'corrupting' the minds of pupils at Malay College. Described in a later issue of the *Bulletin* as 'a clear religious fanatic', he was alleged to be 'the moving spirit in trying to establish throughout Malaya a strong feeling of Muslim Unity and a Muslim Empire....' (*MPBI*, 11, Jan. 1923, Para 60; and 18, Nov. 1923, Para 101; encl. in CO 537/917 and 537/917). The political opprobium attaching to Za'ba did not, however, prevent his appointment as senior translator to the newly formed Malay Translation Bureau, attached to Sultan Idris Training College (with some 400 young Malay students to 'corrupt') the following year. It may be noted that Abdul Majid, too, was among those noted in the *Bulletin* as subscribing to seditious Muslim views (*MPBI*, 15, June 1923, Para. 83, encl. in CO 537/913).

[10] The society was registered under this name on 18 March 1924, Za'ba

objects' the standardisàtion of Malay spelling and Malay grammar. Inche Zainalabidin was the Hon. Secretary of the Society.[11] Shortly after the arrival of Inche Zainalabidin in Kuala Kangsar and his interview with Mr. O'May, I went to Kuala Lumpur. I found Mr. Winstedt very busy in his office writing new books for the Malay schools. He had Daeng Abdul Hamid to assist him and improve or correct his Malay.[12] Daeng Abdul Hamid was considered a great stylist by Mr. R.J. Wilkinson who recommended him to be employed by Mr. Winstedt in his Malay work. I saw that he practically re-wrote whatever Mr. Winstedt drafted. The *Jaya Waras* (Physiology and Hygiene) and *'Ilmu 'Alam* (Geography) were prepared in this way.[13] I remember how the Malay public felt disgusted with the appearance of these new books. Leading Malays in the literary world, like Sheikh Tahir Jalaluddin and one or two others thought they were insulted with the bad Malay of Daeng Abdul Hamid and/openly said so in their letters to the Malay papers. Above all, they declared that no European could be the authority on the Malay language!

Fortunately for the peace of the Education Department, Daeng Abdul Hamid was sent to prison; and the story of his case was

---

having invited a score or so of English-educated government servants in the F.M.S. to come to Kuala Lumpur for the inaugural meeting. For Datuk Setia, see above, Book Two, note 4. In a printed brochure (Za'ba Papers, Arkib Negara Malaysia) Za'ba, as 'One of the Vice-Presidents' is principal signatory; his brother Mohd. Yusuf b. Ahmad, Malay Asst. Inspector of Schools, Selangor, signed as Treasurer, and Mohd. Rustum, Kuala Lumpur, as Secretary. Though Abdul Majid does not record it, the society was reorganized in 1925 as the Persekutuan Kemajuan Pengetahuan (Society for the Advancement of Knowledge) under the presidency of Abdul Majid himself, and from July 1925 published a quarterly journal *Kemajuan Pengetahuan*, of which, however, only two issues appeared. The society itself seems to have become defunct shortly thereafter.

[11]The aims and objects of the Persekutuan Kemajuan Pengetahuan (as distinct from those of the Malay Literary Society) appear to have been to promote education for the Malays generally, but more particularly English education. Much of the content of the journal was in fact written by Abdul Majid.

[12]Daeng Abdul Hamid b. Tengku Haji Muhammad Salleh was a Selangor Malay of Bugis descent.

[13]*Jaya Waras* was published in 1918, and *'Ilmu 'Alam* possibly in the same year.

recorded in my 'Malayan Kaleidoscope' under the heading: A Moot Point.[14]

During the one month I was in the office of Mr. Winstedt at Kuala Lumpur I saw nothing and I heard nothing about my MSS for the Malay Readers which I had forwarded to him before. Nor did I ask him about them as I could see that he was re-organising everything connected with the Malay Schools. I told myself that Mr. Winstedt would go through the MSS and make his decision in time.

Then I was sent to Telok Anson as Assistant Inspector of Schools, Perak. There I found that the best house the District Officer could offer me was one of the quarters for the Customs Out-door Officers on Telok Anson Wharf. I felt very small in going into the house as it was meant for a man getting about/$30/- only p.m. However, there was nothing else to do/but to take it, for the sake of my family. I must say I was very unfortunate about getting Government quarters. Most of the time I was in Kuala Kangsar I had to live in private houses. And the drawback about them was that they were very expensive to rent. Once I had to pay $20/- rent for a house while I was drawing a salary of $60/- only.

So I was not much worried about the unsuitability of the quarters that were given to me. Besides, there was plenty to interest me in my new work; and the time to hold the Annual Inspection of the Schools was coming.

The schools that I had to visit for the Annual Examination were many and distributed in three districts, viz. Lower Perak, Batang Padang and Kinta. I had just returned from the *Ulu*[15] section of Lower Perak and was intending to go to Sitiawan and the few places near it. I found on reaching home that all my children were down with influenza. My wife got the attack on the next day. How was I to go to Sitiawan where I would be away for a week? I could not leave my family as they were since every one of them was ill. I thought of my mother-in-law in

---

[14]*The Malayan Kaleidoscope* (Kuala Lumpur, The Selangor Press, 1935), pp. 69–74. The essay referred to details of a number of alleged defalcations, none of the participants being named or otherwise identified.
[15]*Ulu*, up-river.

Kuala Kangsar who could look after my wife and/children during my absence. So I sent her a telegram asking her to come. But she did not come as I expected. I thought she was not sufficiently impressed with my message telling her that the children were ill and I had to go on duty. So I sent her a second telegram; and this time to make sure that she would come I said in the message: 'Abdul Majid died please come immediately'.

Right enough my mother-in-law arrived in Telok Anson with a friend by car. It was on a Sunday; so there was no train service between Tapah Road and Telok Anson. She had to hire a car at Tapah Road to come to Telok Anson. She was glad to find I was not dead, though she said she felt very sorry and cried most of the time between Kuala Kangsar and Telok Anson. She also told me that when she got to the Railway Station at Kuala Kangsar she met a nephew of Raja Tahir who was going back to Kajang as he also received a telegram that day telling him of the death of Raja Tahir![16]

Next day, in the 'Times of Malaya', Ipoh, was noticed the death of Raja Mohamed Tahir, Assistant District Officer, Kajang, and of Abdul Majid, Assistant Inspector of Schools, Perak.[17]/This public notice of my death brought with it two unpleasant incidents. First, the District Officer, Lower Perak, was asked telegraphically by the British Resident why he did not make his official report about my death and the disposal of Government property entrusted in my hands. Of course, the D.O. jumped on me and asked for explanation as to how the newspaper people came to know of my death when I was still alive, and hale and hearty. Second, a few days later, my father who also heard of my death from one of the Malay papers sent me a telegram enquiring after my health!

There was one good result, however, that came indirectly from this 'death' of mine. The D.O. was informed that all my children with my wife were ill; and so he concluded that the Customs quarters were too small for my needs. So, he allowed me to occupy

---

[16]This was the Raja Mohd. Tahir, who, shortly before, had read Abdul Majid's valedictory address to Hargreaves. See above, Book Two, p. 104 and note 124.

[17]This report has not been traced.

the house formerly given to Mr. Phillips, the Assistant Inspector of Schools, Perak.[18] It was a big house, next to the Church, close by to the Rest House; with two bedrooms and an/annexe at the back. The rent was only $15/- p.m.

But the best advantage to me for occupying the house was that I began to be looked upon by the Telok Anson public as belonging to the higher society. I received more attention and got invitation[s] to several public functions. I was regarded as the successor to Tuan Phillips, and came to know many people who hitherto had looked down upon me.

I must not forget to mention that there was a schoolmate of mine working at that time as a clerk in Grik, Upper Perak. His name was Alang Samin. One afternoon he was working in a padi-field, which was given to him like the other Malay Officers in the town, by the District Officer, Mr. Berkeley, as an encouragement to padi-planting.[19] Who should come to him at that time but Osman, my brother-in-law. He wanted Alang Samin to read for him a telegram which he had just received from Kuala Kangsar. It was the telegram from his mother informing him of my death, sent on the day my mother-in-law received/the news from me.

Alang Samin read the telegram and was so shocked to hear the news that he sat down on the ground exclaiming: 'What! Abdul Majid dead!' He went home, took ill and died after three days! I had never heard of a similar case to this before or since. I wonder if Alang Samin was greatly attached to me! Probably he looked up to me as a sort of hero, so much so that he evidently thought

---

[18] See above, Book One, p. 26, and note 46.

[19] Hubert Berkeley, born in England in 1864, joined the Straits Settlements Police in 1886, serving initially in the Dindings. He transferred to the Perak Civil Service in 1889, first went to Upper Perak in 1891, and remained in charge of that district more or less continuously until his retirement in 1926, resisting all attempts to transfer or promote him. Known popularly among Europeans as the King of Grik, his long service in the district and intimate knowledge of the language and people, together with a flamboyant and eccentric personality, made him a legend in his own lifetime (see, e.g., Victor Purcell, *Memoirs of a Malayan Official* (London, Cassell, 1965), pp. 267-8). It is improbable that Alang Samin was properly speaking a 'Malay Officer' (i.e., a member of the M.A.S.); all the evidence suggests that he was a member of the F.M.S. General Clerical Service.

life was not worth living for him when I was gone!
I do not ever remember Alang Samin to be on very friendly terms with me, while we were in school. He went to Kuala Lipis to work after leaving school. He came back and worked in the Kuala Kangsar hospital as a clerk before he was transferred to Grik. Nor was I ever very intimate with him when he was in the same town with me. Only once I entertained a young man from Pahang because he said that man was his friend! I forget/his name; but I remember he was the eldest son of and heir to the Dato Perba Jelai.[20] This young man had a son, Wan Ali by name, studying in the Malay College. As Wan Ali was a pupil of mine, I considered his father as my guest, though he stayed with Alang Samin.

Poor Alang Samin had a Japanese wife whom he married in Kuala Lipis. She was not an attractive woman; but Alang Samin seemed to be happy with her. I gathered afterwards that she turned Japanese again, after living a Muslim life for so many years! I wonder if Alang Samin is still remembered by his many friends. He was a bit of a clown with full of jokes [sic]. I know none of his people who were said to be in Kota Lama.[21]

The arrival of my mother-in-law in Telok Anson enabled me to leave my family and go to Sitiawan; but I did not go as I expected. I learned on the next day that all the schools in Perak were closed for three weeks. It was the terrible time of the 'flu in 1918!/Hundreds of people died everywhere. Many conjectures were made by various people as to the real cause of the 'flu. But I think the public was satisfied with the theory that all the gas from the smoke of the cannons during the Great War (1914–1918) had travelled from the war area to this part of the world and so contaminated the air that we breathed. Be that as it may, the toll that it took was certainly a big one. All those who caught the 'flu then either died within days or survived if they got over that period![22]

[20]The Datuk Maharaja Perba of Jelai, the Jelai being a major tributary of the upper Pahang River, was one of the principal chiefs of Pahang.
[21]Kota Lama lies just below Kuala Kangsar on the Perak River.
[22]'Epidemic influenza appeared in Malaya in July, 1918. The infection was at first confused with plague, which was prevalent in Kuala Lumpur

How relieved we all felt when the war came to an end. There was a public holiday on the day the Armistice was signed. We all assembled in the public office to celebrate it. There was happiness in every face as the victory was ours. For more than four long years the war had been waged. Everyone was anxious as the war became prolonged. The public helped with all the money they could/spare on Our Days. Many Europeans had gone to the Front, and many of them were reported killed.

My friend, Capt. N.M. Hashim had written to me from Singapore during the war that we should see to it the Malays had their share of the glory in the victory of the war; and following up this sentiment, I had offered to volunteer to go to the Front. I know a number of friends and 'Old Boys' in all parts of Malaya also did the same. But I was rather disappointed when Mr. Hargreaves threw my letter into the waste paper basket and said: 'You are not a fighting man. You will be more useful if you stay where you are'. I had discussed the subject of going to the Front with my wife, and she had made up her mind to go also as a nurse. She said she would be useful in helping the wounded.

Instead, we raised some money once by organising a Bangsawan Show.[23] She made a lot of paper flowers which my daughter, Aminah, sold to the audience. Besides, I also gave a very valuable kris to be sold for Our Day Fund. The kris had belonged to my uncle,/Adam, the eldest brother of my father, and had seen him through many a tight position in the good old days. It was bought

---

at the time, but the doubt was speedily dispelled.... The epidemic reached its peak in September and October, by which time the disease was known to have a world distribution.' *The Institute of Medical Research, 1900–1950* (Kuala Lumpur, Studies from the IMR, Federation of Malaya, Jubilee Volume No. 25, Government Press, 1951), p. 57.

[23] A genre of Malay opera or musical comedy now virtually extinct but extremely popular especially in the towns of the Straits Settlements in the early decades of this century, and usually based on a European play (often by Shakespeare) or Arabian Nights story. The term *bangsawan*, high-born or noble, lent itself to the genre (according to R.J. Wilkinson, *Malay-English Dictionary*) owing to the success of the first opera company, Indera Bangsawan. It is now principally applied to the Malay equivalent (using traditional or pseudo-historical stories) of the radio serial known elsewhere as 'soap opera'.

by Mr. O'May without knowing that it was mine and sent by him to England.

Some months after the signing of the Armistice, I was instructed by telegram to proceed to Matang and act for Mr. A. Keir as Head Master of the Malay Training College there.[24] I am sure this period was the happiest in my life. I remember before I went there I had a dream. I thought I went in a car with my wife to a garden with a lake upon a hill. The scenery all round was grand and we rested a while in the car by the side of the lake. Never had I such a pleasant dream before or since.

When I got to Matang, I found a big house in a big compound as my quarters. There were a lot of flowers in pots as well as some chickens which Mr. H.L. Sumner,[25] the Inspector of Schools, Perak, said to me I could have if I paid $5/- to Mr. Keir for them. But Mr. Keir hoped, he added, that I would look after and feed his dogs and puppies.

Of course I paid the $5/- and detailed one of the College Tamil *kebuns*[26] to look after and feed the dogs. In the compound, there were many coconut trees, so many that I could collect two or three hundred nuts every two months. We made coconut oil from the coconuts we picked, so that with the vegetables grown in the College garden and the fish that could be bought very cheap in

[24]Alexander Keir, born in 1884 and educated at Aberdeen University (M.A. 1905), entered the Education Department of the S.S. and F.M.S. in 1906, teaching at Raffles Institution. He was Inspector of Schools, Selangor, from 1911, and in 1913 was appointed Head of the newly opened Malay Training College at Matang, Perak. He became Inspector of Schools, Perak, in 1920, and on his retirement late in 1938 was Acting Director of Education, S.S. and Adviser on Education, F.M.S. An account of his career appeared in *Warta Malaya,* 28 November 1938, p. 13. The Matang college was set up by the Perak government as a result of disquiet over the small flow of teachers from the central Malacca college, and produced initially fifteen teachers a year, in a two-year course, the number later rising, it appears, to twenty-five. Together with Malacca, Matang was superseded in 1922 by the much larger Sultan Idris Training College, Tanjong Malim, Perak.

[25]Henry Lighbourne Sumner, b. 1880, was appointed European Master, Education Department, Singapore, in 1903, from 1905 serving in Malacca. He was appointed Inspector of Schools, Negri Sembilan, in 1907, and Acting Inspector, Perak, in 1913 (confirmed 1914).

[26]*Kebun,* garden, and hence gardener.

the place, being only a few miles from the seaside, living was very cheap and there was plenty of everything to eat,—chickens, fish, vegetables, coconut and coconut oil! On top of it all, there were the College *kebuns* who could be made to serve us as we wished, and yet keep the whole compound clean.

The work could not be said to be a very heavy one, as there were only 50 students in the College, divided into two classes. There were three assistants under me so that besides the work of supervising the/College I had only three hours a day as my turn to take the classes, viz: two hours in the morning and one in the afternoon, that is to say, from 8 a.m. to 9 a.m.; from 11 a.m. to 12 noon; and from 3 p.m. to 4 p.m. It was between 3 and 4 p.m. that I gave them lessons on gardening, either in the garden itself or in class.

The boys were good and well-behaved; the assistants were intelligent and keen; so my work was a perpetual pleasure. My acting allowance was only $50/-; but when I appealed to the highest authority my salary and the acting allowance was made to amount to $400/-, the minimum salary of a European teacher.

It was at Matang that I wrote the 'Malay Self-Taught' for E. Marlborough & Co., London;[27] and translated into Malay Mr. Keir's book on Gardening.[28] And it was at Matang that I learned the Malay Readers I prepared in Kuala Kangsar would not be used in the Malay Schools; but Mr. Winstedt included a few of my essays and stories in the Series/that he prepared;[29] and for

[27]See above, Book One, p. 16, note 25.

[28]It has not been possible to trace the original English version of Keir's manuscript, if indeed it ever appeared in print. Abdul Majid's Malay translation, which was published as '*Ilmu Tanam-Menanam*, probably in 1920, was revised and reprinted in 1924 by the Malay Translation Bureau as No. 8 in the Malay School Series (cf. Abdullah Sanusi b. Ahmad, *Peranan Pejabat Karang Mengarang* (Kuala Lumpur, Dewan Bahasa & Pustaka,) pp. 23 and 67). The 1917 Winstedt report on vernacular education, which did so much to shape Malay education in the next two decades, laid great emphasis on the inculcation of the virtues of horticulture and handicrafts (see, e.g., Roff, *The Origins of Malay Nationalism*, op. cit., p. 140), and had doubtless been the inspiration for Keir's work.

[29]There were numerous readers for Malay schools produced under Winstedt's aegis. See the list given in Abdullah Sanusi, op. cit., p. 31.

BOOK THREE   131

these I got paid, totalling in all about $200/-!

For a number of years I had been regularly subscribing for the Islamic Review.[30] I found this paper not only instructive in its Islamic message but also constructive to the crumbling House of Islam. Many were the hours of my spare time did I spend on reading its articles and pondering over them. I thought Khwaja Kamaluddin, the founder and editor of this Islamic paper, a very clever man, indeed. He touched politics and criticised British politicians without having his paper banned by the British Government. He infused 'loyalty to the Crown' in his preachings, while he showed that the Islamic ideals as practised by the Prophet and taught in the Islamic doctrines are far superior to the British ideals. I entirely agreed and agree with him that the only hope for the ascendancy of Islam should be based on the principles of working hand in hand with the ambitions of the British Empire. The best brains in any nation would admit that the highest stage in human progress is the establishment of an international law which could secure international or world peace while ensuring to each nation the necessary freedom to develop itself. To me, if the people in any particular village can be made to live in peace by law, it is quite possible that people in the whole world can be made to live in peace by law. But this law should be made not by man or a body of men, like the League of Nations, but by God Himself. And to the best of my judgement and belief such a law is found in the Qur'an!

Recently, I wrote a book called 'Factors for World Peace in Islam', in which I gave my reasons for thinking that Islam would produce peace to the world. But this book is still in its MSS, although the Government on being consulted had declared it to be free from seditious remarks. I found that it had very little public support to justify its publication. My son, Haji Abdul Latiph/keeps the MS.[31]

I also wrote a Malay version of that book. But the Religious Department of Johore thought it was too unorthodox to be read by the 'orthodox' Malays![32]

[30]See above, Book One, note 20.
[31]This manuscript has since been lost.
[32]The religious authorities in Johore had a reputation for strictness

Nevertheless, when I was still in Matang, in the height of my enthusiasm for the ultimate triumph of Islam, as I thought out the various points in the principles of the Faith in its bearing towards the realisation of peace, I had some wonderful dreams which my friends interpreted for me to mean spiritual guidance towards Knowledge of Truth from the Almighty. At first, I would hear, as I lay in the state of half asleep and half awake in the early hours of the morning, the wonderfully sweet voice of a man calling the *azan* (bang)[33] as if he was standing very close to me. This happened many times; and invariably the *azan* stopped immediately I woke up. But once I opened my eyes as I heard the *azan;*/and there I saw close to my head the figure of a man in the act of calling the *azan*. He was dressed like a Malay *haji* with a turban folded round his head. I remember he was a fair and good looking man. I must say I was entranced with the sight of him for about one minute; then he suddenly disappeared.

I heard no *azan,* nor did I see the figure again. It appeared as if he did not like the idea of my seeing him!

At other times, I would dream that I saw the light of dawn in the eastern sky. And once as I got up after the dream, I opened my window and actually saw light in the eastern sky which I took to be the light of dawn. So convinced was I that it was so that I actually went to the bathroom, performed my ablutions and said my *subuh* prayers.[34] When this was over, I heard the clock strike two!

With such a spiritual support, as it were, as I got through my dreams,/what wonder then if I held very tenaciously to my religious views even though the world might tell me they are unorthodox. Besides, they are the convictions of carefully considered opinions on the views advanced by the thinking educated Muslims

---

concerning publications which bore any relation to Islam, a number of magazines being proscribed in the state in the 1930s (see, e.g., William R. Roff, *Sejarah Surat*² *Khabar Melayu* (History of Malay Newspapers) (Penang, Sinaran Press, 1961), p. 34).

[33]The call of the faithful to prayer (Ar. *adhan*; Mal. *adzan* or (from the Persian) *bang*).

[34]The *ṣalāt al-ṣubḥ,* dawn prayer, one of the five daily ritual prayers required of all Muslims, being that for the hour immediately prior to sunrise.

in the Islamic Review.³⁵

With this frame of mind as the background, the reader can easily imagine how happy I was when I heard that Khwaja Kamaluddin was coming to visit Malaya. I learned that he would go to Singapore first, and preparations were being made by the Muslim community to receive him.³⁶ My friend, Inche Zainalabidin, was going there from Kuala Kangsar to translate the lecture he was going to give into Malay. I felt it awkward to leave the College to take charge of itself; so I did not go to Singapore.

In time, he came to Matang from Singapore; as I had asked my friend Inche Zainalabidin to/extend to him my invitation, on behalf of the Muslim community, to come over to Perak. When the Khwaja arrived at Taiping by train, there was a crowd waiting for him at the Station. Dr. I. Md. Ghouse of Taiping garlanded him, after the fashion of Indians, before he got out of his carriage.³⁷ As it was then tea-time, Dr. Ghouse took us all to his house for tea. After that a number of prominent Indians in Taiping came to pay their respects to the distinguished visitor. It was at 5.30 when the Khwaja motored with me to Matang. Next day in the

---

³⁵The reference to 'unorthodox' here arose (as will be seen below) from Abdul Majid's predilection (shared with a number of other English-educated Malays) for what is sometimes called the 'Lahore branch' of the Ahmadiyya movement, as expressed in the writings of Khwaja Kamāl ud-Dīn and Maulvi Muhammad Ali. In the Malay States of the 1920s and 1930s, the Admadiyya movement (so named after Mirza Ghulam Ahmad of Qadian, in India) was widely abhorred by the generality of *ulama* as heterodox, or indeed heretical, and little or no distinction was made between the Lahore and the more extreme Qadian branches, which were alike reviled as 'Qadiani'. In the context of considerable public controversy, a certain defensiveness is frequently found among followers or admirers of Khwaja Kamāl ud-Dīn. See, e.g., the account of M.L. Muallim and K.C. Marican v. J.M.I. Marican and Straits Printing Works, Supreme Court Suit No. 513 of 1925, given at length in Bashir A. Mallal (ed.), *Trial of Muslim Libel Case* (Singapore, printed for the editor by C.A. Ribeiro & Co. Ltd., 1928).

³⁶This appears to have been towards the beginning of 1921.

³⁷Ismail Muhammad Ghouse was born in Tanjore, South India, in 1882, and later studied at the King Edward VII College of Medicine in Singapore, graduating with a Licentiate in Medicine and Surgery in 1917. He went into private practice in Taiping, was honorary physician to certain members of the Perak royal family, became the leading Indian in the public life of the state, and was noted as a devout Muslim.

evening, he gave his lecture to the public in the Taiping Town Hall. It was presided over by the District Officer, Larut and Matang, a Mr. Clayton.[38] Syed Burhan, Editor of the then already defunct 'Perak Pioneer' had refused the honour of taking the presidential chair.[39] A few days after that, we took the Khwaja to Kuala Kangsar. There was some excitement there, as Abdul Hamid, the Qu'ran Visiting Teaching Teacher,[40] was going to ask the Khwaja some questions. But/the Khwaja, on being asked if he was prepared to answer those questions that would be put to him, merely said that it was not his business to try and convert Muslims into Muslims, and thus saved the situation. This happened in the 'Ubudiah Mosque; and I know Inche Zainalabidin could enlighten the reader more about this incident, as he was the mediary through whom the conversation between the parties was made.

Then we went to the Istana Negara where His Highness Sultan Iskandar Shah was waiting for us. I saw the Khwaja presenting a copy of the English translation of the Qur'an by Maulvi Muhammed Ali to His Highness. The Sultan gave nothing in return. So it must be evident that the visit was a failure, as far as its purpose was concerned.[41]

[38] Thomas Watts Clayton (not to be confused with Reginald John Byrd Clayton, who was currently D.O. of the contiguous district of Lower Perak) was born in 1877, educated at Cambridge, and joined the M.C.S. in 1900. He retired as British Adviser, Kedah, in the 1930s, having first acted in this appointment in 1925.

[39] Sayyid Abdul Hassan b. Burhan of Taiping founded the *Perak Pioneer*, the first English-language newspaper in the peninsular states (initially twice-weekly), in mid-1894, preceding and following it with two short-lived Malay papers, *Seri Perak* (weekly, 1893, likewise the first Malay-language journal in the peninsula) and *Jajahan Melayu* (1896–7). The *Pioneer* became a daily in 1905, but ceased publication on the eighteenth anniversary of its inception, 4 July 1912, at which time it was losing $500 a month.

[40] See above, Book One, note 6. His elder brother had been District Kathi for Kuala Kangsar until 1908 or 1909, and it may be assumed that as a member of the religious establishment and bureaucracy Abdul Hamid was likely to have been critical of 'Qadiani'.

[41] The leading figure in the early Khilafat movement in India, and founder of the Khilafat Conference upon his emergence in 1919 from detention by the British, Muhammad Ali first published his translation of the

It must be remembered that Khwaja Kamaluddin was a disciple of Mirza Ghulam Ahmad of Qadian in India,—the man who claimed to be the Mahdi or the Messiah of the last age. In India the/followers of Mirza are known as the Qadianis who are regarded as unorthodox Muslims. Nay! They are even considered as *kafirs*.

The controversy about Qadianism lasted for a long time; the orthodox people do not seem to be able to stamp out the Movement; Qadianis are even to be found in Mecca today. Personally, I spent more than two years pointing out the merits of Khwaja Kamaluddin's works on Islam. My articles appeared in the 'Lembaga Melayu' under the nom-de-plume: *Talib-ul-Haqqul-Mubin*.[42] For my trouble, I came to be known as a Malay Qadiani.

A certain Maulvi Jaafar[43] tried to convince me of my mistaken notions, first by arguing me out in my convictions as they appeared in the papers. Then he made up his mind to speak to me personally. So one evening he took the train to come to Matang. But he never reached Matang; as he got ill when he got half way, and became insane. I read an account of the manner in which he lost his senses, as recorded from the time/he left Singapore till he got to Gopeng and was brought back to Singapore again, by the then Editor of the 'Lembaga Melayu', who was a neighbour of Maulvi Jaafar. From reading the account, I could only conclude that God,—or at least, the spiritual world—was angry with Maulvi Jaafar for condemning Mirza Ghulam Ahmad as a *kafir*. I always feel that God alone has the right to judge anyone and his work. At any rate it does not follow if anyone took a *kafir* or a non-Muslim as a teacher, he also would become a *kafir* or non-Muslim. In any event, I know I do not hold the views that my teacher preaches to me, unless they are accepted by me to be rational.

Qur'ān shortly after his release. Though Sultan Iskandar's coldness to the Khwaja is probably explicable in purely religious terms (in later life Iskandar was noted for the strictness of his views), it is possible that he had also been informed by the Resident or other British officials of Muhammad Ali's political associations in India.

[42]The newspaper *Lembaga Melayu* was published daily from August 1914 to December 1931, under the editorship of Mohd. Eunos b. Abdullah. The articles here referred to have not been traced.

[43]Not identifiable.

Each and every one of us is endowed by the Creator with the reasoning faculties; so it is up to us to test every statement made to us with those reasoning faculties. Personally, I refuse to accept any statement/as the truth, unless my reasoning faculties tell me that it is so. If I am mad and cannot reason out things, then I know that the Almighty God will not hold me responsible for my thoughts!

Khwaja Kamaluddin soon left me to go to Java. On his return, one evening as we sat down after dinner, he offered to take me to England to help him in his missionary work, saying: 'I want a man with the spirit like you. I have heard how doggedly you fought in the Malay papers for our Cause', he added.

'I am sorry', I replied, 'I am not a man with much knowledge to be of much use in your work.'

'Of course', he said encouragingly, 'I shall help. There is very little for you to learn before you become useful.'

'But I am a weak man and will spoil your good work', I said truthfully as a protest against accepting his offer.

'You do not at all look weak', he argued with a laugh, thinking that he had won his point.

'I may not look weak physically', I answered. 'But I know I am weak morally. And England, with her women free, has therefore a lot of temptations for me. I do not want myself to be in any way instrumental in bringing your noble work to a failure.'

'I see!' replied Khwaja. 'Then what about you, Zainalabidin? Can you go with me?'

'If you can guarantee that I get a European wife, I will go!' he answered.

Of course, this silenced the Khwaja who no doubt thought that he never foresaw his work as a Muslim missionary would include the arranging of wives for his assistants!

Personally, I was thunderstruck when I heard these words. I could only think of the low breeding of the man who uttered them in the presence of such a respectable person. I felt ashamed of his company and avoided it ever after![44]

---

[44]The bitterness between the two men is clearly illustrated in a draft letter from Za'ba to Abdul Majid, dated October 2602 (1942), reproduced in facsimile in Ungku A. Aziz, *Jejak-Jejak di Pantai Zaman*

BOOK THREE 137

My happy days in Matang did not last very long, although I was sent there on two/occasions. When Mr. Keir returned from leave, I was sent to Taiping as Assistant Inspector of Schools. After a few months, Mr. Sumner retired from his position as Inspector of Schools, Perak; and Mr. Keir took his place. When this happened, I had to go to Matang again. Altogether I had a total of about 30 months as acting Head Master of the Malay Training College; and I believe during that time, the College did quite well.[45]

When I left the College in 1922 to resume my substantive appointment as Assistant Inspector of Schools, Perak, in Telok Anson, the Inspector of Schools, Pahang, (I forget his name) came to the place. Not long after that, the College was removed to Tanjong Malim, being amalgamated in the process with the Malay Training College, Malacca.[46] Mr. O.T. Dussek Head Master of the Malacca College, became the Head Master of the Tanjong/ Malim (or rather Sultan Idris) Training College.[47] I was sorry that for

(Footprints on the Sands of Time), (Kuala Lumpur, University of Malaya Press, 1975), facing p. 106. Ungku Aziz suggests, pp. 100–7, that the mutual animosity may have dated from the publication in the *Malay Mail* of 1 December, 1923, of Za'ba's article 'The Poverty of the Malays', which drew a critical response a few days later from a pseudonymous letter-writer, 'The Real Malay', who seems certainly to have been Abdul Majid, (cf. M. Said, 'The Problem of Rural Poverty,' letter to *Malay Mail*, 14 June 1957), and that the ill-feeling was fostered by Abdul Majid's subsequent career with the Political Intelligence Bureau.

[45] Abdul Majid appears to have served at Matang from March 1919 to February 1920, and again from perhaps May 1920 (when Keir became Inspector of Schools) until sometime early in 1922. When his father died during Ramadhan 1922 (28 April to 27 May), Abdul Majid had already resumed his post at Telok Anson.

[46] Sultan Idris Training College appears to have opened for business early in August 1922, and was officially opened by Sultan Iskandar on 29 November.

[47] Dussek was born at Greenwich in 1886, son of a timber importer, and took an external degree at the University of London while school-teaching (B.A., ?1910). He joined the educational service of the S.S. and F.M.S. in 1912, and after two years teaching in an English school applied for and was appointed to the headmastership of the Malay Training College at Malacca, subsequently transferring as Principal to the Sultan Idris Training College in 1922, where for fourteen years he exercised a profound influence on a generation of Malay intellectuals, eventually resigning while on leave in 1937. He died in 1965.

my services in Matang, I was not even consulted if I would like to go to Tanjong Malim. I remember Mr. Dussek asked me when I was still in Kuala Kangsar if I would like to work with him, and I said I preferred Kuala Kangsar. I did not know that he would take that answer of mine to hold good for ever!

I have referred to my appointment as Assistant Inspector of Schools. But officially I was known as Malay Assistant Inspector of Schools. Others have been appointed as Malay Assistant Inspectors of Schools too, e.g. Inche Muhammad Zin[48] in Penang and Inche Muhammad Yussuf in Selangor.[49] The latter is a younger brother of Inche Zainalabidin and an Old Boy of mine at the Kuala Kangsar College. The Scheme of Salaries for these Malay Assistant Inspectors of Schools was already drawn up by Mr. Winstedt and published in the Establishment List for public information. The maximum salary for a Malay/Assistant Inspector of Schools provided in that Scheme was only $200/-, which was the same as the amount shown as the maximum salary for a clerk! So, for all the trouble I took to study further in the Kuala Kangsar College and all the good work I rendered to the Education Department, rising as I did to be the Head Master of a Malay Training College,—a position which I think would never be held by a Malay for many generations to come, under the present system of Government—I found myself in 1922 in the same position as regards salary as I was in 1904 when I was a clerk! In fact, Inche Daud bin Muhammad Shah, who joined the Clerical Service together with me in Kuala Lumpur in 1903, was already an Assistant

---

[48]Muhammad Zin b. Ayob, born 1897 in Taiping, where his father was Government Printer, attended Malay School, the Malay Training College in Malacca (1909–11), and King Edward VII (English) School in Taiping (1914–19). He was appointed a Malay Assistant Inspector of Schools in the latter year, taking up his appointment in Penang in 1920, and later serving in Perak from 1924 to 1926. From 1926 he taught at the Anderson (English) School in Ipoh. Among his several publications is the Malay translation of Braddell's *The Legal Status of the Malay States*, undertaken at the instance of Sultan Iskandar and published as *Murtabat (atau Taraf) Negri^2 Melayu pada sisi Undang^2* (Singapore, Ahmadiyyah Press, 1935). He married Abdul Majid's only daughter, Aminah, in 1924 (see below, p. 141ff).

[49]Muhammad Yusuf b. Ahmad, like Muhammad Zin, was first appointed in 1919.

District Officer in Pahang by that time.⁵⁰ He did not leave the Clerical Service, as I did, in order to study further to improve his prospects!

But my interest in my work was never marred by such a misfortune. In fact, I was as jovial as ever when I was with my/friends in the Club. Occasionally, I might be worried by the dishonesty and cheekiness of some of those under me. I recall to mind one such case in particular. He was Visiting Teacher, Telok Anson, named Ali.⁵¹

This man was a bit of a scholar, as he knew some Arabic. I found him first as Head Teacher in the Malay School, Tapah. I recommended him and he was made Group Teacher for the district of Tapah with about 12 to 15 schools under him. On my return to Telok Anson from Matang for the second time, he was already promoted to be Visiting Teacher, Telok Anson. As soon as I arrived in the place, he showed his spirit of insubordination, according to the Malay custom and Malay conventional rules, by sending one of his children to my wife to tell her that his wife expected her to come and see her. Strictly speaking, it was his wife who should come first to see my wife, not so much because he happened to be my/subordinate, but because we were new arrivals in the place. Those who did not come were naturally regarded by the new arrivals as not being friendly disposed towards them.

Of course, I did not allow my wife to go; nor did she want to go! And Ali took this to mean that we considered ourselves too high for him and his wife. So he continued to annoy me further by behaving as if I was his subordinate, instead of he mine. For instance, there was a Government motor boat for the Education

---

⁵⁰Daud was born in 1885, in Singapore, and educated at Malay school there and at the Victoria Institute in Kuala Lumpur. He joined the Selangor Clerical Service in 1903, and was promoted in 1910 to the M.A.S. He retired as Assistant District Officer, Kajang, in 1932, and returned to Singapore to play a leading role in the Kesatuan Melayu Singapura (Singapore Malay Union), the earliest Malay association of political complexion, becoming its president in 1937.

⁵¹No Visiting Teacher of this name appears in the F.M.S., State of Perak, *List of Establishments* for the years 1921 or 1923, and that for 1922 is not in the Arkib Negara Malaysia.

Department which had come under his charge during my absence and the absence of any other Assistant Inspector of Schools in my place. He made me get his 'permission' on one or two occasions before I could use this boat to go on duty! In the end, all the Government motor boats in Telok Anson were placed under the charge of the Harbour Master to whom the application should be made by the officers/of the various Departments when they wanted to go on duty. For the sake of economy, it was further instructed that whenever possible two or three officers should go together in one trip. In this way, Mr. H. Benjafield, the Health Inspector of Malay Schools, often went with me on my inspection of the schools in the *ulu*.

Once, Ali was asked by the Inspector of Schools to get about 200 desks and benches made for a new school in the Sitiawan sub-district. He wrote back to say that the Chinese carpenter wanted $12/- for each desk and bench. Mr. Sumner referred this to me as I was then in Telok Anson, having just come back from Matang. I went to Sitiawan and found to my surprise that a Chinese carpenter there was prepared to make the desks and benches at $5/- each with the additional condition that he would send them to the new school—a distance of about 15 miles—without/further charge! So, I saved the Government $1,400/- plus the cartage. I understand why Ali wanted to be boss in Telok Anson, and not to be bossed by me!

His feelings towards me became more and more bitter as we continued to work together in the same place. At last, I had to inform the Inspector of Schools of the unpleasant 'relationship' between Ali and me and ask, as a favour, either to transfer Ali from Telok Anson or to transfer me. Mr. Keir came to Telok Anson and took me to Bagan Datok. During the walk we had from Bagan Datok to the Malay School at Sungai Nipah, I explained, on being asked, how the trouble arose between me and Ali, not forgetting to mention that Ali's clan, the Mendahiling, was for many generations at enmity with my clan, the Bonjol.[52] Some days after that, I learned that Ali was sent back to Tapah as a teacher!

[52]The reference is to the contiguous parts of Sumatra from which their respective families came, the Mandailing Bataks being just north of highland Minangkabau, where Bonjol is situated.

Socially, I became a popular figure, especially in the Sporting Circles. I was/made the President of the Lower Perak Football League. The Raja Muda (now H.H. the Sultan)⁵³ of Perak gave a silver cup to the League and keen was the competition as shewn in the football matches played between the various teams. I gave eleven silver medals to be won by the players of the winning team. I remember in one match, the players became so excited that they nearly came to blows. I rushed out as the spectators also rushed out to join in the fight and pacified the angry crowd with angry words to the offending player and his supporters as well as with a good display of brandishing my stick. I forgot that it was a *semambu* (malacca cane) stick which the Malays considered as *sial* (bad luck) to be hit with. Anyhow, it served its purpose in restoring peace among the excited crowd; while the players resumed their game. I was congratulated by many friends for the part I played in saving the nasty stuation!

My daughter Aminah had by this time grown into womanhood; and/I noticed that it was a strain on my wife to look after the grown-up girl. I was most of the time away from home on inspection duty; and she told me that there were many young men who came mooching round about the house to have a look at her from the distance. At night, she could hardly sleep, lest something happened 'to cover us with shame, having soot in our face', as the Malay puts it in his language. She could not even go to the bathroom without the daughter following her! There were several enquiries about her from mothers with grown-up sons; but she had told them that the daughter was already betrothed, without consulting me before answering them. She said she thought that their sons would not be suitable to be our son-in-law.

One day I received a letter from Muhammad Zin asking me if I would accept him as my son-in-law. Zin had married a daughter of a wealthy Malay in Taiping, known as Ibrahim Papa.⁵⁴ She was an educated girl; but she died after/the birth of her first and only daughter. She came with Zin to us in Matang, and told Zin

---

⁵³Sultan Abdul Aziz b. Raja Muda Musa (reg. 1938–1948).
⁵⁴Ibrahim Khan b. Ghafoor Khan, of Indian descent but born in Malaya and with a Malay wife, owned a variety of kinds of property in the vicinity of Taiping, ranging from tin mines to rubber estates.

that if she died, she would like to see him marry Aminah! She told him she did not want to see him marry any other girl. So, in obedience to the wish of his dead wife, Zin wanted to marry my daughter.

But I told Zin in reply that it was not according to the established Malay custom for him to ask me in person for my daughter in marriage. I told him I could only reply to his enquiry if he asked me in the usual customary way by sending to me someone responsible from his family. And remembering that in his marriage with the daughter of Ibrahim Papa, he did not even inform, much less get the consent of, his father, I insisted that his father should be present at the *meminang* ceremony[55] as well as at the marriage ceremony. His father was no longer the husband/of his mother: a step-father had taken the place long ago.

Zin complied faithfully to both my conditions; but I regret to note that in his conduct in other matters since then, he was far from observing the wisdom of the Malay saying: '*Biar mati anak, jangan mati adat*'.[56] Probably, he holds the idea that the old customs are all useless and have no national significance. I remember taking him once to the Raja Muda of Selangor, and he shook hands with the heir to the Throne, instead of making the usual obeisance (*sembah*). I am sure even to this day, he greeted me in the manner of greeting a friend not his father-in-law! I wonder what custom he would adopt at the marriages of his own children. Recently, I was told that at the Meeting of the *Sahabat Pena*[57] held in Batu Pahat, he took the seat reserved for the State Commissioner![58] But the worst of it all, I think, was that he

[55]*Meminang* (from *pinang,* the areca nut), the ritual sending of *pinang* and *sireh* (the betel vine leaf in which the nut is folded for chewing) with the formal proposal of marriage, once the preliminaries have been concluded.

[56]'Let your children die, but not the adat (custom)'.

[57]The *Persaudaraan Sahabat Pena* (Brotherhood of Pen Friends), best known simply as *Sahabat Pena,* started as a correspondence club in 1934 in connection with the Penang newspaper *Saudara,* rapidly grew to be the largest pan-Malay organization in the peninsula, with some 12,000 members at its peak in 1938, and numbered among its leaders most of the Malay-educated elite.

[58]District Commissioner is probably intended, the senior Malay administrative official for the district, similar to the District Officers of the

BOOK THREE   143

thought he was the equal of everybody. He did not seem to mind if his mistake was pointed out to him! To him, it was not a mistake!

I shall refer the reader to a few things that occurred about this period to show/the prominent parts I took in the encouragement of sports which won for me the popularity alluded to above. At Matang, a Football League was organised with a few teams from Taiping competing in it; and I was made the Hon. Secretary. Mr. H. Sperling, proprietor of the Matang [Rubber] Estate gave us a silver cup as the League trophy. Mr. Jacques, Manager of the Matang Estate and a State football player, was the captain for the estate team. The College had a team playing in the League, and came out second or third in the list of the League results. Once the Malay Teachers of Penang sent their team to play against the College team, with Zin in charge; and in time the College team went to Penang to play the return match. Capt. N.M. Hashim who was then already promoted to be the District Officer, Balek Pulau, came to Penang to be the referee in this match. As I was in charge of the College team, Captain Hashim took me to Balek Pulau to be his guest./I found his house, the D.O.'s quarters, on top of a small hill, and Che Teh Turki was his wife. Here I met the youngest sister of Che Teh Turki; but though we sat together during meal times as if the purdah system was not known there was no freedom for me, for instance, to go out alone with any of the womenfolk in Captain Hashim's house. So I was free to see my hostess and her sister only in the presence of my host and was restricted to do anything further. I shall mention later about this sister-in-law of Captain Hashim, as she came to my notice in the course of my life.[59]

I also took the College team once to play the Kuala Kangsar

F.M.S. but in Johore assisted (rather than superintended) by parallel British officials known as Assistant Advisers.

[59] No further reference to N.M. Hashim's sister-in-law occurs in the manuscript. One family account is that in 1924 N.M. Hashim tried to persuade Abdul Majid to take his sister-in-law in marriage, and that his failure to do this was part cause of some bad feeling between them in later years. The incident described here must have taken place during Abdul Majid's first period at Matang in 1919/20, at which time N.M. Hashim was appointed Acting District Officer of Balek Pulau.

College team, and was sorry not so much because we lost in the match but because I found that the old spirit so assiduously cultivated by Mr. Hargreaves in the College was there no more. I noticed that at half time when the iced water was brought for
212 the players to drink, the Kuala Kangsar/boys had not the courtesy to allow the Matang boys, as their guests, to have their drink first. I remember Mr. Hargreaves was very particular on this point and often reminded us of this often-forgotten simple rule of hospitality. Another point that I noticed was when our motor cars began to move, a number of the Kuala Kangsar College boys clapped their hands and gave shouts of derision! This, as Mr. Hargreaves was wont to tell us, was nothing short of bad manners, as the idea of cheering at the end of the game was to congratulate the winners for their victory or to encourage the losing side to play the better next time, as the case might be. In any case the cheering should not be given in the spirit of teasing or deriding the losing side for their defeat. After all, the real object of the game is the exercise that it provides to the players and the mild excitement that it gives to those who watch it.

213 When we got back to Matang, on the next day I spent one hour lecturing to the whole College on the objects of playing the game of football together with the best ways of conducting oneself under all circumstances so as to promote 'the sporting spirit'. The lecture was finished up with a warning that I would expect everyone in the College to behave in the ways I had told them towards the Kuala Kangsar boys when they came to Matang to play the return match.

Of course, the Matang College again lost in this match; and perhaps I should say it openly that having seen the Kuala Kangsar College play football for years, none knew better than I did that Matang never had any chance of winning in the match that I proposed.

I know I courted defeat when I arranged to play the Matang College against the Kuala Kangsar College; and I remember
214 feeling mortified when my friend, Inche Mohamed Tahir,[60]/then

[60]Muhammad Tahir b. Setia Raja, of Batu Gajah, born c. 1902, educated at Malay school and Anderson (English) School, Ipoh. He was later employed as a Senior Cooperative Officer.

Sanitary Inspector at Kuala Kangsar, shouted, as if here [*sic*] a schoolboy, from one side of the field to me on the other side of the field, as much as to say: 'How absurd of you to expect to defeat the Kuala Kangsar College team with that rotten team you brought from Matang!'

But my friend did not realise that I came not to defeat the Kuala Kangsar College team, but to see if the spirit that Mr. Hargreaves took so much trouble to inculcate and foster was still there. My short stay had convinced me that the spirit had gone with him. And I was mightily glad to be able to revive it, not in the Kuala Kangsar College itself, but in the College where I was then working. I felt more happy perhaps than receiving a decoration from the Government when I found that the boys behaved just as I/wanted them to do, according to my lecture, to the Kuala Kangsar boys when they came to Matang.

It was at Telok Anson that Mr. H. Fairburn, Intelligence Officer, F.M.S. Police, wanted me to see him at the Bidor Police Station.[61] He phoned up the Police Inspector, Telok Anson, to tell me so; and when the policeman came to my house in search of me I was not in, being away in the Club. When I came home, my wife told me that the Police Inspector wanted to see me. Naturally I asked her why. She said she did not know; but added that she felt that the Government wanted me to go to Mecca. I could not believe this; while she admitted it was only her presentiment: something within her kept telling her that I was to be sent to Mecca.

I was of course asked by the Police Inspector to go to Bidor to meet Mr. Fairburn. And I went by car only to meet him ten

[61] Harold Fairburn was born in 1884 and joined the Malayan police as a young man in 1904. In 1921 he was appointed officer in charge of the Criminal Intelligence Department of the S.S. Police—which despite its name concerned itself almost entirely with political intelligence. A similar section, known as the Criminal Intelligence Branch, was formed within the F.M.S. Police in 1920, and Fairburn moved up to Kuala Lumpur to take charge of this. He retired as Inspector General of Police, S.S., and died in 1973. (For details and discussion, see Alun Jones, 'Internal Security in British Malaya, 1895-1942', Unpublished Ph.D. Dissertation, Yale University, New Haven, 1970, chapters 5 and 6, *passim*). The interview referred to here must have taken place during the first half of 1923.

miles out of Telok Anson. Mr. Fairburn was evidently on the lookout for me and recognised me when our cars passed each other. I had never seen him before.

216 After asking if I was Abdul Majid and/introducing himself, he asked me if I had applied for leave to go to Mecca. Giving him a reply in the affirmative, he asked me why I did not go. I said I could not leave my family as my daughter was grown up, and was at that time betrothed to be married soon. After that he enquired if I could go that year as the Government wanted someone trustworthy to do something for them.[62] I must say that I felt very flattered when I heard that the Government looked up to me as a trustworthy man. So I agreed to go, and was told that the Government would grant me the necessary leave and provide me with the necessary money for the journey.

On the appointed day, I went to see Mr. Fairburn in Kuala Lumpur and received through him from the Government $1000/- to cover my expenses to Mecca.

Meantime, I had arranged with Muhammed Zin to get his marriage ceremony with my daughter performed at once, owing
217 to my proposed departure for Mecca. He of course/willingly agreed to expedite matters, as he had asked for an early marriage, only I put it off for a year at the *meminang* ceremony.

In due course, the marriage took place; and I must say it was a grand affair for me in my position. Everybody whom I knew was invited, and the attendance was quite a big one. There were

[62]Essentially, to act while in Mecca (inaccessible to non-Muslim British consular officials) and Jeddah as an agent of the Political Intelligence Bureau of the S.S. and F.M.S. Police, and to safeguard the welfare of pilgrims from British Malaya (the importance attached to the latter aim is forecast in, e.g., the Report on the Pilgrimage written by R.J. Farrer and W.M. Lee-Warner in 1920, encl. in Conf. Desp., Governor of the Straits Settlements to Colonial Office, 24 Nov. 1920, in CO 273/503). The duties of the newly appointed pilgrimage officer were set out in a memorandum by René Onraet, head of the Political Intelligence Bureau, dated 10 October 1924: (i) registration of pilgrims; (ii) registration and retention of return tickets; (iii) assistance to pilgrims; (iv) check against female slavery; (v) assistance to British Agent, Jeddah; and (vi) 'assistance in detecting and countering any political movement, e.g. the possible communist activities of the newly-established Soviet agency in Jeddah' (copy in Kelantan Files, 'K' series, No. 1039/1924).

Malays, Chinese, Indians and Europeans as guests, each community being entertained separately. The District Officer, Telok Anson, Mr. R.J.B. Clayton,[63] whose wife was a granddaughter of the well-known English novelist, Charles Dickens, was also present. The *bersanding*[64] took place at about 10 p.m.; and the wedding presents from the guests, placed on tables before the bride and bridegroom as they sat on the *pelamin* were varied and numerous. Notable among these were the gold locket and chain with a gold watch and chain from the Malay teachers, silk cloths for lady's *bajus* from Sheikh Ahmad of Seremban, gold sovereigns from Mr. Tyte, Manager of the Eastern Smelting Co. Ltd., Kampar, a Chinese scroll embroidered in gold letterings from the Chinese Club, Telok Anson, and a fairly large sum of money in cash. Only one friend was not present, and this was Mr. T.F.H. Kemp of the F.M.S. Police.[65] He was away home on long leave.

Mr. Kemp knew me when I was in Matang where he was Police Officer when he first came to this country. He often came to my house then for Malay *makan*; and once we went together for a picnic in Pulau Sembilan at the mouth of the Perak river. Mr. Tyte also came; and some of the Malay teachers accompanied us, proving themselves useful in many ways. There was plenty of fishing, bird-shooting and turtle-eggs collecting which we all enjoyed. There was a small hut on one of the big islands, and we all slept in it. There were a few coconut trees growing here and there which we saw as we went round the islands; and I planted some durian seeds, as if to commemorate our visit there. I must not omit to mention that my son, Abdul Latiph, also went to

---

[63]Reginald John Byard Clayton, born 1875, joined the M.C.S. in 1898 and spent most of his early years of service in Perak. He was appointed D.O. Lower Perak in 1920, and served in this capacity until 1926. He retired as British Adviser, Kelantan, in 1930.

[64]The public enthronement or sitting in state of a newly married Malay couple. The *pelamin* (see below) is the decorated and garlanded dais or throne on which they sit.

[65]Thomas French Hewitt Kemp, born 1900 and educated at Bedford School, served in the First World War and came to Malaya in or around 1919, being posted initially, it appears, in Perak. He was made an Assistant Commissioner of Police in 1921, and rose steadily to become Superintendent of Police, S.S., in 1937, holding this post until the war.

Pulau Sembilan with us. He was then only ten years of age.

On our return voyage, we had a bad time. The wind was in front of us; and instead of taking two hours to cross back, as we did on going out, we took eighteen. Our provisions ran short, and our water-supply was entirely exhausted. Someone suggested that we should boil some of the turtle eggs we were taking home with us in the salt water. This increased our thirst. Only God knows our sad plight when we found, as the big junk went aground, that we had to wade in the water for three hours before we touched solid ground. We had another hour to walk before we reached a Chinese coffee shop; and here everybody had something to eat and drink. From the coffee-shop, there was a walk of another two hours before we got back to our motor-cars. This walk was in the mud, caused by the rain which was then pouring, on the unmetalled road.

220 When the marriage ceremony was over, the bridegroom returned to his place at Butterworth in Province Wellesley, taking with him his bride. My cousin, Sheikh Ismail Naim[66] who was also my brother-in-law (he was the husband of my sister, Haji Eshah) and my mother-in-law, accompanied my daughter to her new home. When they returned, I made arrangements to get my son, Hashim, circumcised. He was then ten years old.[67] Abdul Latiph was circumcised when he was a little over a month old, due to a sickness which, it was believed, he had owing to a vow (niat) I made shortly before he was born.[68] I left for Mecca on the same day that Hashim was circumcised. In fact, he fainted three times after the operation and I went away during his third swoon to catch the train for Singapore.

My journey to Mecca and back was a very unpleasant one. The Namazie boats by which I travelled to and fro took 22 days to go

[66] Syaykh Ismail, from Minangkabau, a religious teacher living in Kuala Lumpur, was Eshah's second husband.

[67] The age held to be appropriate for circumcision varied, but it was often done in conjunction with the ceremony known as 'berkhatam Qur'ān', finishing the Qur'ān, the point in time at which a boy completed reading through the entire Qur'ān with his teacher. The prepubertal age of ten or so was therefore a common one.

[68] The reference here is unclear. A niat (Ar. niyyah) is a vow of intent, which, if for any reason not fulfilled, may be held to result in some ill.

from Singapore to Jedda or vice versa, instead of the 14 or 15 days taken by the Blue Funnel boats.[69]/I chose this line because I was given to understand that food was provided to the pilgrims on board these ships. But I found that food was supplied only to the (Dutch) Javanese pilgrims from the Netherlands East Indies. The Namazie ships carried both the Javanese pilgrims from Batavia and the Malay pilgrims from Singapore. Thus when I got on board I found myself without food. Luckily for me, the man in charge of the food for the Javanese pilgrims was a good man and he gave me such food as he could spare from the canteen, getting in return for his supplies and service a number of stories from me every evening. His name was Ali ....,[70] his father being an Arab and his mother a Javanese. He had with him his mother who was going on pilgrimage and he proved himself to be very dutiful to her. I met him in Batavia in 1929 when I stayed with Syed Ismail Al-Attas on my way back from Jedda to Malaya.

At other times I had my meals with Haji Babu of Malacca. Haji Babu's father was a Sikh who turned Muslim on marrying his mother./He had his wife and two sons, Abdul Rahman and Tambi with him. Tambi's wife, Haji Rahman, and Haji Ahmad, her brother, with Yunus, her brother-in-law (husband of her elder sister) were also in the party. Haji Babu's wife died in Mecca.

When we arrived at Jedda, I had only a few cents left. The fact was there was only $100/- balance out of the $1000/- I received from Mr. Fairburn; and after paying for my train fare and passages I had only $10/- with me when I boarded the pilgrim ship, and this amount was spent on cigarettes during the voyage. I went to the British Consulate and asked Mr. Grafftey Smith,[71] the Vice-

---

[69]These were the two principal companies plying the pilgrimage route from Singapore to Jeddah—the Ocean Navigation Co. of Hongkong, owned by Haji Mohd. Hassan Namazie (with his nephew Mohd. Ali Namazie, J.P., as Singapore agent), and the British-owned Blue Funnel line, whose local agents were Mansfield & Co. Blue Funnel fares were thought by some British officials to be rather high, in the face of growing Japanese competition (Report by R.J. Farrer and W.M. Lee-Warner, cited in note 62 above), but it is clear that they offered better conditions than Namazie.

[70]Name omitted in original.

[71]Laurence Grafftey-Smith, b. 1892 and educated at Repton School,

Consul acting as Head of the post, to write to the Government of the Straits Settlements for a loan of a few hundred dollars for me. Haji Babu who saw me going to the Consulate was given to understand that I remitted my money through the Government and expected to receive it at the Consulate. When he was told that the money had not yet come, he advanced me with $100/-. My Sheikh, Osman Shabana, likewise agreed to postpone the payments of my pilgrimage dues to him.[72] So, in due course I got to Mecca along with the others.

Very soon, my friends organised a picnic in one of the gardens in Mecca; and there we stayed for three nights. We had Qu'ran-reading every evening followed by *Qasidah*[73] which lasted till very late at night. Of course, there were several sheep slaughtered every day to feed the company. It was then the month of June when Mecca was very hot.[74] The people in Malaya have no idea

---

joined the Levant Consular Service in 1914, and after two years' language training at Cambridge University was sent to Egypt. In December 1920 he was posted to Jeddah as Vice-Consul where he served (with two periods as Acting Consul, Dec. 1921–April 1922, and February–June 1923) until transferred to Constantinople in May 1924. For some account of Jeddah during these years, see his autobiography, *Bright Levant* (London, Murray, 1970), pp. 139–77.

[72]Expenses for Malayan pilgrims in 1924, the ensuing year, were as follows: M$105 for lodgings in Singapore or Penang, fares, and quarantine on arrival; $5 for boat hire, porterage, and house rent in Jeddah; $20 for camel to Mecca and back; $36 for house rent in Mecca, plus tent hire and food in Arafat and Muna; $24 for camel to Arafat and Muna and back; $71 for camel to Medina and back; and $7 for transit of Jeddah on return; total M$268. This did not include food in Mecca or Medina, accommodation in the latter, or sundry payments to Bedouin and others. Fees to one's *syaykh* for personal services were also separate. It was estimated that the minimum required was M$400. For discussion, see Abdul Majid's first report, 28 September 1924, encl. in the memorandum by Onraet cited in note 62 above.

[73]*Qasida*, one of the basic forms of classical Arabic poetry, in modern times often sung and frequently of secular content.

[74]The pilgrimage month (Dzu'l-Hijjah) in 1923 ran from 15 July to 13 August. Though it is not clear when Abdul Majid arrived in the Hejaz, the principal caravans from Mecca to Medina, preceding the pilgrimage proper, left in the weeks after the fasting month of Ramadhan (which had ended on 16 May). As Abdul Majid does not mention fasting on board ship, it seems likely that he had arrived in Mecca in early June, left for Medina in one of the last caravans to go north, and returned

how hot it is in summer there. The walls of the houses are like the chimneys of a burning lamp; and clothes from the washing become dry if put in the shade for five minutes. In such a heat very few people work or even move about. Many Malays and Javanese try to cool themselves by having a bath or covering themselves with a wet towel. So they get ill very often. The Arabs get over this by using very thin clothes and allowing their perspiration to dry on/their bodies. They take their bath only either in the morning or in the evening when the sun is not hot. Certain fruits are also not to be taken in the day-time, but only at night.

Being a fool like most of my countrymen in these respects, I did nearly all the things I should not do and became very ill within a few days of my arrival in Mecca. For six long days, I lay tossing with fever in bed, taking no food whatsoever, nor drink except an occasional draft of *zemzem* water.[75] Indeed, I only knew that I had lain six days from Sheikh Osman Shabana who came on the sixth day and asked me if I wanted to go to Medina as the caravan was leaving on the next day.[76] I was very annoyed with the Sheikh for making that enquiry since he should know that I was unfit to do the journey. But the Sheikh in the true spirit of his profession took my censure very calmly and remarked: 'None knows better than I that you have been ill for the last six days; but in this holy land, unlike/in Malaya, things happen in the most extraordinary manner. For example, a sick man like you recovers in no time if he puts his faith in God and believes that everything happens according to His will. So, if you will only make up your mind to pay a visit to the Prophet and leave it to God to decide whether you will pay the Prophet that visit, God will see to it that your wish is fulfilled if it is so fated for you. Caravans for Medina do not go every day; so pray to

---

after 45 days (see below) just before the pilgrimage ceremonies.

[75] I.e., water from the sacred Zemzem well within the precincts of the Masjid al-Ḥarām in Mecca, traditionally held to possess curative powers.

[76] Medina, some 250 miles from Mecca, is the burial place of the Prophet Muhammad, and is usually visited by pilgrims (though not an obligatory part of the *haj*) before the ceremonies in and around Mecca. In the mid-1920s, the journey took upwards of 8 to 10 days in each direction, travelling by camel caravan.

God to allow you to go with one that is going tomorrow; and if He be pleased you will find yourself healthy again and fit to go'.

At hearing these words, I found that I had nothing wherewith to contradict him; so I told him that I wanted to go to Medina; and inwardly prayed to the Almighty to enable me to go.

Right enough, on the very next morning I found that I had sufficient strength to do the necessary packing for the trip and to perform the/*tawaf wida'* in the afternoon.[77] As the sun was very hot, the heated marble flooring round the Ka'aba blistered my feet awfully before the *tawaf* was over; but the happy prospect of visiting the Prophet in his last resting place relieved me somewhat of the pain from the blisters. Nevertheless, the blistered feet became swollen for some days.

When the caravan was ready to take us along, I found myself sharing the same *shaqduf*[78] with Abdul Rahman bin Haji Babu. The camel for our *shaqduf* was a big, highly-spirited one with a tendency to turn its head frequently to right and left thereby throwing down the wooden structure from its back with all that was on it. In this way, I was thrown down no less than ten times from Jiad,[79] where our quarters were, to Shuhada, our first halting place. The distance was only about two miles; but Shuhada was the station where/the competent Authorities inspected the *koshan*, that is to say, the tax payable by each and every pilgrim to the Hejaz Government for the journey.[80] Here we stopped for one whole day and night.

It was at Shuhada when the caravan was again moving off on the next day that the camel carrying my *shaqduf* suddenly scamp-

---

[77] *Tawāf*, ritual circumambulation of the Ka'ba in the Masjid al-Ḥarām is performed at various stages of the pilgrimage. The *ṭawāf al-wadā'* is a (non-obligatory) circumambulation of departure, made before leaving Mecca.

[78] A shelter or canopy placed on the camel's back.

[79] The fort of Jiyad is on a hill outside Mecca to the north-east.

[80] Eldon Rutter, who made the journey between Mecca and Medina in 1926, described these dues as amounting to four pounds sterling (M $32) on each camel bearing a *shaqduf*, the owner of the animal being entitled to a further four pounds (*The Holy Cities of Arabia*, London & New York, 2nd (one vol.) ed., 1930, p. 459).

ered off two or three times of its own accord and thus threw me down from its back as if it refused to carry me entirely. I was disgusted with this extraordinary behaviour of the animal and told the Sheikh that I refused to go any further unless he gave me a new camel and a good one in place of this bad one. Of course, the Sheikh could not do this; but in his reply to me he said that he was willing to do it and that he would do it immediately. This of course make me happy as I mounted again into the *shaqduf*; but I did not know that I/was having all the time [*sic*]. Any way, I had no trouble again from the camel and enjoyed my ride like the other pilgrims ever after that. I learned afterwards that my camel was of a type noted for its strength, but through long disuse the animal had developed a spirit which would take one or two days to break. Two or three other camels in the caravan suddenly collapsed during the journey and died; but my camel remained healthy and strong all through.

My discomfiture at being thrown down from the *shaqduf* in Shuhada was seen and laughed at by a fellow-pilgrim named Abdul Halim; and strange to say as if rebuked for getting fun out of another's misfortune his camel suddenly scampered off for about 50 yards and threw him down from his *shaqduf*. This man met me afterwards in one of the halting places on the journey and related to/me what had happened to him while asking for my pardon for what he believed was his sin by laughing at me in my fall.

I discovered that Haji Abdul Halim was a Malacca Malay doing business in Singapore and living at 275 Joo Chiat Place.[81] He and I became very good friends ever since.

The journey was a very memorable one as it was full of unusual incidents. In the first place, it was an experience to find in the desert as we stopped at the various halting places so many grocers' and butchers' 'shops' where the travellers could buy anything and everything for their needs to satisfy the inner man. Besides the hustle and bustle to prepare the food on reaching these temporary stations, there was also music, both Indian and Arabic, on every

---

[81] Abdul Halim b. Habib (c. 1888–c. 1943), a general trader in Singapore, was also a pilgrimage *syaykh*, specializing in pilgrims from Cambodia and Thailand as well as the Malay states.

side with much singing sung in the highest pitch of the voice of the singers, thus making the whole encampment a very lively scene,/indeed. One can imagine how active everybody was during these hours of rest when it was realised that when the caravan was on the move everyone was compelled to rest as he or she lay cramped up in the *shaqduf*.

In the second place, the Bedouins of the desert who were entitled to a certain percentage of the *koshan* collected by the Hejaz Government but did not receive their dues thought it essential to show their authority by stopping the caravan and demanding their money for the passage through their territory.[82] In this way, we were stopped in three or four places and our journey delayed. At Bir Abbas, three days journey distant from Medina where the biggest tribe, Beni Ahmadi, lived, we had to stay no less than eight days. I understood that it took the Sheikhs or their Agents some time to collect the ten riyals from each *shaqduf* to satisfy the demand of this tribe.[83]/And what hot days they were those eight days at Bir Abbas as it was then already late in the month of May.[84] The winds that blew in our faces as we lay there without any tent but with only the *shaqduf* to give us any shelter felt like fire from a furnace nearby. I know my wife told me on my return home that I was very much sun-burnt and looked much darker than when I went away.

When we got to Medina at last, I again fell ill and therefore was unable to go with the others to visit Baki'[85] and the other interesting places round about that holy city, usually visited by pilgrims. I had to be content with going only to the mosque where the grave of the Prophet is.[86] And this I did with great difficulty

---

[82] After the final deposition of Husain by Ibn Sa'ud in December 1925, passage dues were regularized and the rights of the Bedouin recognized but brought under strict control.

[83] The *riyal* at this time was worth about two shillings sterling.

[84] This may be in error for early June. See above, note 74.

[85] *Baḳī' al-Gharḳad,* or *al-Baḳī',* the cemetery to the south-east of the town. After the Wahhābi occupation of Medina in early 1926 the thousand of tombs—many of them those of members of the Prophet's family or leading Companions—were destroyed from motives of puritanically orthodox iconoclasm (see, e.g., Eldon Rutter, op. cit., pp. 562-3).

[86] The Masjid al-Ḥaram in Medina, also known as the Prophet's Mosque,

as I was still ill, only the Sheikh told us that we would be going back in two days' time. I remember going alone to the mosque which was only about 500 yards away from the house where I stayed. I saw that the city itself was much smaller than Mecca, and so was the mosque. But the people in Medina were not so noisy and quarrelsome as those in Mecca. Even the *muzawwirs* were less persistent in offering their services to take you round and show you what to do in the mosque than the *mutawwifs* of Mecca.[87] There was an air of gentility in everybody in Medina that you did not find in Mecca. Once I spoke very harshly to a *muzawwir* coming to offer his services to me and I found all faces in the mosque scowling at me. Harsh words and rough conduct were foreign to everyone in Medina so much so that the Bedouin camel-drivers following their example during their short stay there became totally different persons in their behaviour towards you. I remarked this good behaviour of the people in Medina to a friend, and was told by way of explanation/that it was a legacy of the Holy Prophet whose own genteel conduct and behaviour had set the example to the whole city. That this personal example of the Holy Prophet should last during these 1300 and over years among a people who is noted for their lawlessness and rowdiness like the Arabs is indeed very remarkable and speaks volumes for the divine origin of His teachings!

On our way back to Mecca, we took a different route, known as the Jalan Ghir, the former route being known as the Jalan Sultan.[88] This route was shorter than the former route by a few

---

was in its reconstructed and completed form only some eighty years old in 1923. The tomb of the Prophet, together with those of the Caliphs Abu Bakar and 'Umar, and possibly that of Muhammad's daughter Fatima, are situated within the mosque.

[87] The *muzzawir*, or visitors' guides, in Medina are so styled in distinction to the *mutawwif* of Mecca, one of whose principal responsibilities is the induction of the pilgrims into circumambulation, *ṭawāf*, of the Ka'ba.

[88] Eldon Rutter (op. cit., p. 477) describes the *Darb al-Sultāni* (Mal. '*Jalan Sultan*', Sultan's Road) as the more direct of two main caravan routes between Medina and the coastal town of Rabigh, the other being the *Darb al-Far'i*, which appears to have struck westwards towards Medina's port of Yanbu before heading south to Rabigh. Richard Burton, *Personal Narrative of a Pilgrimage to Al-Madinah and Meccah* (London, Bohn's Popular Library ed., 1913), Vol. II, p. 58, refers to

stages, so that one could cover the distance by camel in nine or ten days whereas it took us twelve days to do it by the Jalan Sultan. We saw large areas planted with date palms in two or three places along this route; and in one place we came [upon] a small stream of water in which I took a bath for a few hours in the/hot sun,—and got ill as the result.[39]

This time my illness lasted for some days until we reached Rabigh, where the caravan rested for two days. At this place, I was so very ill that I had to stay in one of the coffee-shops and hire one of the long chairs that looked like charpoys[90] for me to sleep on. Presently, an Arab who was serving in the caravan passed by; and when he saw that there was no one attending to me in my illness he brought some medicine which he bought with his own money from one of the shops in the place and began to apply it on me as he thought would suit the case, saying as he did so that I would be all right in a few hours. He went away as he came, without telling me who he was or asking me who I was.

It was very characteristic of the Arabs to do a good turn without expecting any return for their service, particularly/to the pilgrims whom they call 'the guests of God'. I must say if ever men did anything *for the sake of God,* this man was one of them. And I can only pray that some day he will get his reward from the Almighty for what he did for me.

I said it was characteristic of the Arabs to help the pilgrims whenever and wherever possible because during my short stay in Medina I found this attitude so prevalent there. On many occasions, I got fresh, cold water brought to me by unknown persons just in time to save me from falling in a swoon due to the terrible heat. When I lost my way going back from the mosque to my

---

four principal 'roads' in use in the 1850s: the *Darb al-Sultāni* (taken by his immediate predecessor Jacob Burckhardt), the *Tarīk al-Ghabir* (a mountain path), the *'Wadi al-Kura'* route, and the *Darb al-Sharki* ('Eastern Road') which appears to have led more or less due south through the Nejd. What the *Darb al-Ghir* referred to by Abdul Majid was is not clear.

[89] Eldon Rutter refers to the predilection of Malay pilgrims for bathing *en route* whenever possible (op. cit., pp. 463–4), which he attributes to their being unaccustomed to living without water.

[90] Indian rope beds.

house, the Imam Shafie[91] of the Medina mosque invited me to his shop and gave me tea, before directing me back to my house.

At another place along this Jalan Ghir, we were shewn the grave of a certain Sheikh,/(I forget his name) who died there while he was on his way to Medina. It is said that this Sheikh came all the way from his native town on foot, singing the praises of the Prophet all the time. The unfortunate part of it all was that he never reached the city of the Prophet, having died only within a few more days' journey of his cherished destination.[92]

A few days after Rabigh, we came to Doff, and here while we sat down to our breakfast that morning immediately after our arrival there, a number of the local Bedouins came and with rifles and swords robbed all the camels from our party so that when the rest of the caravan moved on towards Mecca that evening we of Osman Shabana's pilgrims numbering about 40 persons in all had to remain one more night in the place. However as the Sheikh of Doff came that same evening and offered to supply us the required number of camels to enable us to proceed on/the next day, we eventually left Doff and reached Mecca in due course. We discovered on arrival in Mecca that we spent 45 days on the journey to Medina and back with a stay of 7 days in that Holy City, instead of the usual 30 days. None regretted the end of the journey as the Bedouin camel-drivers left us with their string of animals to return to their homes in the desert.

Perhaps one of the Bedouins would remember that journey with curses to the end of his days for he swallowed urine on that occasion. The manner he did it happened in this wise. It was customary for every pilgrim to be supplied with a *sherba*[92] which he kept tied up at the back of his *shaqduf* in such a way that he could easily get at it to drink from it whenever he wanted it. The *sherba* would of course be filled before the caravan started from every halting place. My fellow traveller, Abdul Rahman bin Haji Babu, found to his disgust/that every time he took his *sherba* to drink it was empty. And by keeping a watch he discovered that his cameldriver was in the habit of taking the *sherba,* drink[ing] all the water

---

[91]Imam of the Shafi'i school of law and its adherents.
[92]Water gourd.

that was in it and put[ting] it back in its place—empty. So, one day Abdul Rahman filled his *sherba* with his own urine, instead of with water. Thus, when the thief stole the *sherba*, he swallowed urine, instead of water. You should hear him cursing and swearing as he spat it out of his mouth when he discovered what it was he was drinking.

[The autobiography ends at this point, with some half-dozen pages of the notebook left empty.]

BIBLIOGRAPHY OF ABDUL MAJID'S PUBLISHED WRITINGS

Jalan Belajar Bahasa Inggeris yang Senang: Vocabulary and Grammar for Beginners. Singapore, Methodist Publishing House, ca.1910. (This English primer had reached its 7th edition by 1941)

Rahsia Mengajar. Muar, publisher unknown, 1912; 2nd ed., Singapore, Methodist Publishing House, 1914. (Selected translation from either *A New Manual of Method* (1896) or *A Primer of School Method* (1905), by Alfred Hezekiah Garlick.)

Anak Kunchi Pengetahuan. Singapore, Methodist Publishing House, ?1913.

Malay Self-Taught. London, E. Marlborough & Co., 1920. (This is still in print, the 14th impression having appeared in 1958.)

Ilmu Tanam-Menanam. Tanjong Malim, Malay Translation Bureau, rev. ed. 1924; Malay School Series, No. 8. (Translated from a manuscript or publication on gardening prepared by Alexander Keir of the Education Service, this was probably first published about 1920.)

'A Peculiar Custom in Kuala Kangsar', *Journal of the Malayan Branch Royal Asiatic Society, (JMBRAS),* III, 1 (April 1925), 85–86.

'A Malay's Pilgrimage to Mecca', *JMBRAS,* IV, 2 (October 1926), 269–87. (An account of Abdul Majid's own first pilgrimage in 1923 in the context of more general discussion of the *haj.*)

'Random Notes on Current Malay Beliefs', *JMBRAS,* V, 2 (November 1927), 360–61.

'Some Malay Superstitions', *JMBRAS,* VI, 4 (November 1928), 41–45.

The Malays in Malaya, By One of Them. Singapore, Malaya Publishing House, 1928. (Published anonymously, this was written, 'by a Malay', in response to the appearance of L. Richmond

Wheeler's *The Modern Malay,* London, Allen & Unwin, 1928.)
The Malayan Kaleidoscope. Kuala Lumpur, The Selangor Press, 1935. (Most of the 25 short articles brought together in this volume had appeared previously in the *Malayan Police Magazine.*)

In addition to the foregoing, Abdul Majid contributed regularly from about 1908 to the Malay and the English press in Malaya, always, so far as is known, under pseudonyms, and from 1940 to 1941 he edited and wrote extensively for his journal *The Modern Light.*

INDEX

ABBAS (ABDUL MAJID'S SON), 35
Abdul Aziz b. Raja Musa, Sultan, 33n, 141 &n
Abdul Halim b. Habib, Haji, 153 &n
Abdul Hamid b. Tengku Haji Muhammad Salleh, Daeng, 123-4
Abdul Hamid, Haji, 6-7 &n, 9-10, 134 &n
Abdul Hamid, Sultan (of Kedah), 38n, 109n
Abdul Hassan b. Burhan of Taiping, Sayyid, 134 &n
Abdul Jalil ibni Almerhum Sultan Idris, Sultan, 25 &n, 117n
Abdul Latiph, Haji (Abdul Majid's son), xiii, xv, 3, 17 &n, 32, 33, 34, 36, 38-9, 50, 86, 131, 147-8
Abdul Majid bin Zainuddin, Haji: birth and childhood, viii, 45-7; attends Victoria Institution, viii ix, 46; at Malay Residential School (Malay College), ix, 5, 52, 56, 60-8, 74-7, 92-108; as Malay Assistant Inspector of Schools, x, 10-11, 25-6, 88, 89, 93n, 124-9, 137, 138; and as Acting Head Master of Malay Teachers' Training College, x-xi, 88-9, 129-37; his pilgrimage to Mecca and Medina, xi, 148-58; and appointed first Malayan Pilgrimage Officer, xii, xiii, 53, 89n, 146n; as political liaison officer, xii; his religious views, xiii-xiv, 21-3, 62-4, 66-7, 112, 131-2, 135-6; founds *The Modern Light*, xiii-xiv; on his illness, 1-3, 14-15; death of his father, 10-12; on death, 12-15; on the importance of being useful, 15-16; on money and business ventures, 17-20, 27, 43-4; his wives, 24, 27-39, 49, 57, 115-17; and children, 17n, 33-6; his house in Kuala Lumpur, 42-4; and education of, viii-ix, 46-8, 54, 56; on kindred spirits, 49; and on gratitude, 51-2; his abortive love affair with Haji Muhammad's niece, 54-6, 57-8; as a teacher, 60-5, 67-8, 92; articles and translations of, 65-6, 97, 130; and football, 68-9, 86, 141, 143-5; and clubs, 69-71, 77, 79, 80-1, 86; on Sultan Idris, 71-4 91-2; billiards and skittles, 77-9, 86; Silver Jubilee celebration of Sultan Idris, 79-84, 87, 90; on women and love affairs, 84-5, 110-11, 113-17, 118-20; card games, 86; on *'anak dagang'*, 87-9; on Malay volunteer force, 90-2; and teachers' salaries, 92-4, 95; and Mr Rowlands, 94-6; books written by, 97-8, 130-1; and new Malay Readers, 97-100, 124, 130; appointed Malay Assistant Inspector of Schools, 100; organizes Hargreaves' Farewell Dinner, 100-5; and farewell address to, 105-6; and Inche Zainal Abidin as his successor at Malay College, 106-8, 120-1; applies for job of Inspector of Schools, Pahang, 108; and refuses head-

mastership of Alor Star English School, 108-9; Zainal Abidin stays as guest in house of, 120-2; and plans to start Literary Society, 121-2; sent to Telok Anson as Assistant Inspector of Schools, 124-5; his mother-in law arrives in Telok Anson, 124-5, 127; and public notice of 'death' of, 125, 126; First World War and, 128-9; appointed Acting Head Master at Malay Training College, 129-37; and Khwaja Kamal-ud-Din's visit, 133-6; his relationship with Ali, Visiting Teacher, 139-40; becomes President of Lower Perak Football League, 141; his daughter Aminah's marriage to Muhammad Zin, 141-3, 146-7, 148; sports encouraged by, 143-5; invited by Fairburn to go to Mecca as pilgrimage officer, 145-6; and pilgrimage to Mecca, 145-58

Abdul Malek b. Yusof, Inche (now Tun Haji Abdul Malek), 61 &n
Abdul Manap (Bilal), 64
Abdul Qadir, Sir, 40
Abdul Rahman b. Haji Osman (Malay Writer, Education Office, Singapore), 99
Abdul Rahman b. Haji Babu, 149, 152, 157-8
Abdul Rahman, Tengku (latterly Prime Minister, Malaysia), 38n
Abdul Rahman b. Tunku Muhammad, Tunku, 61n
Abdul Rashid b. Sultan Abdul Aziz, Raja, 101 &n, 118
Abdul Razak b. Haji Abdul Ghani, Inche (Datuk Setia of Selangor), 53 &n, 122n, 123n
Abdullah (Abdul Majid's son), 35
Abdullah, Haji (Visiting Teacher, Kuala Kangsar), 73
Abdullah, Raja (of Kota Lama Kanan), 77-8 &n
Abdullah b. Tunku Mahmud, Tunku, 109
Abdullah b. Jaafar, Datuk (Prime Minister of Johore), 104 &n
Abdullah b. Muhammad, Datuk (Johore Bahru), xv
Abdullah b. Tahir, Datuk, 6 &n
Abdullah Singgora, Sheikh, 29, 30-1&n
Abu Bakar, Sultan (of Johore), 84 &n
Adams, T.S., 18n
Agoes Salim, Haji, 34 &n
Ah Teng (Sultan of Perak's head Boy), 102
Ahmad b. Yahya, Inche (Johore Bahru), 18-19, 58 &n, 59
Ahmad Kamil b. Nik Mahmud, Nik, 2
Ahmad of Qadian, Mirza Ghulam, 41 &n, 133n, 135
Ahmad, Syaykh (Seremban), 147
Ahmadiyya movement, xiii, 13n, 48n, 133n
Aishah Bee (Abdul Majid's first wife), 24, 28, 29, 31-4, 36-7, 42, 44, 50
Akad nikah (marriage contract), 63 &n
Akhirat (the hereafter), 12 &n
Alang Samin (Grik), 126-7
Ala'uddin Mansur Shah, Sultan, 33n
Alhady, Sayyid Alwi b. Sayyid Syaykh, 58 &n
Ali (Visiting Teacher, Telok Anson), 139-40
Ali, Wan, 127
Ali b. Ahmad (Abdul Majid's brother-in-law), 33n
Alor Star, Government English School at, 76, 77; Abdul Majid refuses offer of headmastership of, 108-9
Alsagoff, Salleh b. Sayyid Ahmad, Captain Sayyid, M.B.E., 38 &n
Aminah, Hajjah (Abdul Majid's daughter) ,xi, xv, 36, 128, 141; her marriage to Muhammad Zin, 141-3, 146-7, 148

INDEX

Anak dagang (foreigners in Perak), 80 &n, 82–3, 84, 87–9
Anak Kunchi Pengetahuan (Key to Knowledge), 94 &n, 97
Anderson, Sir John (High Commissioner of the F.M.S.), 56n, 76
Anglo-Chinese School, Telok Anson, 17n
Al-aqā'id al-imān (articles of faith), 22 &n
Arab Irregulars (regiment in Hyderabad), 40
Al-Attas, Syed Ismail, 149
Azan (Islamic call to prayer), 132

BABU, HAJI, of Malacca, 149, 150
Baki' al-Gharkad (al-Baki'), 154
Balek Pulau, 32, 33
Bangsawan Show (Malay opera), 128 &n
Bee see Aishah Bee
Beni Ahmadi tribe, Bir Abbas, 154
Benjafield, H. (Health Inspector of Malay Schools), 140
Berkeley, Hubert, 126 &n
Berzanji, 67 &n
Billiards, 77–9, 86
Bir Abbas, Hejaz, 154
Birch, J.W.W. (Resident of Perak), 58n, 83n
Blue Funnel (taking pilgrims to Jeddah), 149 &n
British Navy, H.M.S. *Malaya* given to, 118 &n
Buka puasa (daily breaking of fast at sundown), 7 &n, 9, 10
Bukit Chandan, Sultan's palace at, 6
Bukit Kanching, 10
Bulan Puasa (fasting month), 5 &n
Butterworth, Province Wellesley, 148

CAMBRIDGE UNIVERSITY Local Examination Syndicate examinations, ix, 46–7
Card games, 86
Carimon Islands, 17
Ceylonese burghers, 95 &n

Chan Kim Loon, 70 &n
Che Teh Turki (Captain N.M. Hashim's wife), 143
Che Wan, Dato Panglima Kinta, 71 &n, 78–9
Chettyars (Chetties: Indian Tamil caste of businessmen), 44–5, 83–4
Chinese, 45, 95, 147
Chulan b. Sultan Abdullah, Raja Sir, 69n, 78 &n, 86
Circumcision, 148 &n
Clayton, R.J.B., 147 &n
Clayton, Thomas Watts (D.O. Larut and Matang), 134 &n
Clifford, Sir Hugh, 31n
Coconut trees/oil, 42, 129, 130
Colgan, Mr and Mrs, 103
Collinge, H.B. (Inspector of Schools, Perak), 95 &n

DAUD B. MUHAMMAD SHAH, 93n, 138–9 &n
D'Cotta, Dr, 3
Din, Bilal, 6, 7n
Dussek, O.T., 137 &n, 138

EDUCATION, xi, 17n; Abdul Majid's, viii–ix, 46–8, 54; article on 'Education in Egypt', 54; Seventh Standard examination, 61, 63; religious, 62–5, 66, 67–8; teachers' salaries, 92–4, 95, 106, 121, 138; Abdul Majid's new Malay Readers, 97–100, 124, 130
Ehsan Qadir, Lieutenant, 40
Elcum, John Bowen, 97 &n, 98–9
Ellerton, H.B. (District Officer Kuala Kangsar), 81–2 &n, 102
Ellerton Club, 69 &n, 77
Eshah (Abdul Latiph's wife), 34
Eshah bte Sayyid Othman Abu Sarir, Sharifah, of Mecca, 17n
Eu Tong Seng, The Hon., 82 &n

'FACTORS FOR WORLD PEACE IN ISLAM' (Abdul Majid), xiii, 131 &n
Fairburn, Harold, 145–6 &n

Fatimah bte Colonel Muhammad, 17n
Federal Scholarships, 47 &n
F.M.S. (and S.S.) Police, xii, 17n, 145 &n, 146n; Abdul Majid employed as liaison officer with Political Intelligence Bureau of, 89 &n
F.M.S. public services, Malays employed in, 43 &n
F.M.S. Volunteer Rifles, 17n
Fitrah, 218n
Football, 68–9, 86, 101, 102, 141, 143–5
Fruits, fruit trees, 42–3

GARLICK, ALFRED HEZEKIAH, 62 &n
Ghouse, Dr. Ismail Muhammad, 133 &n
Ghusl wajib (Muslim mandatory bath), 63n
Government English School, Telok Anson, 17n
Grafftey-Smith, Laurence (Vice-Consul, Jeddah), 149–50 &n
Great War (1914–1918), 127, 128

HAAD YAI (THAILAND), 18–19
Hargreaves, William, Head Master of the Malay College, 47, 56 &n, 60–1, 62, 64, 69, 74, 75, 96, 109, 110, 128, 144, 145; Farewell Dinner for, 100–5
Hari Raya (feast after Ramadhan), 5 &n, 6, 94, 109
Hashim (Abdul Majid's son), 14, 17 &n, 29, 34, 36, 37, 148
Hashim, Captain N.M., 81 &n, 90, 128, 143 &n
Hasnah (Abdul Majid's daughter), 35
Hejaz, xi, xii, xiii, 40, 41, 49, 154 (*see also* Mecca)
Hussain, Sheriff, 40
Hutan Melintang, 45
Hyderabad, 40

IBRAHIM KHAN B. GHAFOOR KHAN (Ibrahim Papa), 141 &n, 142
Ibrahim b. Wan Suloh, Datuk Wan, xv
Idris b. Raja Iskandar, Sultan of Perak, ix, 5 &n, 8, 71–4, 90, 118 &n; his quarrel with wife, Raja Permaisuri, 8–9; Silver Jubilee of, 79–84, 90; against Malay volunteer force, 90–1
Ilmuddin, Professor, 40
Imports of goods from Middle East, 19–20
India, Indians, 39–41, 147; Chettyars, 44–5, 83–4
Influenza epidemic (1918), 127 &n
Iskander Shah, Sultan of Perak, 101n, 134, 135n
Islam, xiii, 39 &n; Abdul Majid's views on, xiii–xiv, 21–3, 131–2, 135–6; Ahmadiyya movement, xiii, 13n, 48n; education, 62–5, 66, 67–8; patron saints, 112 &n; world peace and, 130–2;'Ubudiah Mosque opening ceremony, 117–18; prayers, 132 &n; Qadianis, xiii, 41 &n, 133n, 134n, 135 (*see also* Mecca; Qur'ān; Ramadhan)
The Islamic Review, 13 &n, 131, 133
Ismail b. Sayyid Syaykh al-Khairat, Sultan of Siak, 83n
Ismail Effendi (Oriental Secretary, British Legation, Jeddah), 31
Ismail Naim, Syaykh, 148 &n
Istana Negara, Kuala Kangsar (state palace), 24 &n, 70 &n, 101, 102, 134; Silver Jubilee Ceremony in, 82–4

JAAFAR, MAULVI, 135
Jacques, Mr, (Manager of Matang Estate), 143
Jajahan Melayu, 134n
Japanese occupation of Malaya, 17n
Javanese pilgrims, 149, 151
Jelai, Datuk Maharaja Perba of, 127 &n
Jeddah, xii, 28, 29, 35, 40,146n; siege of (1925), 34 &n; pilgrim-

INDEX

age route to, 149 &n *(see also* Mecca)
Johore Bharu, 17n, 58 &n, 59
Johore Malay Literary Society, 107–8 &n

KAHAR, TUNKU (later Tunku Laxamana of Negri Sembilan), 49–50
Kak Bedah, 113–17, 119–20
Kamāl ud-Dīn, Khwaja, xiii, 13 &n, 131, 133–6
Kanagapathi Pillay, 70 &n
Kassim, Haji (Qur'ān teacher), 64–5
Kassim, Megat, 32 &n, 33n
Kastan Zarian Club, 69, 70–1, 77, 79–81, 84, 87n
Kechik (Abdul Majid's Chinese driver), 10
Kedah, 108–10
Keir, Alexander, 12n, 67–8 &n, 129 &n, 130 &n, 137, 140
Kemajuan Pengetahuan, 123n
Kemp, T.F.H., 147
Kempe, John Erskine, 77 &n
Kenion, A.N., 68–9 &n
Khalid b. Abdullah Munshi, Inche, 59 &n, 83n
Khilafat movement/Conference, 134n
King Edward VII School, Taiping, 17n, 60n, 94, 95
Kitab literature, *kitab* classes, 64 &n, 67–8
Kota Bharu, 17n
Kuala Kangsar, Perak, 27, 35, 52, 138; Abdul Majid's life in, ix–x, 5–10, 56; Government English School, 17n; Khwaja Kamāl ud-Dīn's visit to, 134; college football team play Matang team, 143–5, *(see also* Malay College)
Kuala Kangsar Mosque, Qur'ān-reading parties in, 6–10
Kuala Lumpur, viii, 38, 108, 138; Abdul Majid attends Victoria Institution in, viii–ix, 46; Methodist Boys' School, 17n; Abdul Majid's house at No. 2, Treacher Road, 42–4; Abdul Majid leaves Kuala Kangsar for, 123, 124; plague in, 127n
Kuala Pilah Rest House, 49

LAHORE PARTY (of Ahmadiyya Movement), 41n
Laidin, Inche (Alor Star), 2
Latiph, Haji *(see* Abdul Latiph)
Lotfiah (Abdul Majid's daughter), 35
Laxamana, Tunku *(see* Kahar, Tunku)
Lembaga, 58n
Lembaga Malayu, 58 &n, 135 &n
Linehan, W., 65 &n
Long Ja'afar, Inche, 58 &n
Lower Perak Football League, 141

MCLEAN, L.S. DR., 33–4n, 111
Mah, K.L. Dr., 2, 15
Mahdi, Imam ('The Divinely Guided Leader'), 40–1
Mahmud b. Sultan Ahmad Tajuddin, Tunku, 108–9 &n
Mahmud Iskandar Shah, Sultan, 79n
Maimunah (Abdul Majid's daughter), 35
Malay Administrative Service (M.A.S.), 43n, 57n, 61n, 87n, 93n &n
Malay Art School, Kuala Kangsar, 7n, 121
Malay College (formerly Malay Residential School), Kuala Kangsar, Perak, 17n, 47, 52n, 56n–7n; Abdul Majid at, viii, ix, xiii, 5, 52, 56, 60–8, 74–7, 92–108, 120, 138
Malay College, Telok Belanga, 59 &n
Malay Company of the Singapore Volunteer Infantry, 90 &n
Malay Football Association of Singapore, 81 &n, 83, 90
Malay Literary Society, 122–3
Malay Mail, 92 &n
Malay Nationalist Party (MNP), 17n

Malay Officers' Scheme *see* Malay Administrative Service
Malay Self-Taught (Abdul Majid), 16 &n, 130
Malay States Guides, 90–1n
Malay Teachers' Training College, Matang, Perak: Abdul Majid employed as Acting Head Master at, x–xi, 12, 26, 67 &n, 88–9, 129–37, 138
Malay Training College, Malacca, 137 &n
Malay Volunteer Force, 90–2
Malaya, H.M.S., given to British Navy, 118 &n
Malayan Civil Service (M.C.S.), 43n, 47n, 61n
The Malayan Kaleidoscope (Abdul Majid), 6 &n, 92 &n, 124 &n
Manap, Bilal, 6 &n
Mansur Shah, Sultan, 79n
Marks, Oliver, 102 &n
Marriage: *akad nikah* contract, 63 &n; of Abdul Majid's daughter, Aminah, 141–2, 146–7, 148; *meminang* ceremony, 142 &n, 146; *bersanding*, 147
Mas'ood, Haji ('Bapa'), 11–12
Mat Noor, Haji, 74, 84
Matang, Perak: Malay Teachers' Training College at, x–xi, 12, 67 &n, 88–9, 129–37, 143; Khwaja Kamāl ud-Dīn's visit to, 133–4; football team, 143–5
Maulud, 67 &n
Maxwell, William George (British Adviser to Kedah), 110 &n
Medina, 150n; Abdul Majid's pilgrimage to, 151–7
Mecca, 40, 145; Abdul Majid's pilgrimage to, xi–xii, 34n, 53, 89n, 148–58; and his role as friend and adviser to pilgrims, xii, xiii, 49 &n; Latiph's visit to, 17n; Abdul Majid's wife from, 29–31, 34, 36, 37–9; Mosque, 41; Abdul Majid invited by Fairburn to go as pilgrimage officer to, 145–6; expenses for Malayan pilgrims, 150n

Merican, Ismail, 109–10 &n
Methodist Boys' School, Kuala Lumpur, 17n
Minyak attar, 112 &n
The Modern Light, 2n; founded by Abdul Majid, xiii–xiv; and Latiph becomes editor of, 17n
Mohamed, Encik (Principal, Malay College, Telok Belanga), 59n
Mohamed Sa'id, Haji, 7, 8–9
Mohamed Tahir (Senior Co-operative Officer, Pahang), 1
Mudzaffar Shah b. Sultan Mahmud Shah, Sultan, 79 &n
Mudazaffar Shah III, Sultan, 79n
Muhammad Ali, Maulvi, 133n, 134 &n
Muhammad b. Haji Ilyas, Inche (Head Official Translator, Johore), 107 &n
Muhammad Eunos, The Hon. Inche, 6 &n, 58 &n, 66 &n, 135n
Muhammad Nur, Haji, 5 &n, 6, 7 &n, 64, 72, 82
Muhammad Shah, Sultan, 79n
Muhammad Shah b. Yam Tuan Antah, Tunku, 90 &n
Muhammad Sheriff b. Awang Osman, Haji, 110 &n
Muhammad Tahir, Haji, 6–7 &n
Muhammad Tahir b. Jalaluddin al-Azahari, Shaykh, 7 &n, 80, 83, 84, 123
Muhammad Tahir, Raja, 104 &n, 125 &n, 144–5
Muhammad Talkah b. Mohd. Arif, Inche, 82 &n
Muhammad Yatim, Penghulu, 83 &n
Muhammad Yusuf b. Ahmad, 123n, 138 &n
Muhammad Zin b. Ayub, xv, 138 &n, 141–3; his marriage to Aminah, 141–3, 146–7, 148
Muhammad, Haji (Visiting Teacher, Selangor), 54 &n, 57, 58, 59
Muhammad Omar b. Haji Bakar,

Inche (editor of *Jajahan Melayu*), 59 &n
Musa, Haji (Imam of Matang), 12
Musa b. Raja Haji Bot, Raja, 61 &n
Musa'eddin, Tengku, Raja Muda of Selangor, 18 &n, 19
Mustafa b. Datuk Menteri Satu, Haji, 7, &n, 8

NAMAZIE SHIPS (Ocean Navigation Company), 148-9 &n
Netherlands East Indies, 149
Ngah Ibrahim, Mentri of Perak, 58n
Nik Mahmud b. Haji Wan Ismail, Datuk, 49n
Noordin, Dato Stia of Perak, 1
Nurdin b. Abdul Karim, Haji, 59 &n

OMAR, SHEIKH, 109
O'May, John, 33n, 75 &n, 76, 77, 105-6, 111, 120, 121, 123, 129
Osman, Haji (Visiting Teacher, Province Wellesley), 59
Osman b. Megat Ali, Megat, 32n
Osman Shabana, Sheikh, 150, 151, 157

PAHANG, 108, 127; Abdul Majid applies for job of Inspector of Schools in, 108
Pakatan Bahasa Melayu Persuratan Buku Di-Raja (Johore), 108n
Pakatan Belajar Mengajar Pengetahuan Bahasa Melayu (Johore), 108n
Pandak Kamal, Inche, 7 &n, 8, 121
Pangkor Engagement, 63n
Pawang (Malay spirit-doctor), 45-6
Peel, Sir William, 89
Penang Free School, 56n, 109-10
Perak: title of Bendahara of, 32-3n; and position of *anak dagang*, 87-9; Abdul Majid appointed Assistant Inspector of Schools in, x, 10-11, 25-6, 88, 89, 93n, 124-9; 'flu epidemic in, 127 &n

(*see also* Malay College, Malay Teachers' Training College)
Perak Pioneer, 134 &n
Persekutuan Kemajuan Pengetahuan (Society for the Advancement of Knowledge), 123n
Phillips, C.M., 26n, 97 &n
Phillips, W.M., 26 &n, 97n, 126
Physiognomy: Abdul Majid's views on, 23
Political Intelligence Bureau (of F.M.S. Police), xii, 89 &n, 145n, 146n
Polygamy, 21
Permaisuri, Raja: quarrel with husband, Sultan Idris, 8-9
Port Swettenham: Abdul Majid employed as clerk in Marine Office, 53-4
Pudu village, near Kuala Lumpur: birth and childhood of Abdul Majid in, viii, 45
Pulau Sembilan, 147-8
Puteri, Tengku, 38 &n

QADIANISM, xiii, 41 &n, 133n, 134n, 135
Qāris (Qur'ān Readers), 5-6, 31, 74, 109
Qasida (Arabic poetry form), 150 &n
Qur'ān, 14, 15, 21, 22, 109 &n, 112 &n; 'The Cow' (*ul-Buquru*: 2nd sura), 13 &n; *al-Fātiḥah* (opening sura), 13 &n, 112; *al-Iklās* (112th sura), 112 &n; *berkhatam Qur'ān* ceremony, 148n
Qur'ān-reading, 6-10, 31, 63, 64, 74, 118, 150

RAFFLES INSTITUTION, SINGAPORE, 26n, 53n, 97, 108n
Rahsia Mengajar (The Secrets of Teaching), 62 &n, 97
Rajah, Professor, 51
Ramadhan, 5, 109, 112 &n, 150n; Qur'ān-reading parties in Kuala Kangsar mosque, 6-10; illness and death of Abdul Majid's father during, 10, 45

Ramli bin Haji Ali, 23 &n, 43, 44
Razman b. Raja Abdul Hamid, Raja, xv
Religion (see Islam)
Riba, 21
Ronggeng (Malay dancing girl and show), 105 &n
Rowlands, R.C.W., 60 &n, 70, 94–6, 104
Rubber production, 27 &n
Rukun iman (elements of faith), 39 &n
Rukun Islam (fundamental principles of Islam), 39 &n
Rukun sembahyang (essentials and rituals of prayer), 39 &n
Rutter, Eldon, 155n, 156n

SABAK BERNAM, 10, 45
Sabīl ul-Rashād (Latiph), 17n
Safar (Abdul Majid's son), 36
Sahabat Pena (Friends of the Pen), xii, 142 &n
Samuels, Dr., of Johore, 2
Saudara, 142n
Selangor Clerical Services, 92n, 93 &n, 138, 139n
Selangor Secretariat; Abdul Majid employed as clerk in, 53
Selangor Tin, Ltd., 19
Serban (turban), 9–10
Seri Perak, 134n
Setapak, 19
Shamsuddin b. Kassim, Dr., 82 &n
Shaw, Bennett, Head Master of Victoria Institution, 46n, 47
Shuhada, Hejaz, 152, 153
Singapore, 17n, 19n, 26n, 108, 128, 133, 139; Abdul Majid's visit to (1911), 81 &n; pilgrimage route to Jeddah from, 149 &n
Singapore Royal Naval Volunteer Reserve, 17n
Singapore Volunteer Infantry/Corps, 17n, 90 &n
Singgora (Songkhla), 18–19, 30
Sitiawan, Perak, 124, 127, 140
Skittles, 86
Smiles, Samuel, 52

Sperling, H., 143
Sports, 68–9, 75–6, 77–9, 86, 141, 143–5
Sri Menanti, 90, 92n
Straits Echo, Penang, 66 &n
Straits Settlements Customs Service, 17n
Stuart, E.A.G., 75–7, 109n
Sulaiman, Haji (Johore), 6
Suleiman, Sultan of Selangor, 18n
Sultan Idris Club, Kuala Kangsar, 105
Sultan Idris Training College, Tanjong Malim, 137 &n; Translation Bureau at, 106, 107n, 122n
Sumatran traders, viii
Sumner, Henry Lightbourne, 129 &n, 137, 140
Sungai Nipah Malay School, 140
Swettenham, Frank Athelstane, 8 &n, 31, 71

TAHIR JALALUDDIN, SHEIKH, 80, 83, 84, 123
Taiping, 137; Khwaja Kamāl ud-Dīn's visit to, 133–4
Tanjong Malim, Sultan Idris Training College at, 137
Teh (Abdul Majid's sister-in-law), 33 &n
Telok Anson, Perak, 45; Abdul Majid in x, 10, 11, 25–6, 88, 89, 124–9, 137, 139–40, 145; Anglo-Chinese School, 17n; mosque, 25; Rest House, 26
Teraweh, Megat, Bendahara of Perak, 33n
A Text-Book of the Malay Peninsula; Abdul Majid's translation into Malay of, 97
Thailand (Siam), 18
Thambipillay, Mr. (teacher at Victoria Institution), 20–1
Thompson Optical Company, 3
Times of Malaya, Ipoh, 66 &n, 125
Tin-mining, 18–19 &n
To' Rakna, Dato, 113 &n
Towers, A.C.J., 47
Treacher, W.H. (Resident-General

of the F.M.S.), 56n
Turkish cigarettes, imports of, 19–20
Tyte, Mr., Manager of Eastern Smelting Co. Ltd., 147

'UBUDIAH MOSQUE, BUKIT CHANDAN, 134; opening ceremony, 117–18
Uda b. Raja Muhammad, Raja, 61 &n
Ulu Langat, 19
Usury (*riba*), 21
Utusan Melayu, 66 &n, 73, 90

VANRENAN, F.A., 74 &n, 104
Victoria Institution, Kuala Lumpur, 20, 59; Abdul Majid's education at, viii–ix, 46 &n, 47, 93
Vocabulary and Grammar for Beginners (Abdul Majid), 15–16, 60, 97
Voice of the People, 17n

WAHHABISM, xiv
Walker Cup Football matches, 68 &n
Watson, James, Inspector of Schools, Pahang, 108 &n
Wembley Empire Exhibition, 7n
Wilkinson, R.J., Federal Inspector of Schools, ix, 52 &n, 56 &n, 60, 92, 99n, 123
Winstedt, R.O., Assistant Director of Education, x, 25n, 67, 99–100 &n, 123, 124, 130 &n, 138

YAACOB, TUNKU, 2
Ya'akub b. Ismail (Ya'akub Perak), Shaykh, 12 &n, 29, 37–8, 85
Ya'akub b. Raja Bilah, Raja Haji, 59 &n
Yahya Afifi, Sheikh, 1
Yahya b. Awaluddin of Johore, Datuk, 19n
Yap Ah Loy (Kapitan China of Selangor), 18 &n
Yap Tai Chi, 18
Yusof b. Sultan Abdullah Muhammad Shah, Raja, 83 &n

ZAGHLUL, SA'D, PASHA (Egyptian nationalist leader), 96 &n
Zainal Abidin bin Ahmad, Inche (Za'ba), 35 &n, 48n, 66n, 106–8, 120–3, 133, 134, 136 &n, 138